Dedication

This book is dedicated to my Lord,
Jesus Christ, who is the same
yesterday, today, and forever.
Because He lives and is coming again,
we have hope!

Table of Contents

continued overleaf

APPENDICES

Acknowledgments

I would like to express my gratitude to the following individuals whose many hours of research helped make this work possible. They are symbolic of thousands of concerned Christians around the world who rarely receive the credit they deserve for their years of dedicated service: Carl Teichrib, Dona Lackman, Milton Cragg, Shirley West, Samantha Smith, Berit Kjos, Gail Todd, Willy Peterson, Scott Pearson, Dennis Cuddy, Peggy Cuddy, Nancy Fitzgerald, Richard Phelps, Irvin Baxter, J. R. Brestin, and Brian Weiss.

I also wish to thank the following persons whose invaluable assistance, prayers, and moral support helped sustain us during the course of this project: Norma Butler, Barbara Singleton, Cheri Ellstrom, Karen Fearnow, our friends at the Indianapolis Messianic Fellowship and at Harbour Shores Baptist Church, along with Grant Jeffrey and his committed staff at Frontier Research Publications.

In addition, a special thanks to the many prayer partners and supporters who have undergirded this effort. You have played a major role in seeing this project through to completion, and you are greatly appreciated!

Throughout the course of writing this book, the Lord used various Christian songs to inspire and comfort me. The meaningful songs of Twila Paris, Michael Card, and Steve Green ministered to me and challenged me on a daily basis. Thank you for being obedient to the Lord's call on your lives! I was also tremendously blessed by the music of Ray Boltz, Steve Millikan, Jacqueline Barker, Bill Murk,

Joy McClain, and the group Rapture. May the Lord bless you all, as you have blessed me.

Along with drawing from the music of these gifted artists, there are several individuals whose sound biblical teachings influenced me greatly during the writing of this book. I have benefited regularly from the Christ-centered messages and godly wisdom of my pastor, Don Jennings II, as well as the insightful and challenging sermons of John MacArthur, David Jeremiah, and Erwin Lutzer. Thank you for standing firm for the Lord and for not compromising his Word. You are making a difference!

Finally, I would like to thank my devoted family, especially my loving wife, Audrey, who has been a continuous source of encouragement. She is a true gift from the Lord and is a living example of a Proverbs 31 woman. Her unwavering faithfulness and perseverance will some day be rewarded!

Foreword
by
Grant R. Jeffrey

It is a pleasure to introduce to you *The New World Religion*. This unique source of in-depth documentation reveals the philosophical and religious roots of the occult movement to establish a new world order. Gary Kah is an excellent and dedicated researcher who probes behind the headlines to discover the hidden spiritual motivations leading the political and intellectual elite to bring about the world's first truly global government. His timely exposé provides a penetrating look at spiritual and political trends that will profoundly affect all of us in the years ahead.

A new world religion is rapidly taking shape as an increasing number of organizations and denominations, representing a large spectrum of religious beliefs, are striving to create a worldwide ecumenical system. Gary's fascinating book will take you behind the scenes to show you the key personalities, issues, and dangers of this growing religious movement. It will also explore the mystical teachings of the major New Age leaders who have provided the intellectual foundation for the present movement to flourish.

Several years ago I met Gary as a speaker at a Bible prophecy conference in Florida. I was very impressed with his integrity as a serious researcher and writer. Ever since, I have admired his dedication to uncover the truth about these critical spiritual issues. Gary is deeply committed to Jesus Christ in his ministry and personal life. Together with his wife Audrey and their children, he has been leading a crusade to defend our biblical faith. His years of exhaustive research into the underlying philosophy and spiritual teachings of the New Age movement have given him a detailed understanding of the pressing spiritual issues facing our nation as we enter the new millennium.

Gary Kah is the highly respected editor of the bi-monthly newsletter *Hope For The World Update* that I have utilized as a valued and accurate research source for a number of years. His newsletter provides penetrating analysis of global economic, religious, and political developments that affect all of our lives. With his extensive background in government—in the area of international trade—Gary is in a unique position to evaluate world trends. He is a well-respected guest on hundreds of radio programs and is a gifted speaker in demand at conferences throughout the world.

I highly recommend *The New World Religion* to anyone who wishes to understand the true story behind the superficial coverage of international events in our media. The only way we can effectively resist the New Age assault on the fundamental truths of Christianity is to understand the movement's real agenda and motivation. If we will prayerfully and knowledgeably prepare our families through biblically-based teaching, we can achieve personal victory over this serious attack on the foundations of our faith.

Gary Kah's insightful study will provide you with a biblical understanding of vital issues that will enable you and your family to resist the coming deception by trusting in the wisdom of our Lord Jesus Christ.

Grant R. Jeffrey
Author of *Surveillance Society*

Introduction

More than seven years have come and gone since the publication of my first book, *En Route to Global Occupation*, which warned America of the coming push for a one-world society. Much has happened in the arena of world affairs since that time. Many of the scenarios discussed in *En Route* are now quickly coming to fruition. The United Nations of today, for example, is significantly more powerful than the U.N. of a few years ago.

Each year new international treaties and agreements are ratified, giving the United Nations more direct control over national and local government plus our personal lives. This recent "empowerment" of the U.N. will affect all of us, as new international laws and regulations become fully enforceable in the new millennium. The U.N. recently proposed the introduction of a global income tax on every human on earth to establish its independence from national dues. The organization needs massive increased budgets to implement its new environmental and population control policies, its growing peace-keeping forces, and the huge bureaucracies being established to oversee its newly formed agencies. Along with these political and economic changes, we will soon experience the impact of the U.N. 's spiritual agenda, which is quite intolerant of Bible-believing Christians and Jews.

Since the release of *En Route to Global Occupation*, I have had the opportunity of traveling throughout North America as well as overseas, appearing on hundreds of talk shows and fielding questions from many concerned listeners. To my surprise, the most-often-asked questions have pertained to spiritual matters as they relate to the unfolding end-time events of Bible prophecy—particularly the spiritual agenda of the coming global government, the movement toward a one-world ecumenical religion, and the signs pointing to the soon return of Jesus Christ.

Therefore, my purpose in writing this book is to address these issues. My first book presented an overview of the three major areas where globalists are making the greatest inroads towards influencing our lives—summarizing developments in the political, economic, and religious realms. This new book will probe deeply into the New Age/interfaith movement, explaining the pagan and anti-Christian motivation of the elite who are planning our spiritual future.

The New World Religion presents a unique glimpse at the personal lives and strongly held beliefs of those individuals who, during the past century, have had the greatest influence in shaping the New Age movement of today—people such as Helena Blavatsky, Carl Jung, Teilhard Chardin, and Edgar Cayce, along with Mikhail Gorbachev and other contemporary "ecumenical" leaders. In examining these key lives, the book will unveil the chronological history of this deceptive spiritual movement. It traces the New Age movement from its ancient dark beginnings, through the centuries to its current activities, and its religious plans for the new millennium. In the process the research will point out the pitfalls and dangers of its seductive but spiritually empty teachings.

A special focus will be given to Alice Bailey, the founder of Lucis Trust, a mysterious but powerful organization whose occult concepts continue to influence key members of the United Nations and the globalist organization known as the Council on Foreign Relations. We will also take an in-depth look at the teachings and activities of the renowned mystic, politician, and educator, Robert Muller. He is the central figure in today's U.N.-sponsored global education reforms and plays a significant role in the interfaith religious community. We will review his timetable for the establishment of a complete world government. In addition, the book will examine the phenomenon of so-called spirit guides, the current widespread fascination with angels, and the growing curiosity about paranormal spiritual activity.

This book is not intended to be an exhaustive study on the emerging world religion. Rather, it is designed to be a practical handbook investigating the religious motivation and associations of a dangerous and rapidly growing occult movement. This information will benefit both Christians and non-Christians alike by assisting the reader to understand the clear differences between biblical Christianity and the mystical teachings of the New Age.

We are entering a perilous time known as the "last days" which will produce massive global upheaval and spiritual changes as foretold by the prophets in ancient Scripture. We need to be aware of the spiritual deception surrounding us so that we do not unwittingly fall prey to its false doctrines. As we begin to understand the tactics of our ultimate enemy, Satan, and learn to trust in the promises found in the Word of God, we will be able to withstand the challenges during the difficult days that lie ahead.

Fortunately, the Book of Revelation declares that Jesus Christ will one day descend from Heaven to defeat the forces of evil. My prayer is that you will be compelled to take a stand for righteousness and will be faithful to the teachings of Jesus Christ as we expectantly await His return! With the Lord's help, we will be overcomers against the spiritual darkness of the new world religion!

1

Laying the Foundation

"Everyone who hears these words of mine and does not put them into practice is like a foolish man who built his house on sand."
Matthew 7:26 (NIV)

"For no one can lay any foundation other than the one already laid, which is Jesus Christ." *1 Corinthians 3:11 (NIV)*

One can view our world and its history of the rise and fall of nations, its wars and conflicts, and its ever-changing ideas and philosophies as a crazy quilt of happenstance—unplanned, unrelated events. Or we can discern in all of this a pattern, a slow moving forward of human history toward a goal, a climactic event, or as some refer to it, the Omega Point.

Presuming there is such a goal, agenda, or plan for absolute control of the world by a global authority—massive deception would undoubtedly have to be employed to achieve it. This deception would eventually have to engulf all of the earth.

One person or group of persons could never orchestrate something of this magnitude. But the Bible tells us there is a being capable of such an undertaking. His name is Lucifer (Satan). He was a member of God's highest order of created beings, an angelic prince, whose name means "light-bearer." Isaiah 14:12–15 and Ezekiel 28:11–19 tell us much about the corruption of his character and of God's judgement against him.

When Lucifer was cast from the mountain of God (Ezek. 28:16), he lost his high and holy position before the Ancient of Days, but he lost none of his supernatural intelligence and power. It merely became perverted. His sin was in coveting God's place and desiring, as a created being, the worship that is due the Creator, the Most High, alone (Isa. 14:13–14). When he failed to get a majority of the angels to worship him instead of God, he turned his eyes toward earth. Ever since, his desire has been to gain the worship of men.

Lucifer, known as Satan after his rebellion, understands our fallen human nature very well since it is he who corrupted Adam and Eve's originally pure and sinless ways. He does not need a wide array of deceptions and lies to achieve his goal. Two primary lies serve his purpose well enough.

The first is to cast doubt on God's Word, to change it to mean something entirely different from what God intended. The Lord has promised eternal life in heaven for all who believe in his Son (John 3:16). Those who reject God, on the other hand, will be separated from Him for all eternity in hell. But Satan has twisted this system of eternal rewards and punishments into the false belief that man will never truly die, that he just keeps coming back in different life forms (reincarnation) and will face no final judgement by God.

Satan's second tactic is to convince us that we have the right, the ability, and the power within us to transcend our humanity and become like God. He knows very well that this is no more possible for us than it was for him. Still, the lie has continued through the ages, with man vainly embracing this seductive delusion in one form or another. All of this is recorded in the book of Genesis, along with the disastrous results for the first man and woman who were deceived by Satan's convincing lies.

Very few people perceive the fact that human history has been, and continues to be, a spiritual battleground. Satan and his legions are waging war against our Creator. The prize in this war is our souls and the final outcome depends upon the decision in our hearts as to whom we will give our loyalty and worship. If any should doubt the reality of this battle, remember that Satan even tried to get Jesus to worship him. That was two thousand years ago. The battle is now in its final stages, and mankind is consciously or unconsciously choosing sides.*

---

* In discussing the spiritual battle being waged between God and Satan, Christians sometimes inadvertently create the impression that Satan is on an equal footing with God, when, in reality, he is no match for God at all. Satan is a created being who is more comparable in his spiritual power to the archangel Michael than to God. However, of all our adversaries—consisting of the legions of fallen angels—Satan is the most powerful, relentless, and determined. He sits atop this hierarchy of evil spirits. Hence, he has become the principle target of Christians exposing the realm of darkness.

Satan has successfully elicited devotion to himself through the ages by introducing—via human vessels—a variety of false religions and cults, including outright Satan worship. It is not my purpose here to give a detailed history of his activity in ages past, but rather to focus on the events of the last one hundred years or so, since much of the groundwork for the climax of this battle has been laid during the past century. As we shall see, Satan's efforts during this period have been relentless.

False Religions and Cults of the 1800s

With much of the world already steeped in the occult, America would do its share to contribute to Satan's plans by birthing numerous false religions during the 1800s. The first of these "new" religious systems had its beginnings in the 1820s and would eventually become known as Mormonism. Mormonism today is one of the fastest growing religions in the world, and is quite possibly the wealthiest on a per capita basis. One of the beliefs of the Mormon Church, as found in their book *Pearl of Great Price* is that Jesus was the spirit brother of Lucifer before he entered the world.[1] The late apologist Dr. Walter Martin wrote: "If one peruses carefully the books of Abraham and Moses as contained in *the Pearl of Great Price* (allegedly 'translated' by Smith), as well as sections of Ether in *The Book of Mormon, Doctrine and Covenants*, and *Discourses of Brigham Young*, the entire Mormon dogma of the preexistence of the soul, the polygamous nature of the gods, the brotherhood of Jesus and Lucifer, and the hierarchy of heaven . . . will unfold in a panorama climaxing in a polygamous paradise of eternal duration."[2]*

Spiritism, on the other hand, with its emphasis on contacting the dead—actually, contacting demonic spirits posing as the spirits of dead humans—became an organized religion known as Spiritualism in 1848. In our generation it has gained acceptance among many of the world's elite and is responsible for leading millions astray by introducing them to forms of divination.

Between 1860 and 1870, Mary Baker Eddy began teaching her occult doctrine that became known as Christian Science. Followers of this religion believe that it is impossible to understand the Bible apart from Mrs. Eddy's teachings as found in her book *Key to the Scriptures*.

---

* On page 219 of his book, *The Kingdom of the Cults*, Dr. Walter Martin comments: "In Mormon theology, Christ as a pre-existent spirit was not only the spirit brother of the devil (as alluded to in the *Pearl of Great Price*, Moses 4:1-4, and later reaffirmed by Brigham Young in the *Journal of Discourses*, Vol. 13, p. 282), but celebrated his own marriage to both 'the Marys and Martha, whereby he could see his seed before he was crucified'" (apostle Orson Hyde, *Journal of Discourses*, Vol. 4, pp. 259-260).

According to this thinking there would have been little point in even reading the Bible previous to Mrs. Eddy's enlightenment!

Theosophy had its beginning in 1875 under the leadership of Helena Blavatsky. The influence of this organization remains powerful throughout the New Age movement of today. We will examine Blavatsky and her teachings more closely in the following section.

The Jehovah's Witnesses came into being in 1879. This group denies the doctrine of the Trinity and the divinity of Jesus Christ. It prints its own version of the Bible called *The New World Translation*. Key passages in this translation have been altered to fit the group's teachings. Here again we see the subversion of God's Word. Who in this country has not had a well-meaning Jehovah's Witness at their doorstep at some point, ready to share with you their "new truth"?

The Unity Church was organized in 1886 under the leadership of Charles and Myrtle Fillmore. Of the "new" religions that had their origins in the nineteenth century, the Unity Church (along with Theosophy) is probably the most representative of New Age thinking.

Truly Satan was busy laying his foundation of deception during this period of time. But this was only the first phase. The work was just beginning. Before we look at the next phase of his plan we will examine the teachings of some of his choice instruments from the last century. At the top of the list is Helena Blavatsky, founder of the Theosophical Society.

Helena Petrovna Blavatsky (1831–1891)

In studying the teachings of any religion, it is always helpful to take a close look at the religion's founder. One would expect to discover a life that is at least somewhat consistent with the founder's beliefs. Madame Blavatsky's life seems to be a perfect match with her teachings, which are located in the volumes of material she wrote.

Blavatsky has been described by her various biographers as

> [having a] restless and very nervous temperament, one that led her into the most unheard-of, ungirlish mischief . . . attraction to, and at the same time fear of, the dead; her passionate love and curiosity for everything unknown and mysterious, weird and fantastical.[3] . . . from her earliest youth [she] attracted the attention of all with whom she came in contact. . . . She rebelled against all discipline, recognized no master but her own good will and her personal tastes.[4]

(She was) one of the most evil and immoral women who ever

lived . . . [with] personal duplicity and profound contempt for humanity.[5]

Helena Petrovna Blavatsky was born in Russia on August 12, 1831. After the death of her mother when she was eleven years old, Helena passed back and forth between her father and other relatives, for it seemed that no one could manage her. As her mother was dying, she was heard to comment, "Ah well! perhaps it is best that I am dying, so at least I shall be spared seeing what befalls Helena! Of one thing I am certain, her life will not be as that of other women..."[6]

As a child, Helena conversed with animals and birds and frightened the other children with terrible and captivating stories. From an early age she demonstrated the abilities of a medium and, while in a trance, claimed that she frequently saw the majestic figure of a Hindu in a white turban. She called him her protector and believed that he saved her from danger on many occasions. She later described an alleged face-to-face encounter with that same "master" in England at the age of twenty, at which time he instructed her to leave for India to organize the Theosophical Society.

Helena acquired the name Blavatsky at the age of seventeen when she married an elderly general as a result of a dare from a governess who challenged her "to find any man who would be her husband, in view of her temper and disposition."[7] The marriage lasted only three months. Helena deserted her new husband and ran away to begin a life of world travel in service to "her master." Of all this she stated, "I wouldn't be a slave to God Himself, let alone man. . . . Woman finds her happiness in the acquisition of supernatural powers. Love is but a vile dream, a nightmare."[8]

So we see that Madame Blavatsky—an immoral individual heavily steeped in the occult—was hardly a candidate to be chosen as an instrument for bringing God's light and truth to mankind. However, she was perfectly suited for the purposes of the "great deceiver." Thus, Blavatsky drew many deluded followers to herself and her organization during her lifetime. Her "chelas," or disciples, were devoted to her and were more than willing to help spread her doctrines, many of which she acquired from "enlightened" mystics during her travels to Egypt and India.

Many of Blavatsky's beliefs can be found in two extensive works entitled *Isis Unveiled* and *The Secret Doctrine. The Secret Doctrine,* written in 1888, is a 1,474-page occult classic that initiated many prominent figures into the realm of spiritual darkness, leaving them convinced that they were receiving special, hard-to-find "truth." This material was allegedly dictated to her through her "masters" who were called by the various names of Koot Hoomi, Morya, or simply "the Ascended Masters of Wisdom." These "masters" were, she believed, more highly evolved beings who, after going through numerous reincarnations, had left the earth's plane and were now guiding mankind.

In the New Age movement of today, automatic (demon-manipulated) writing (in a trance) is very popular. The names of these so-called ascended masters, or spirit guides, are often as well known as the human authors themselves. The spirit "Seth," for example, supposedly writes through Jan Roberts, and the popular Ruth Montgomery books are supposedly written by her many spirit guides. The controversial J. Z. Knight, on the other hand, communicates the revelations of her special guide, Ramtha. Of course, their message is always a "cosmic gospel" that is diametrically opposed to orthodox Christianity.

If we look at what the "masters" have taught the world through Theosophy, we find that they have "depersonalized God and created various planes of spiritual progression culminating in universal salvation and reconciliation through reincarnation and the wheel concept of progression borrowed unblushingly from Buddhism."[9] The central teachings of Theosophy are summarized in the book *Elementary Theosophy*, by L.W. Rogers:

> God and man are but two phases of the one eternal life and consciousness that constitute our universe! . . . This conception makes a man a *part* of God, having potentially within him all the attributes and powers of the Supreme Being. [Author's note: This is also the core belief of pantheism, the underlying belief system of the Eastern mystery religions, including not only Buddhism, but also Hinduism and Shintoism, among others.] It is the idea that nothing exists except God and that humanity is one portion of Him—one phase of His being.

> . . . If the idea of the immanence of God is sound then man, as a literal fragment of the consciousness of the Supreme Being, is an embryo god, destined to ultimately evolve his latent powers into perfect expression.

> . . . It is an unqualified assertion that humanity is a part of God, as leaves are a part of a tree—not something a tree has created in the sense that a man creates a machine but something that is an emanation of the tree, and is a living part of it. Thus only has God made man. Humanity is a growth, a development, an emanation, an evolutionary expression of the Supreme Being.[10]

It is illogical that an impersonal God-force has created beings of intelligent thought, creativity, and individuality. In contrast, the Scriptures teach us that God can speak (Acts 28:25), and that he has a mind (Romans 8:27). The god of Theosophy is certainly not the God of the Bible.

If Lucifer (Satan) were going to use a mortal person as a channel to cast doubt on the Bible and weaken the Christian faith, what teachings would he most want to attack? Let us look at *Isis Unveiled* to see what he had to say through Madame Blavatsky.

> Like Buddha and Jesus, Apollonius was the uncompromising enemy of all outward show of piety, all display of useless religious ceremonies and hypocrisy. If, like the Christian Saviour, the sage of Tyana had by preference sought the companionship of the poor and humble; and if instead of dying comfortably, at over one hundred years of age, he had been a voluntary martyr, proclaiming divine Truth from a cross, his blood might have proved as efficacious for the subsequent dissemination of spiritual doctrines as that of the Christian Messiah.[11]

In this statement, Blavatsky denies the unique sacredness of Christ's death, bringing the atoning blood of Jesus down to the level of any martyr or religious leader. What a contrast we find in the Book of Revelation, where it states that it is Jesus' blood that actually overcomes Satan: "And the great dragon was cast out, that old serpent, called the Devil, and Satan, which deceiveth the whole world: he was cast out into the earth, and his angels were cast out with him. . . . Now is come salvation, and strength, and the kingdom of our God, and the power of his Christ: for the accuser of our brethren is cast down, which accused them before our God day and night. And they overcame him [Satan] by the blood of the Lamb, and by the word of their testimony . . ." (Rev. 12:9–11).

This passage of Scripture unfortunately meant nothing to Blavatsky, who denied the legitimacy of the Bible. Although publicly she often restrained herself, not allowing her full hatred for Christ and Christianity to manifest, her private views were completely damning. The following calculated statement reflected only her "public" views on the subject, yet was still condemning of Christianity and the Bible.

> It is but fair to say at once that the last of the *true* Christians died with the last of the direct apostles. Max Müller forcibly asks: "How can a missionary in such circumstances meet the surprise and questions of his pupils, unless he may point to that seed, and tell them what Christianity was meant to be?

Unless he may show that, like all other religions, Christianity too, has had its history; that the Christianity of the nineteenth century is not the Christianity of the middle ages, and that the Christianity of the middle ages was not that of the early Councils; that the Christianity of the early Councils was not that of the Apostles, and that what has been said by Christ, that alone was well said?"[12]

With one swoop of the pen, Blavatsky and her "masters" cleverly try to do away with over two-thirds of the New Testament, including all the teachings of the Apostle Paul. This is not surprising. Since they want no personal God to whom they are accountable, occultists would hardly want to listen to the words of the Apostle Paul, who makes such powerful admonishments as to how the Christian life should be lived.

It should be explained that the New Age movement of today publicly espouses the religion *"of* Jesus, not *about* Jesus." That is, it does not point out the attributes that are unique regarding Jesus Christ. Rather, it teaches that Jesus was only one of many great masters and that we can all ultimately attain the same "Christ-consciousness," becoming gods ourselves. It twists the words of Jesus to mean the exact opposite of his original, logical statements.

Blavatsky goes on to say, "Thus we may infer that the only characteristic difference between modern Christianity and the old heathen faiths is the belief of the former in a personal devil and in hell."[13]

It is very difficult to fight a war if you do not know anything about the nature of the enemy. It is impossible to fight a war if you do not even believe there is an enemy. Satan would like nothing more than to convince the masses that he does not exist, thus leaving him a free hand to go about his work of deception and destruction. But Jesus described Satan in words that cannot be mistaken: "He was a murderer from the beginning, and abode not in the truth, because there is no truth in him. When he speaketh a lie, he speaketh of his own: for he is a liar, and the father of it" (John 8:44b).

In spite of Blavatsky's public denial of Satan's existence, upon examining her statements in *The Secret Doctrine*, it is obvious that she believed in the "father of lies" and knowingly helped spread his false light. On page fifty-three she states, "Better be man, the crown of terrestrial production, and king over its opus operatum, than be lost among the will-less Spiritual Hosts in Heaven."[14] She goes on to boast,

Satan is that Angel who was proud enough to believe himself

God; brave enough to buy his independence at the price of eternal suffering and torture; beautiful enough to have adored himself in full divine light; strong enough to still reign in darkness amidst agony, and to have made himself a throne out of this inextinguishable pyre . . . the prince of anarchy, served by a hierarchy of pure spirits.[15]

Madame Blavatsky, in *The Secret Doctrine*, says that Eliphos spoke with unparalleled justice and irony when he wrote: "It is this pretended hero (Satan) of tenebrous eternities, who, slanderously charged with ugliness, is decorated with horns and claws, which would fit far better his implacable tormentor."[16] She sums up her ideas on the devil saying, "And now it stands proven that Satan, or the Red *Fiery* Dragon, the 'Lord of Phosphorous' (brimstone was a Theological improvement), and *Lucifer*, or 'Light-Bearer,' is in us: it is our *Mind*—our Tempter and Redeemer, our intelligent liberator and Saviour from pure animalism."[17]

The following statements by Helena Blavatsky further demonstrate her personal hatred for Jesus Christ and glorification of Satan:

"*Lucifer* is divine and terrestrial light, the 'Holy Ghost' and 'Satan,' at one and the same time." (*The Secret Doctrine*, Vol. II – *Anthropogenesis*, H.P. Blavatsky Collected Writings, 1888), The Theosophical Publishing House, 1979, p. 513.

"There is a whole philosophy of dogmatic craft in the reason why the first Archangel, who sprang from the depths of Chaos, was called Lux (Lucifer), the 'Luminous Son of the Morning,' or manvantaric Dawn. He was transformed by the Church into Lucifer or Satan, because he is higher and older than Jahovah, and had to be sacrificed to the new dogma." (*An Abridgment of the Secret Doctrine*, Edited by Elizabeth Preston & Christmas Humphries), Quest Books, The Theosophical Publishing House, 1966, p. 38.

"Thus 'SATAN,' once he ceases to be viewed in the superstitious, dogmatic, unphilosophical spirit of the Churches, grows into the grandiose image of one who made *terrestrial a divine* MAN; who gave him, throughout the long cycle of Mahâ-kapla the law of the Spirit of Life, and made him free from the Sin of Ignorance, hence of death." (*The Secret Doctrine*, Vol. I – *Cosmogenesis*, originally published in 1888), Theosophical University Press, 1988 edition, p. 198.

"Theosophy was founded as a nucleus for Universal Brother-

Exhibit A

In order to regularly voice her contempt for God and disdain for Jesus Christ, Blavatsky founded Lucifer Magazine, *a monthly publication promoted and circulated by the Theosophical Society from 1887 to 1897. A groundswell of public outrage from Christians of the day reportedly forced the magazine out of print. The image above depicts the front cover of one of the* Lucifer Magazine *issues, sent to us courtesy of Dennis Cuddy, a North Carolina researcher and author of numerous books on the secret societies.*

hood. So was Christ. The latter was a complete failure and is a sham. . . . Don't let us do as the Christians do. Our Society was established to bring together people as searchers after truth, independent thinkers, one having no right to force his opinion on the other: or meddle in his religious views." (*The Letters of H.P. Blavatsky to A.P. Sinnett*, Compiled and introduced by A.T. Barker, Theosophical University Press, 1925), Theosophical University Press, 1973, p. 221.

"Take away from Christianity its main prop of the Fallen angels, and the Eden Bower vanishes with its Adam and Eve into thin air; and Christ, in the exclusive character of the One God and Saviour, and the victim of Atonement for the Sin of animal-man, becomes forthwith a useless, meaningless myth." (*The Secret Doctrine*, Vol. II – *Anthropogenesis*, The Theosophical Publishing Company, Limited, 1888), Theosophical University Press, 1988, p. 497.

Blavatsky believed she received her directions telepathically from the Enlightened Ones or Initiated Adepts (synonymous with spirit guides or masters). In occultism, an adept is one who has reached the stage of initiation and become a master in the "science" of Esoteric Philosophy (secret occult doctrines and practices).

One would think that these teachings of a rebellious and depraved woman of the last century would have little bearing on the lives of people today. But it is interesting to note that from his jail cell shortly after the murder of Sen. Robert Kennedy, Sirhan Sirhan requested a book by Blavatsky entitled *Manual for Revolution*. In this particular book, she called for the assassination of national leaders as an instrument for revolution. Blavatsky's life was lived for revolution and the overthrow of the present social world order.

Another well-known follower of Madame Blavatsky was Adolf Hitler. This evil revolutionary kept a copy of *The Secret Doctrine* at his bedside. The margins of his copy were full of comments and notes in his own handwriting.

Joseph Carr, in his book *The Twisted Cross*, makes the following insightful observation:

The Foundations of both Nazi and New Age Movement philosophy are in the occultic doctrines that were made popular in the late nineteenth century by the theosophical movement. Both Naziism and the New Age Movement depend heavily upon the teachings of Helena P. Blavatsky (*The Secret Doctrine* and *Isis Unveiled*). From theosophists Hitler derived his genesis theories and the notion of a controlling hierarchy of initiates. Both the theosophists of the time and the Nazis believed that mankind was guided by superior beings, Ubermenchen (supermen), who live in remote areas of the world—such as the Gobi Desert (Western China) and the Himalayan nation of Tibet. There was a substantial Tibetan and Chinese community in Berlin because of the occultic interests of German society, and Hitler augmented them with new émigrés after he came to power. By 1941, there were more than one thousand Tibetans living in Berlin.[18]

No serious student of history would deny the widespread influence of the Theosophical Society on world events during the past one hundred years. The global anti-Jewish/anti-Christian sentiment that enabled Hitler to carry out his atrocities was spawned and nurtured by the spiritual ideas of Theosophy and its leaders. Had Blavatsky been alive to witness the Holocaust, she would probably have taken at least some of the credit for its "success."

Exhibit B
The Theosophical Society Logo.
Like Hitler's Nazi Party and the New Age movement of today, Blavatsky's Theosophical Society relied heavily on the use of symbols to convey its secret occult tradition. Notice the inverted swastika near the top of the seal. This well-known occult symbol is believed to have originated in ancient India and has been carried forward by the Hindu religion; it is considered "sacred" by occult orders in both Eastern and Western society. The Theosophy logo contains other occult symbols as well. The Egyptian ankh cross, for example, is surrounded by two interlocking pyramids, representing the union of heaven and earth. They, in turn, are encircled by the alchemical symbol of a serpent.

Helena Blavatsky had many close associates and followers in her lifetime. However, when she died at the age of sixty, she was alone and estranged from even her closest friends. Nevertheless, she remained loyal to her spiritual masters to the end.

Notes

1. Walter Martin, *The Kingdom of the Cults* (Minneapolis: Bethany Fellowship, 1965), p. 218.

2. Ibid., p. 208.

3. Mary K. Neff, *Personal Memoirs of H.P. Blavatsky* (Wheaton, IL: Theosophical Publishing House, 1937), p. 23.

4. Ibid., p. 17.

5. John Steinbacher, *The Man, the Mysticism, the Murder* (Los Angeles: Impact Publishers, 1968), p. 5.

6. Neff, *Personal Memoirs*, p. 17.

7. Ibid., p. 33.

8. Ibid., p. 37.

9. Martin, *The Kingdom of the Cults*, p. 247.

10. L. W. Rogers, *Elementary Theosophy* (Pasadena, CA: Theological University Press, 1950), pp. 23–25.

11. Helena Petrovna Blavatsky, *Isis Unveiled*, Vol. II. Theology, originally published in 1877 (Pasadena, CA: Theosophical University Press, 1976), pp. 341–342.

12. Ibid., p. 10.

13. Ibid., p. 10.

14. Steinbacher, *The Man, The Mysticism, The Murder*, p.29. Quotation from Helena Petrovna Blavatsky.

15. Ibid., p. 31.

16. Ibid., p. 31.

17. Helena Petrovna Blavatsky, *The Secret Doctrine*, Vol. II. Anthropogenesis, originally published in 1888 (Pasadena, CA: Theosophical University Press, 1988), p. 513.

18. Joseph J. Carr, *The Twisted Cross* (Lafayette, LA: Huntington House, 1985), p. 275.

2

Unveiling the Plan

"There is a way which seemeth right unto a man, but the end thereof are the ways of death." Proverbs 14:12

Unfortunately, after Helena Blavatsky's work ended, others were eager and ready to pick up the banner of spiritual deception and carry on. The next in line for a short time was Dr. Annie Besant (1847–1933). Drury's *Dictionary of Mysticism and the Occult* describes her as

> an English theosophist and social reformer who became president of the Theosophical Society in 1891. . . . Originally an intellectual force rather than a spiritual one, she experienced a dramatic illumination by making contact with the Tibetan Mahatma Master Morya and became his disciple. . . . Dr. Besant was a leader in the Co-Masonic movement and a prolific author.[1]

Although Annie Besant and her contemporary Theosophical allies were extremely influential, due to a series of scandals the Society's leadership underwent major changes. Eventually, Alice A. Bailey would emerge as the leading figure in this occult movement.

Alice Ann Bailey (1880–1949)

Of the major Theosophists, Alice Bailey was probably the most instrumental in developing the infrastructure and presenting the strategies of today's New Age movement. By the time she had finished her work in 1949, she had established a number of organizations, including Lucis Trust, World Goodwill (an organization linked to the leadership of the World Constitution and Parliament Association; see *En Route to Global Occupation*, pp. 77, 83), Triangles, the Arcane School, and the New Group of World Servers. She had also compiled twenty-four books, a total of 10,469 pages, most of which were allegedly written in a trance state through her spirit guide, known as Djwhal Khul, or the Tibetan.

Bailey founded Lucis Trust, the parent organization in 1922, under the name Lucifer Publishing Company (Exhibit C). Today it boasts a membership of approximately six thousand people. Some of the world's most renowned financial and political leaders have belonged to this organization, including individuals such as Robert McNamara, Donald Regan, Henry Kissinger, David Rockefeller, Paul Volker, and George Schultz. This is the same group of people that runs the Council on Foreign Relations, the elite organization responsible for founding the United Nations.

Not coincidentally, Lucis Trust was headquartered at United Nations Plaza for many years. It finally moved to a new location in the 1980s after receiving some unexpected adverse publicity. Its current address is on Wall Street in New York: 120 Wall Street, 24th Floor, New York, NY 10005.

Bailey, like her Theosophical predecessors, held extremely vicious anti-Christian and anti-Jewish views. Some of her most revealing statements on the subject appear in Appendix A: "The Tibetan's Views on Jews and Christians—As Channeled through Alice A. Bailey." Upon examining these writings one realizes that many of Alice's plans and predictions—all of which were made prior to 1949—are currently coming to fruition. She was a far more significant force in modern occultism, and in shaping the new world religion, than most people realize or would care to admit.

Alice Ann Bailey was born to a family with high social standing in Manchester, England, on June 6, 1880. Although her parents both died when she was young, she wanted for nothing and was raised by relatives in a protective environment. As a young woman, she spent a number of years in Christian work. However, in reading her autobiography, one senses that she "served" the Lord without ever really knowing him. It can be tiresome to work in Christian service if you don't have a personal relationship with Jesus Christ. Lacking the indwelling power of the Holy Spirit, Alice soon burned out.

All alone in a strange country with three young daughters after a difficult and painful marriage, she was ripe for the same deceptive spiritual forces that had used Helena Blavatsky in establishing the Theosophical Society. She was contacted by two English ladies who

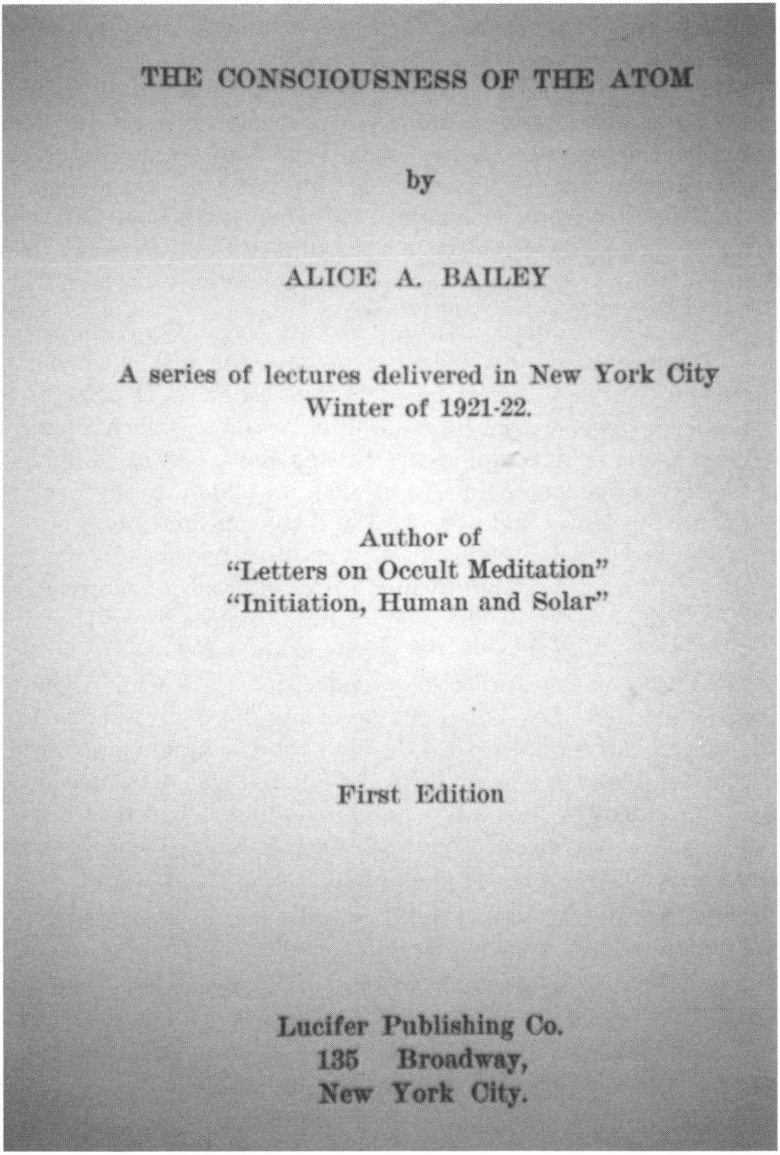

THE CONSCIOUSNESS OF THE ATOM

by

ALICE A. BAILEY

A series of lectures delivered in New York City
Winter of 1921-22.

Author of
"Letters on Occult Meditation"
"Initiation, Human and Solar"

First Edition

Lucifer Publishing Co.
135   Broadway,
New York City.

Exhibit C

Thanks to Willy Peterson, a researcher from the Kansas City area, we are able to prove that Lucifer Publishing Company did in fact exist under that name. Mr. Peterson has obtained an original copy of one of Alice Bailey's first books entitled The Consciousness of the Atom. *Notice that the name Lucifer Publishing Company appears on the title page pictured above. Bailey changed the name of the organization to Lucis Trust two years after the book's publication.*

lived in Pacific Grove, California, who originally came from the same social background in England. They were deeply involved in the occult teachings of Theosophy.

Bitter over an abusive marriage and confused about her purpose in life, Alice rejected Christ and began a metamorphosis that transformed her into a master teacher of the occult. She became one of the most receptive channels of demonic influence the world had yet known. After becoming acquainted with Blavatsky's book, *The Secret Doctrine*, Bailey described her spiritual seduction away from Christianity toward the pagan ideas of Theosophy:

> My mind woke up as I struggled with the presented ideas and sought to fit my own beliefs and the new concepts together. . . . I sat up in bed reading *The Secret Doctrine* at night and began to neglect reading my Bible, which I had been in the habit of doing. . . . I discovered, first of all, that there is a great and divine Plan. . . . I found that race after race of human beings had appeared and disappeared upon our planet and that each civilisation and culture had seen humanity step forward a little further upon the path of return to God. I discovered, for the second thing, that there are Those Who are responsible for the working out of that Plan and Who, step by step and stage by stage, have led mankind on down the centuries. I made the amazing discovery, amazing to me because I knew so little, that the teaching about this Path or this Plan was uniform, whether it was presented in the Occident or in the Orient, or whether it had emerged prior to the coming of Christ or afterwards. . . . I learnt that when I, in my orthodox days, talked about Christ and His Church I was really speaking of Christ and the planetary Hierarchy.[2]

After Alice Bailey rejected the Christ of Calvary, she was willing to embrace a different view of Christ presented by a supernatural occult belief system.* This doctrinal transformation allowed her to be used for thirty years as a channel for transmitting all that Satan desired humanity to accept as truth. She died on December 15, 1949,

---

* Technically, one could argue that only God is supernatural, with everything that God created—including angels (some of which became fallen angels)—being part of the natural realm, part of God's creation. However, for most people the term "supernatural" has widely come to be used as a direct reference "to any being or phenomena having to do with spiritual matters or relating to the spirit realm." Hence, my use of the term supernatural in this book should be understood to be synonymous with the latter definition.

just thirty days after she claimed the Tibetan had finished writing through her. Apparently, her usefulness to the hierarchy of evil had ended.

Before we take a closer look at what these "masters" taught, we need to understand who they claimed to be and how they were able to work so effectively through a human channel.

The Ascended Masters

In their own words, "The spiritual Hierarchy of the earth is the aggregate of those of humanity who have triumphed over matter, who have achieved the goal of self-mastery by the same path that individuals tread today. . . . They are no longer centered in the individual consciousness but have entered into the wider realization of the planetary group life. . . . They work according to plan and are known as 'The Custodians of the Plan.'"[3]

In other words, they claim to be a group of human beings who, having experienced the process of reincarnation, are now so highly evolved spiritually they have somehow gained the right, or ability, to watch over and guide the progress of humanity.

> The senior members of the Hierarchy are the masters of the Wisdom. A Master of the Wisdom is one who has through self-mastery achieved mastery over the whole field of human evolution. Having done so, his understanding is no longer limited or bounded by the human kingdom but also encompasses that kingdom of pure consciousness termed the kingdom of souls. . . . Because of an individual natural predisposition to certain lines of work, they each have a special contribution to make towards human progress in one of the seven major fields of world work: political, religious, educational, scientific, philosophical, psychological or economic.[4]

From the state of our world today, it looks as if these satanic spirits have been quite busy. However, their success seems to be more in creating chaos than in bringing about genuine progress and peace.

New Age occultists refer to these spirits by a variety of names, including: Spirit Guide, Guide, Instructor, Adviser, Director, Master, Enlightened One, Adept, Initiated Adept, Hierarchy of Initiates, Spiritual Hierarchy of the Earth, Planetary Hierarchy, the Hierarchy, Übermenschen (German), and Custodians of the Plan.

The most powerful or highest-ranking members of this so-called hierarchy are known as Ascended Masters of the Wisdom. More typically they are referred to as Masters of Wisdom, Ascended Masters, the Tibetan Masters, or simply, Masters. All are references to the same beings.

The generally accepted view among New Agers is that these beings are humans who have gone through numerous cycles of reincarnation, having evolved to a higher level of spiritual perfection each time. Some mystics believe that these creatures physically walk the earth, or have possessed bodies who can. They are supposedly concentrated in the region of the Himalayas (Tibet, Nepal, and western China) because this is alleged to be the part of the world that has been most receptive to their occult teachings. Others believe that these "more highly evolved beings" exist purely on a spiritual plane, being accessible only through occult meditation.

The "Tibetan Master," Djwhal Khul, allegedly explained his own existence directly to Alice Bailey. Bailey published his explanation in several of her books, including *The Externalisation of the Hierarchy* and *Esoteric Psychology I*. The Tibetan said:

> I am a brother of yours, who has travelled a little longer upon the Path than has the average student, and has therefore incurred greater responsibilities. I am one who has wrestled and fought his way into a greater measure of light than has the aspirant who will read this article. . . . I am not an old man, as age counts among the teachers, yet I am not young or inexperienced. My work is to teach and spread the knowledge of the Ageless Wisdom wherever I can find a response, and I have been doing this for many years.[5]

Regardless of which explanation New Agers accept, it is understood that these beings are able to communicate telepathically with those individuals who open themselves up to their "enlightened teachings." This is accomplished by going into a trance, or an altered state of consciousness, which apparently gives the Masters a license to "come through." My personal belief is that these entities are nothing more than demonic beings or fallen angels who can take on the appearance of humans to those who enter into altered states while practicing occult meditation.

I believe that at some point Theosophy's most advanced occultists, such as Blavatsky and Bailey, realized that these beings were actually demonic spirits serving Lucifer. There are too many references to Lucifer in their writings for anything else to have been the case. But whatever explanation occultists give for the existence of these beings, the impact is always the same: People are led away from

God's truth by accepting the false hope that they too can overcome death and be as gods.

Angels and Altered States

The belief in reincarnation is particularly useful in rationalizing the existence of these spiritual beings. However, individuals who do not believe in reincarnation may have the same "spiritual experiences" if they unwittingly open themselves up to the occult.

For example, an atheist who goes into an altered state while experimenting with self-hypnosis, not aware of the fact that he is involving himself in a spiritual rather than a scientific matter, may have a similar encounter. However, since he does not believe in the existence of a spirit realm, these beings are more likely to take on the appearance of extraterrestrials, leading him to believe that they are more highly evolved beings from other worlds who are able to communicate in ways he is not yet able to fully understand. In fact, such an explanation would seem to be acceptable to anyone believing in evolution and life on other planets, whether he is of an atheistic or a religious persuasion. I am personally aware of people working for NASA and the U.S. Department of Defense who claim to have had such experiences. Even U.S. President Bill Clinton has taken an interest in extraterrestrial life. (See the article "Clinton, Rockefeller and UFOs" in Appendix B.)

Those persons, on the other hand, who come from a Christian background but have naively allowed themselves to enter into altered states of consciousness may at some point be approached by beings posing as angels, or even as Mary or "the saints" in the case of Catholics. Such explanations would most likely by accepted by an individual who has some Christian family roots but who is not firmly grounded in the biblical faith. After all, who doesn't believe in angels? (Satan's angels usually don't volunteer the fact that they are "fallen" angels.)

It stands to reason that Satan's fallen angels, being spiritual entities with intelligence superior to humans, would know where we are most vulnerable for deception and would approach us in whatever form is most acceptable if a person opens himself up to the occult via altered states.

It is no coincidence that books on extraterrestrials and angels (fallen angels) are typically found in the New Age/Occult section of bookstores. In fact, angels seem to be the latest craze. As I am writing this book, the world appears to be enthralled with the subject. Some of the most popular books on these spirits, from a New Age perspective, have included *Your Guardian Angels*, by Linda Georgian (from the Psychic Friends Network), and *The Angels Within Us*, by John Randolph Price (author of *The Superbeings*).

The current best-selling New Age book on angels is *The Messengers*, written by Nick Bunick, a millionaire businessman who believes he is a reincarnation of the Apostle Paul. Bunick received many of his so-called "revelations" during hypnosis and past-life regression therapy sessions. A similar book, *Mary's Message to the World*, by Annie Kirkwood, supposedly conveys Mary's enlightened wisdom for humanity. It is currently very popular in Catholic circles.

To keep all of this in perspective, we must remember that God's holy angels outnumber Satan's angels two to one. However, God's angels cannot be summoned whenever people wish. Rather, we must pray to God (in the name of Jesus Christ), who decides their purpose, along with when and where to send them. Unlike fallen angels who crave attention, God's angels give the glory for their deeds to God alone, not drawing attention to themselves. These angels, more often than not, are invisible to the human eye, but we know by faith, according to God's Word, that they exist (Hebrews 13:2).

I should also mention that most individuals who go into a trance do not have supernatural encounters on their first attempt. In fact, some people may practice occult meditation for years without having such an experience. Perhaps they have a Christian parent or relative who is fervently praying for their protection and salvation. I do not know how else to account for the fact that some people have these experiences while others do not. However, based on personal testimonies, I do know that going into an altered state dramatically increases one's chances of having a demonic spiritual encounter. I also know that it is never God's will for humans to induce an altered state, since this is the first step of spiritism, a practice strictly forbidden in Scripture. In fact, altered states of consciousness and ritual magic are the two principle "gateways" to the occult. Deuteronomy 18:10–12 warns us against becoming involved in any kind of occult activity:

> Let no one be found among you who sacrifices his son or daughter in the fire, who practices divination or sorcery, interprets omens, engages in witchcraft, or casts spells, or who is a medium or spiritist or who consults the dead. Anyone who does these things is detestable to the Lord, and because of these detestable practices the Lord your God will drive out those nations before you. (NIV)

Additional passages forbidding occult practices include: Leviticus

19:26b, 31; 20:27; Deuteronomy 13:1–4; 1 Chronicles 10:13–14; Revelation 21:8; 22:15.

The following diagram depicts some of the most popular techniques for inducing altered states of consciousness. Please notice the active brain wave activity of a person in a normal, alert state of consciousness (beta waves) as opposed to the reduced brain activity of an individual in an altered state.

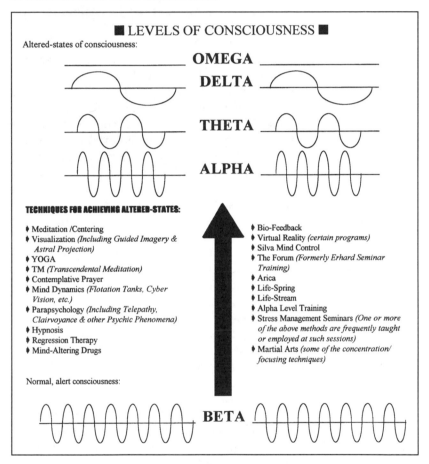

When a person is in a normal, alert state of consciousness he possesses the ability to discern or "screen out" deception by using logic and his ability to reason. However, going into an altered state strips away a person's defense mechanisms, allowing spirit entities to bypass the screening process to communicate directly with one's subconscious mind.

This is incredibly dangerous for obvious reasons. It can

potentially skew one's entire view of reality, planting untrue thoughts that may lead to unjustified actions or spiritual rebellion. If, for example, while in a trance you are told that you were molested by your parents as a child, upon coming out of the trance you would most likely believe this to have been the case, regardless of the actual truth.

In Western society hypnosis has become the most accepted technique for inducing a trance. Demonstrations by hypnotists have become so popular they are being performed in public.

A few years ago a prominent hypnotist came to my niece's high school to demonstrate his "powers." After carefully selecting several students to be his victims, he proceeded to put them "under." He had the entranced students crawl on the floor barking like dogs and displaying other uncharacteristic behavior, while the rest of the students laughed hysterically. It all seemed like such innocent fun.

Sometime later the same hypnotist returned to the same school to do another demonstration. Without any warning he spoke his "trigger" word. Those students in the audience whom he had hypnotized a few semesters earlier immediately fell into a trance, slumping over in their seats. None of these teenagers had seen or spoken with the hypnotist since his previous visit! At this point many of the students, especially those from Christian homes, became spooked and proceeded to inform their parents and community leaders of what had taken place. Fortunately, the Christians in this rural Indiana community banded together to make sure this hypnotist would not be back anytime soon.

The bottom line: Contrary to popular belief, hypnosis is not a science; it is a spiritual phenomenon that activates, or taps into, the forces of the occult. Hypnosis and all other methods of achieving altered states should be avoided at all costs!

The Plan of the Hierarchy

Jesus Christ is sometimes portrayed by the Hierarchy as being one of the ascended masters, or "Christs," but they present Buddha with this title as well, and place him in a superior position. (It should be pointed out that the Hierarchy considers "Christhood" a position that can be attained. Their reference to "Christ" therefore is not always to the person of Jesus.) They tell us that Christ came to show us the love of God, but Buddha came to bring us enlightenment. They go out of their way to suggest that the Bible has been misinterpreted and its true meaning lost through the centuries. But they claim this has never happened to the "sacred" scriptures of the East, so they can still be trusted.

The Hierarchy has revealed to occultists that the teachings intended to condition the world for the New Age (also known as the Aquarian Age or the New World Order), fall into three categories: (1) preparatory, given from 1875–1890, written down by Helena Petrovna Blavatsky; (2) intermediate, given from 1919–1949, written down by Alice Bailey; and (3) revelatory, emerging after 1975, to be revealed on a worldwide scale via the radio and television (meaning that some of the major film producers and script writers, as well as television personalities—whether they be politicians, religious leaders, or merely paid actors—would have to be tapped into the same occult forces and be privy to the same demonic "enlightenment" as their predecessors at the Theosophical Society).

A Return to Atlantis

At great sacrifice to themselves, occultists are told, the Hierarchy plans to some day enter again onto the physical plane of human affairs.

> Its appearance, expression and activity will be upon the physical plane for the first time since it withdrew into the subjective side of life and focussed itself on the mental plane (instead of the physical) during the days of ancient Atlantis and after the war between the Lords of the Shining Countenance and Lords of the Dark Face, as *The Secret Doctrine* calls it.[6]

Atlantis was supposedly the most advanced occult society in history and was destroyed by the Great Flood. According to occult legend, Atlantis existed at the helm of a world government based on ten geopolitical regions and containing elements of democracy. However, because of rampant and universal involvement of humans in the occult, fallen angels had been invoked to the point where they were apparently enabled to physically manifest themselves and even to have sexual relations with women, producing a part human/part supernatural offspring (parallel to the teaching of Genesis 6).

A growing number of Bible scholars believe that it was the widescale birth and multiplication of these supernatural human beings that precipitated God's intervention via the Flood. Some theologians also speculate that the spirits of these "hybrid beings" became known as demons after the Flood destroyed their physical bodies. Ever since, it is believed, these demonic entities have been seeking to inhabit or "possess" human bodies to once again be able to experience the full realm of senses unique to human life. Whatever the case, it is safe to conclude that demons as well as these hybrid beings were of satanic origin.

The Bible supports the fact that such beings dwelled for a time upon the earth. Genesis 6:4 states: "There were giants in the earth in those days; and also after that, when the sons of God came in unto the daughters of men, and they bare children to them, the same became mighty men which were of old, men of renown" (AKJV). *The Living Bible* translates the passage, "In those days, and even afterwards, when the evil beings from the spirit world were sexually involved with human women, their children became giants, of whom so many legends are told."

The *New International Version* refers to these "giants" as the Nephilim. *Unger's Bible Dictionary* offers the following explanation of Nephilim:

> The Nephilim are considered by many as giant demigods, the unnatural offspring of the "daughters of men" (mortal women) in cohabitation with the "sons of God" (angels). This utterly unnatural union, violating God's created orders of being, was such a shocking abnormality as to necessitate the worldwide judgement of the Flood.

The biblical reference here to "sons of God" has an obviously negative connotation, referring only to those angels who had rebelled against God. We know they were evil beings because their appearance is the last thing recorded in the Bible prior to God sending the Flood. God painfully realized that mankind had reached the point of no return. There had to be a new beginning to break man's infatuation with the occult and intermingling with these sexually perverted fallen angels (unclean spirits). By sparing Noah and his family, God allowed humanity to start again.

In spite of this lesson from history, our generation has witnessed an amazing resurgence of occult activity. People are once again invoking spirits in massive numbers. These developments cause Jesus' words to take on a more literal meaning. Concerning the time immediately preceding His return to put an end to this evil, Jesus said: "As it was in the days of Noah, so it will be at the coming of the Son of Man" (Matt. 24:37, NIV).

In spite of all the pointed warnings of Scripture, occult leaders are intent on taking the world back to the so-called "enlightened state" of Atlantis. Masonic leaders of the past, such as Manly P. Hall and Albert Pike, had much to say about Atlantis, the Flood, and the resurrection of occult activity after the Flood during the time of Nimrod and the Tower of Babel. Pike referred to Freemasonry as the "custodian" or special guardian of this secret occult history and knowledge. He also revealed the hidden agenda of his institution—the eventual "re-forming" of a Luciferic one-world government. (See pp. 121, 124, 144, and 145 of *En Route to Global Occupation.*) It is worth noting that Alice Bailey—like Blavatsky, Besant, and other top Theosophists—was a well known leader in the women's Masonic movement of her day.

Not long ago, the featured movie on a local cable network was *Cocoon.* For months this movie, which contains a mystical plot, aired almost daily. Its occult themes weren't difficult to spot, even though they were presented through a well-directed, entertaining plot. The main characters were from the legendary, sunken continent of Atlantis; they were beings of pure light; they had returned and held out the promise to humanity that if we would follow them, we would never die. "And the serpent said unto the woman, Ye shall not surely die" (Gen. 3:4).

Many films today have an underlying New Age theme. *Star Wars* teaches us about the "Force;" *E.T.* is a sweet little creature from another world; *The Never Ending Story* teaches children that they can create their own reality; the movie *Contact,* starring Jody Foster, promotes the view that extraterrestrials exist and guide us from one stage of life to the next—no heaven, no hell, only the comforting assurance of a continued existence in some higher form. Not surprisingly, this film was dedicated to the late New Age philosopher, Carl Sagan.

The Work of the Hierarchy

Lucis Trust describes the patient strategy of the occult Hierarchy.

> Hierarchical work is so quietly and smoothly developed and so effectively expressive of expanding human consciousness, that when it is well advanced it appears quite natural and reasonable. In the early stages, however, it is generally considered radical and even revolutionary and often meets determined opposition. . . . The Masters work slowly and with deliberation, free from any sense of speed, toward their objective, but they do have a time limit. . . . There are periods of major opportunity of which the Hierarchy takes advantage and this present period is one of major opportunity.[7]

The greatest time of opportunity for demonic forces was foretold two thousand years ago when Jesus described the tribulation of the last days to the Apostle John. "And the great dragon was cast out, that old serpent, called the Devil, and Satan, which deceiveth the whole world: he was cast out into the earth, and his angels were cast out with him. . . . Woe to the inhabiters of the earth and of the sea! for the devil is come down unto you, having great wrath, because he knoweth that he hath but a short time" (Rev. 12:9, 12b).

The Tibetan, Djwhal Khul, provides further details about the Hierarchy's strategy.

> Members of the Hierarchy do not as a rule intermingle largely with the public or walk the streets of our great cities. They work as I do from my retreat in the Himalayas, and from there I have influenced and helped far more people than I could possibly have reached had I walked daily in the midst of the noise and chaos of human affairs. . . . I reach this vast number of human beings through the medium of the books which I have written, through the groups which I have started and impulsed, such as Men of Goodwill [World Goodwill] and the Triangles, and through my disciples who talk and spread the truth as I have sought to present it.[8]

In a publication of Lucis Trust, this demonic spirit reveals, "In 1919, during the month of November, I made contact with Alice Bailey and asked her to do some writing for me."[9] In Bailey's book *The Unfinished Autobiography,* her husband, Foster Bailey, explains how this was done:

> Mrs. Bailey gets in touch with the Tibetan . . . he communicates with her telepathically. The information is given with very great rapidity and the detail teaching is impressed upon her consciousness with such clarity that she is enabled to write it down, so that no word is changed.[10]

Many psychologists have been fascinated with this form of writing and have sought to explain it in their own language. The psychologist Carl Jung, whom we will study next, believed that the Tibetan represented Bailey's personified "higher self." When the reality of Satan is denied, another explanation is always sought. The concept of the "higher self" is very popular today and is often used to explain away what is in reality demonic channeling.

Teachings of the Tibetan Master

There are four pillars upon which the New Age movement is built; the writings of the Tibetan through Alice Bailey reinforce all four. These pillars are evolution, reincarnation, astrology, and occult meditation.

Evolution

In her *Unfinished Autobiography* Alice states, "All evolutionary development in all fields is an expression of divinity and the static condition of theological interpretation is contrary to the great law of the universe, evolution."[11] Occultists and pantheists almost universally use the theory of evolution to explain away the existence of a personal Creator, suggesting that humanity is part of an evolving god-force.

Reincarnation

The entire concept of the occult Hierarchy is one of progress up the ladder of reincarnation until perfection is reached and one can move beyond the physical plane of existence. Of her own life, Alice states, "I know that I am today what many, many lives of experience and bitter lessons have made me."[12] Reincarnation is a demonic substitute for the resurrection promised to all who belong to Jesus Christ.

Astrology

One of the twenty-four books dictated by the Tibetan is *Esoteric Astrology*. A few of the chapter titles in this work are: The Zodiac and the Rays, The Sacred and Non-Sacred Planets, and The Nature of Esoteric Astrology. Seeking guidance through the stars and planets is Satan's substitute for the guidance of the Holy Spirit in a Christian's life.

Meditation

The Tibetan also placed great importance on the New Age practice of meditation. One of the books he wrote through Alice Bailey was called *Letters on Occult Meditation*. The concepts promoted in this book have completely permeated the popular culture of our day. In this work the Tibetan stated,

> One powerful stimulation to the mental rapport between East and West may be an increasing tendency for the Westerner to cultivate the science of meditation, long practiced in the East as an essential part of religious and spiritual experience. In this day and age, and as we enter into the mentally-oriented Age of Aquarius, with increasing numbers of men and women transferring from an emotional to a mental focus, the science of meditation as a mind training technique in concentration and invocation will become increasingly practiced in the West.[13]

Djwhal Khul went on to predict that the growing influence of the "science" of meditation will eventually lead to the establishing of schools of meditation under the guidance and instruction of initiated disciples. Today these schools are flourishing in major cities throughout the world. Transcendental Meditation, forms of yoga, and other "centering" techniques are now being taught to our children even in some public schools.

In the field of music, the latest trend is New Age "meditative" music, which is designed to facilitate listeners in achieving altered states of consciousness. Virtual reality is another new technology attempting to fuse science with spiritual/occult phenomena. Some of the programs now available can automatically induce altered states of consciousness (hypnotic trances) in individuals using them. Researchers are dubbing this technology "the LSD of the future."

Organized Meditation

One of the organizations established by Alice Bailey to promote the science of meditation is called Triangles. A triangle is a group of three people who link each day in thought for a few minutes of "creative meditation." Many of these triangles involve people in more than one country. During the time of this "linkage," they believe that they are invoking the energies of light and goodwill. They visualize these energies as circulating through the three focal points of each triangle and pouring out through the network of triangles surrounding the planet. At this time they repeat the Great Invocation, which we will discuss a bit later.

A paper put out by Lucis Trust makes the following statement about the concept of triangles:

> Men have the power, through focused united invocation to affect world events. The massed thought power of men and women of good-will can create a channel of communication between God and man through which spiritual energies can flow to heal and rebuild a troubled world. It is this power, properly used and directed, that can be humanity's "saving force."[14]

As we will see in a later chapter dealing with global unity, the plan of the Masters to involve the whole world in the use of mind power through occult meditation is being fulfilled.

One of the techniques widely used in New Age groups, and, increasingly, in our public schools, is that of focused, or meditative, visualization. Even some churches are teaching that it is important to visualize the answer to our prayers if we hope to get results. In other words, technique is everything! This is also the basis of most positive mental attitude seminars. The subtle message is that you can create your own reality through visualization.

When we consider what the Masters said through Alice Bailey more than fifty years ago it appears as if "their Plan" is rapidly falling into place: "The teaching on the New Discipleship includes the newer type of meditation emphasizing visualization and the use of creative imagination."[15]

The Bible has much to say about meditation, especially in the Psalms. We are to meditate (or reflect) upon God's Word, his goodness and mercy, and the wonders of his creation. The biblical concept of meditation means to think about or to dwell upon; it involves an active thought process. This is far different from Eastern meditation, which puts the mind into a passive, neutral trance state, open to any spiritual forces choosing to enter. There is much beauty to behold in God's creation, but visualizing what isn't there will not bring it into being. It does, however, open a door to demonic forces to work more directly in our lives. The initial results may seem to get us what we desire, but the long-term consequences are deadly, leading us away from a biblical faith in God.

Divine Energy

Along with redefining meditation, occultists have given new meanings to other words. Everywhere one turns in the New Age movement, one is confronted with terms such as "energy" and "vibrations." While these words are not new, they have been given new meanings. For example, to the Christian, God is Sovereign Creator, Father, and Redeemer. But to the New Age mind, God is the sum of all life; he is the "energy," or "life-force," that flows through all things. The Tibetan explains the significance of this energy:

> The esotericist of today is a practical worker. His illumined consciousness makes available to him a source of energy supply which is inexhaustible and which originates within the circulating energy of the One Life. He thus becomes a center of energy transmission between Hierarchy and humanity. . . . Spiritual impression has been interrupted and there has been interference with the divine circulatory flow. It is the task of disciples of the world to restore this flow and to stop this interference.[16]

Today, Lucis Trust continues to further the work of Djwhal Khul and the Hierarchy. They distribute volumes of material and run a flourishing correspondence school to educate disciples in the esoteric teachings of the Masters, including their ideas on meditation, energy, and how to invoke the appearance of "the Christ" and his New Order.

The Great Invocation

One of the most widely publicized writings of Lucis Trust is "The Great Invocation," allegedly given to Alice Bailey by Djwhal Khul as an invocatory prayer to "the Christ" and his Hierarchy. It has appeared as an advertisement in *Reader's Digest* and is included as a special insert in all of the Bailey books. The following is the most often used section of this invocation:

> From the point of Light within the Mind of God
> Let light stream forth into the minds of men.
> Let Light descend on Earth.
> From the point of Love within the Heart of God
> Let love stream forth into the hearts of men.
> May Christ return to Earth.
> From the centre where the Will of God is known
> Let purpose guide the little wills of men–
> The purpose which the Masters know and serve.
> From the centre which we call the race of men
> Let the Plan of Love and Light work out
> And may it seal the door where evil dwells.
> Let Light and Love and Power restore the Plan on Earth.[17]

This well-publicized section was given to Alice in 1945. A lesser-known section, given in 1940, is most revealing. Part of this section states:

> Come forth, O Mighty One.
> The hour of service of the Saving Force has now arrived.
> Let it be spread abroad, O Mighty One.
> Let Light and Love and Power and Death
> Fulfill the purpose of the Coming One.[18]

The "Mighty One" or "the Christ" mentioned here by Bailey is actually a reference to the future appearance of the Antichrist, who some Bible scholars believe may cleverly come in the name of Christ, pretending to be the prophesied Messiah. This event is described in 2 Thessalonians 2 and Revelation 13–14, as well as passages of Daniel and 1 John. The Antichrist, or Beast, will be Satan personified—just as Jesus Christ was God manifested in the flesh. He will briefly rule the world during a seven-year period known in the Bible as Daniel's seventieth week. The latter half of this seven-year period is called the Great Tribulation (Rev. 7:14, also 11–18), a three-and-one-half year

LUCIS TRUST

3 Whitehall Court	113 University Place, 11th Floor	1 Rue de Varembé (3è)
Suite 54	P.O. Box 722, Cooper Station	Case Postale 31
London SW1A 2EF	New York, NY 10276	1211 Geneva 20
England	Tel: (212) 982-8770	Switzerland

August 1995

Dear friend,

Since it was released in 1945, promotion of the Great Invocation has been a constant and central feature of the service activities of the Lucis Trust. For 50 years we have done what we can to ensure worldwide use of the Invocation, and to encourage friends and co-workers to see that it becomes more widely known. Looking ahead we are confident that its potency and usefulness will inspire increasing efforts to extend its availability to all parts of the world. For at a time of great spiritual crisis and opportunity such as we are experiencing today, the Great Invocation embodies in a powerful and simple formula the vision of humanity's higher potential. It expresses a vision of the oneness of life; it affirms the promise of the reappearance of the Christ; and stresses the reality of the Plan of love and light. However, in this letter we would like to focus attention on one particular idea of the Great Invocation--that it is through humanity itself that the Plan of love and light will work out.

In the writings of Alice Bailey the Plan, as it is presently sensed, is defined as *the production of a subjective synthesis in humanity and of a telepathic interplay which will annihilate time.* If telepathic interplay is considered as the sharing of creative mental energy towards a particular objective, we can recognise this occurrence--or at least imagine its presence--in the power generated by many minds when applied to the resolution of such world problems as armed conflicts, the eradication of diseases, and the improvement of education.

The goal of a subjective synthesis will not be achieved through the formation of a world state or government. It will be the result of a widespread global recognition of the unity of the whole and the interrelatedness of all parts of that whole. Only in this way can right human relationships, characterized by individual, group, and national unselfishness, be established.

Neither will a subjective synthesis inevitably lead to the founding of a world religion. Rather, it will evoke the recognition by people of goodwill everywhere that all formulations of truth and belief are only partial, formed to suit the psychology and conditions of a particular time and people. Adherence to a particular approach to the truth can nevertheless accommodate the realisation that other approaches and interpretations of divinity can be equally correct, forming other facets of a whole which is greater than humanity's present state of understanding can comprehend. This is the spiritual core of tolerance and it is significant that the United Nations has designated 1995 the Year for Tolerance.

In this year of Emergence/Impact on Public Consciousness, in the three-year cycle of the new group of world servers, an understanding of public consciousness as the essence of true citizenship is urgently needed by humanity. We can see the growth of this understanding in perhaps the single most outstanding characteristic of these later years of the 20th century: the fact that people of goodwill in their millions are taking responsibility for creating better relationships in every area of activity in their environment. Humanity is at a turning point in human affairs because it has gone so far from its true spiritual centre and sufficient human beings now search so deeply for a new direction. Today there are visionary people in every field of service who call for spiritual values to be given priority, and who challenge the materialistic world view with alternative possibilities that are life-enhancing and oriented towards a spiritual world view.

Exhibit D-1

This letter (continued overleaf), sent to Lucis Trust supporters in August 1995, explains the importance of "The Great Invocation." As stated, the wide scale promotion of this occult prayer continues to be a major activity of the organization. Notice how the letter speaks openly about the United Nations, "the Christ" and his hierarchy as if they are all part of the same spiritual agenda. This is no coincidence. The U.N., as we shall see, has a very strong "religious" motive behind its political and economic plans.

In the 1920's and 30's Alice Bailey gave emphasis to three words which she foresaw would eventually come to have special meaning to us. These three words didn't stand for much then but they certainly do now-- wholeness, interdependence, networks. The awakening sense of responsibility in humanity is demonstrating in particular through the realisations that these three words embody. We are starting to understand that if we want security, if we want a future based on freedom and liberty, then the gross inequalities in our world must be put right. We are recognising that we are interdependent and expressing that interdependence in the many networks dedicated to service.

A significant number of human beings now realise the fact that a better way of life for all people depends on the thoughts and actions of the individual. We can each make a difference. Our human kingdom is part of a great Chain of Being in which humanity has its place and its responsibilities, and it is through the intelligent thoughts, actions and cooperation of people of goodwill that love and wholeness manifest. This is true cooperation with the Christ through expression of the Christ principle which exists in every human heart. Through recognition of all workers on behalf of the Plan who share underlying values based on unity, love, and a true harmlessness, we can help to strengthen their hands. A meditation formula on Strengthening the Hands of the New Group of World Servers, which many throughout the world use on the day of the new moon, is enclosed with this mailing.

Other ways in which we can cooperate with the Christ and aid those who are actively working to prepare his way include the Special Meditations given in *Discipleship in the New Age, Vol.II*, pp. 22-31, by Alice Bailey, on Attracting Money for Hierarchical Purposes (used on Sunday) and on Reflective Meditation Upon Preparation for the Reappearance of the Christ (used on Thursday), with which many of you are already familiar. If you would like copies of these meditation outlines, please return the enclosed reply form.

The World Goodwill Symposium in all three centres will be held, as usual, in the lower interlude of the year. In New York the theme is **Let the Future Stand Revealed: Envisioning the World We Choose** (October 28th). In London the theme is **The United Nations and the Path to Unity and Right Relations** (November 18th). In Geneva the theme is **Religion and Tolerance** (November 25th). We hope you will be able to attend but whether you can be present or not, we count on your subjective support.

We also want you to know of the impending relocation of New York headquarters' offices on or about September 1, 1995 to a building with space designated for non-profit organizations and, therefore, exempted from real estate taxes. The new address will be 120 Wall Street, 24th floor, New York, New York 10005. After Labor Day please send all mail to our new address, although our current post office box will also be kept active until November.

In group service,

LUCIS TRUST

Exhibit D-2

time span immediately preceding the true physical return, or second coming, of Jesus Christ at the end of this age. During this period, the Antichrist will temporarily succeed at gaining the worship and allegiance of man, in defiance of God.

Thousands are already engaged in occult prayer invoking "the Christ" (Antichrist) to come and reign. In one publication of Lucis Trust, in a section entitled Deeper Meaning of the Great Invocation, disciples are told,

> The great Invocation if given widespread distribution, can be to the new world religion what the Lord's Prayer has been to Christianity. . . . First, the general public will regard it as a prayer to God Transcendent. They will not recognize Him yet as immanent in His creation. . . . Secondly, esotericists, aspirants and spiritually-minded people will have a deeper and more understanding approach. To them it will convey the recognition of Those Who stand subjectively behind

world affairs, the spiritual Directors of our life . . . an era of spiritual propaganda, engineered by disciples and carried forward by esotericists, will mature.[19]

There is a lesson here for the Christian. If the forces of darkness place such importance on this invocation or prayer, there must be great spiritual power involved. Unfortunately, it is being utilized to call forth the forces of evil. How much more should Christians be praying to their heavenly Father, with whom all power resides. How many of us are so busy with "Christian service" that we never find time to be alone with God? The Scriptures tell us that we are in a spiritual battle and that "the weapons of our warfare are not carnal, but mighty through God to the pulling down of strong holds" (2 Cor. 10:4). The greatest of these weapons is prayer!

Determine to Do Right

Everyone reading this book is urged to take a stand against the dangerous false teachings of the occult. Exposing anti-Jewish and anti-Christian teachings and actions, such as those promoted by Alice Bailey and Lucis Trust, should be a part of every Christian's life. It is because so few people speak out to warn others that our adversary is able to achieve success today. We should all be disturbed by the fact that many of the preceding views have gained widespread acceptance, even in some Christian circles.

Jesus warned us that times such as these would come prior to His return:

. And as [Jesus] sat upon the mount of Olives, the disciples came unto him privately, saying, Tell us, when shall these things be? and what shall be the sign of thy coming, and of the end of the world? And Jesus answered and said unto them, Take heed that no man deceive you. For many shall come in my name, saying, I am Christ; and shall deceive many. . . . And then shall many be offended, and shall betray one another, and shall hate one another. And many false prophets shall rise, and shall deceive many. (Matt. 24:3-5, 10–11)

Even though these things have been prophesied to occur, we should not passively sit back and do nothing. To the contrary, we must expose the works of darkness while sharing the hope we have in Jesus Christ with everyone who is willing to listen, even if this constitutes only a minority of the world's people.

The fact that Jesus prophesied these events means only that He knew these evil times would eventually come. It does not mean that He condones this evil, nor does it mean He wants his people to help bring this evil about by becoming apathetic. Ephesians 5:11 commands us to "have no fellowship with the unfruitful works of darkness, but rather reprove them."

The day may soon come when Christians will need to lay down their lives for their faith. But regardless of the cost, we must continue to raise a standard, proclaiming the truth of Jesus Christ. The eternity of billions hangs in the balance.

Notes

1. Nevill Drury, *Dictionary of Mysticism and the Occult* (San Francisco: Harper & Row, 1985), p. 28.

2. Alice A. Bailey, *The Unfinished Autobiography* (New York: Lucis Trust, 1951), pp. 137–140.

3. *The Spiritual Hierarchy* (New York: World Goodwill, booklet), pp. 3–4.

4. Ibid., p. 4.

5. Alice A. Bailey, *The Externalisation of the Hierarchy* (New York: Lucis Trust, 1957), p. vii. This statement was made by the Tibetan in August 1934.

6. Ibid., p. 519.

7. *The Spiritual Hierarchy*, pp. 9–10.

8. Bailey, *The Externalisation of the Hierarchy*, p. 682.

9. Alice A. Bailey, *My Work by the Tibetan* (New York: Lucis Trust, 1943), p. 2.

10. Bailey, *The Unfinished Autobiography*, p. 259.

11. Ibid., p. 123.

12. Ibid., p. 91.

13. Alice A. Bailey, *Letters on Occult Meditation*, as quoted in *Thirty Years Work, The Books of Alice A. Bailey and the Tibetan Master Djwhal Khul* (New York: Lucis Trust, booklet), p. 15.

14. *World Service Through the Power of Thought* (New York: Lucis Trust, booklet).

15. *The Tibetan Master's Work* (New York: The Arcane School, World Goodwill, booklet), pp. 3–4.

16. *Thirty Years Work, The Books of Alice A. Bailey and the Tibetan Master Djwhal Khul* (New York: Lucis Trust, booklet), p. 17.

17. Bailey, *The Externalisation of the Hierarchy*, p. v.

18. Ibid., p. v.

19. Compiled by Wilma Leftwich, *A Profile of a Tax-Exempt Foundation* (New York: Lucis Trust, report), p. 81.

3

Presenting Occultism as a Science

"Where is the wise man? Where is the scholar? Where is the philosopher of this age? Has not God made foolish the wisdom of the world?" 1 Corinthians 1:20 (NIV)

"See to it that no one takes you captive through hollow and deceptive philosophy, which depends on human tradition and the basic principles of this world rather than on Christ." Colossians 2:8 (NIV)

Although the writings of Blavatsky and Bailey may convey the appearance of scholarly endeavors and to this day are accepted by some of the world's most powerful elite, the majority of the followers of these occult traditions have not been among the highly educated in the intellectual community. However, while these foundation stones for the new occult order were being put in place, the groundwork was simultaneously being laid in the academic world. The next two people we will examine were scholars who not only believed themselves to be theologians of sorts, but who were also involved in the sciences. The followers of Carl G. Jung and Pierre Teilhard de Chardin come from among the educated. Their disciples are among the most highly respected in the fields of psychology and philosophy and include leaders from the mainstream "academic" churches.

In *The Aquarian Conspiracy*, a best-selling book endorsing the New Age movement, author Marilyn Ferguson took a survey of the practices and beliefs of top New Agers. When asked to name those individuals whose ideas had influenced them the most—either through personal contact or written materials—the two most often named were Carl Jung and Teilhard Chardin.[1] In addition, Ferguson noted that 81 percent of those responding were no longer active in the religion of their childhood. This rejection of one's childhood faith also holds true for most of the individuals we are studying in these first few chapters, including the famous psychologist, Carl Jung.

Carl Gustav Jung (1875–1961)

Carl G. Jung was born in Kesswil, a small Swiss village on Lake Constance, on July 26, 1875, the same year that Helena Blavatsky started the Theosophical Society. As is so often the case, when Satan finds a willing vessel for furthering his web of deception, there is evidence of occult activity in that person's family background. Carl Jung was no exception.

Jung reported that his maternal grandfather, who was the vicar of Kesswil, had "second sight" and carried on lively conversations with the dead—although he was a minister. The vicar always believed himself to be surrounded by ghosts. Jung explains, "My mother often told me how she had to sit behind him while he wrote his sermons because he could not bear [to have] ghosts pass behind him while he was studying. The presence of a living human being at his back frightened them away!"[2]

It seems that this inclination toward the paranormal was passed on to Carl's mother. In his autobiography, *Memories, Dreams, Reflections*, Carl relates that at night the atmosphere in his parents' house would thicken.

> From the door to my mother's room came a frightening influence. At night Mother was strange and mysterious. One night I saw coming from her door a faintly luminous indefinite figure whose head detached itself from the neck and floated along in front of it, in the air like a little moon.[3]

In spite of all this, or possibly because of it, Jung felt close to his mother. He felt that she was rooted in a deep invisible spiritual ground that had nothing to do with the Christian faith. That ground seemed more connected to the things of nature such as animals, trees, meadows and running waters. He felt a close affinity for all of this in his own life. Later Jung admitted that he never realized how pagan this foundation was. He would spend many hours sitting on a large rock behind his house, and at times would have trouble distinguishing if he was the boy sitting on the rock or the rock being sat upon by the boy. In short, he felt an unusual oneness with nature.

One day his mother read to him from a richly illustrated children's book that contained accounts of exotic religions, including that of the Hindus. There were illustrations of the Hindu gods—Brahma, Vishnu, and Shiva—which were for him an inexhaustible source of interest. He would return to these pictures repeatedly.

His understanding of Jesus became distorted at an early age. He associated Jesus with death and the men in black coats and top hats who put people in a box in the ground. His preacher-father told him that the Lord Jesus had taken them unto himself. Carl also associated Jesus with a Jesuit priest who once had frightened him.

Carl's views of Jesus were affected in a more personal way by a strange dream he had when he was a boy. It was an alluring dream of an occult underground temple with a throne room and erotic symbolism. Apparently, this mystical dream portrayed Jesus Christ in a negative light, as one would expect. In his autobiography, Carl relates the importance of this dream.

> Through this childhood dream I was initiated into the secrets of the earth. What happened then was a kind of burial in the earth, and many years were to pass before I came out again. Today I know that it happened in order to bring the greatest possible amount of light into the darkness. It was an initiation into the realm of darkness. My intellectual life had its unconscious beginnings at that time.[4]

John's Gospel tells us there is no darkness associated with Jesus, only light: "In him was life; and the life was the light of men. And the light shineth in darkness; and the darkness comprehended it not. . . . And this is the condemnation, that light is come into the world, and men loved darkness rather than light, because their deeds were evil" (John 1:4–5; 3:19). Clearly, Jung's experience was not from God, but from Satan.

Rejection of Christianity

Perhaps because of his family's spiritual hypocrisy, Jung finally rejected the established doctrines of Christianity for a mystical religion based upon experience. He often stated that he does not believe, he only knows, based upon his own experience. He gained this experience from a life lived in the internal regions of his own so-called psyche. His internal world of dreams and visions was always more real to him than the external world of objective reality.

Carl despised the Christianity of his father. He considered his father to be a weak and tragic failure who preached a shallow message about the love and grace of God. His rebellion sent him in search of a new belief system that could explain his existence. But Carl's new found religion represented a cataclysmic shift from one of revealed biblical truth to one of myth, from Christianity to psychology, and from the conscious to the unconscious.

The Bible tells us that God's household is "built on the foundation of the apostles and prophets, with Christ Jesus himself as the chief cornerstone" (Eph. 2:20, NIV). Having rejected that cornerstone, Carl Jung built his philosophy upon a faulty foundation from the beginning. Tragically, thousands of people today study his teachings with almost a religious fervor and reverence. Most major cities have Friends of Jung study groups, going by that name or some other, and Jungian analysts can be visited to help one "explore one's inner depths."

The New Age movement, like Jung, bases its "spiritual truth" upon personal experience, not upon established fact and biblical truth. This experience is gained from "going within." Carl Jung, more than anyone else, created the atmosphere for this concept to flourish. In a city close to where I live the local Jungian analyst had at one point been the pastor of a Christian church. However, after studying for five years at the Carl Jung Institute in Switzerland—which one biographer refers to as "the mystical body of Carl Jung"—this young pastor abandoned his faith to join Jung in the subjective world within.

Not surprisingly, there are at least twelve references to Carl Jung and his concepts in Nevill Drury's *Dictionary of Mysticism and the Occult*, confirming his involvement in the occult. On page 137 of that dictionary, Drury states, "In his later years, Jung became absorbed with ancient cosmologies and spent a considerable time analyzing Gnostic, alchemical, and mystical systems of thought. He provided commentaries for Richard Wilhelm's translations of the *I Ching*.[5]

Jung's Personal Theology

For a period of about six years, Jung worked closely with Sigmund Freud. Although the works of Freud are more widely known (mainly because of his ideas on human sexuality), Carl Jung had the most influence on intellectuals embracing mysticism. His ideas and teachings on the collective unconscious, the archetypes, and their symbolism paved a broad path leading people away from the beauty and simplicity of God's created order and the Bible.

The Jungian concept of the collective unconscious holds that each individual is like an island, joined together by a sort of underwater continent of unconscious thought. Picture a hand with the tips of the

Following in the tradition of Carl Jung, the C.G. Jung Bookstore promotes a variety of materials on the occult—ranging from alchemy to astrology. Exhibits E-1 and E-2 depict the front cover and title page of the store's catalogue, while Exhibits E-3 and E-4 list some of the books available through the catalogue's occult section. Other occult materials offered in the catalogue—but not shown here—include books and videos on Eastern Mysticism (Buddhism, Kundalini Yoga, Taoism, etc.), Kabbalism, Angels/Spirit Guides, Dream Studies, Healing, Mother Goddess Fertility Rites, "Snake Charm," and the Spiritual and Magical Powers of Animals.

"Crow Seeking the advice of a master"   Kirsten-Daiensai

C. G. Jung Bookstore
of Los Angeles

WINTER REVIEW 1996-1997

Exhibit E-1

C.G. Jung Bookstore

10349 W. Pico Blvd., Los Angeles, CA 90064
PHONE (310) 556-1196 · FAX (310) 556-2290
e-mail: junginla@earthlink.net
web site: http:\\websites.earthlink.net/~junginla

HOURS

12 noon – 5 PM   Monday – Saturday
(Also, one half-hour before lectures held at the Institute)

OVER 1,000 TITLES

Alchemy, Archetypes, Art Therapy, Body/Mind Healing, Death/Aging, Dreams, Folklore/Fairytales, Gay/Lesbian Studies, General Psychology, Journals, Men's and Women's Issues, Myths, Relationships, Religion, Sandplay, Social Issues, and Symbols.

LECTURES ON TAPE

We offer a wide selection of audio tapes of lectures given under the auspices of the C. G. Jung Institute, the Analytical Psychology Club of Los Angeles, the C. G. Jung Bookstore, and *Psychological Perspectives*. In addition we offer a variety of audio tapes by notable speakers, both public and professional.

GIFT CERTIFICATES

Our mail order form may be used for gift certificate purchases.

ORDERING

See the last page for order form. Order by mail, phone, fax, or e-mail and use your Mastercard, Visa, American Express, or Discover Cards. We ship world-wide – U.S. mail, UPS, or Federal Express.

Reviews by Greg Reyna and Bobbie Yow. Desktop publishing by Charlene Sieg.

Exhibit E-2

Alchemy, Astrology & Occult Matters

Through examples such as the lives of Buddha, St. Anthony and Jesus and classic stories and fairytales, Wieland-Burston describes the space we need to develop as individuals and yet not become separated from and closed off to the world.

192 pages, paper $12.95

Alchemy,
Astrology &
Occult Matters

BRADFORD, ROBERT
I Ching: The Bradford Professional Deck emulates the statistical probabilities of tossing the coins with the use of cards. Easy to learn and use, this deck is an ideal method of carrying the I Ching with you at all times. Comes with a small instruction booklet. The optional video clearly demonstrates the use of the deck.

24 minutes, video $22.00
misc $40.00

DE PASCALIS, ANDREA
Alchemy: The Golden Art gives an account of the vicissitudes of alchemy's fascinating quest, the historical figures who have marked its progress, and the theories which have been constructed over the centuries. Richly illustrated with blackand-white and color plates, Alchemy is an historical account that is authoritative and eminently readable.

192 pages, cloth $32.50

GRASSE, RAY
The Waking Dream: Unlocking the Symbolic Languag of Our Lives presents and develops the insights of a network of ideas and laws that have historically attempted to explain the hidden workings of reality. This "symbolist" worldview is drawn from the oral and written teachings of esoteric schools from around the world.

315 pages, paper $16.00

GREENE, LIZ
The Astrological Neptune & the Quest for Redemption explores Neptunian themes in myth, literature, religion, politics and fashion. Liz Greene, a Jungian analyst and professional astrologer, confronts the spectrum of opposites which Neptune symbolizes, from the extremes of psychic and physical disintegration to the life-transforming light of inner revelation.

506 pages, cloth $30.00

GUTTMAN, A. & JOHNSON, K.
Mythic Astrology: Archetypal Powers in the Horoscope allows the reader to explore the connection between mythology and astrology in depth-without having a background in either. The authors show how the

4

characteristics of the gods and goddesses transformed into the meanings associated with particular planets and signs and develop a way to gain a deeper and more spiritual perspective on the art of astrology.

384 pages, paper $17.95

IDEMON, RICHARD
The Magic Thread: Astrological Chart Interpretation using Depth Psychology is an innovative presentation synthesizing depth psychology, myth, archetypal imagery, dreams and astrology within the framework of a symbolic labyrinth. Idemon discusses the dominant and inferior functions, shadow issues, death and polarities and incest as these issues unwind within the birth chart.

263 pages, paper $14.95

KOFF-CHAPIN, DEBORAH
Soul Cards is an exquisite set of 60 full-color cards and a 36 page manual which guides participants into a living relationship with the images through silent contemplation, dream incubation, visualization and story-telling. Dynamic instructions for using the cards with another person are included.

cloth $22.95

MOOKERJEE, A. & M.
The Tantric Way deals with the astronomy, astrology, alchemy and cosmology in tantrism. Ajit and Khanna Mookerjee discuss the different viewpoints of "left-hand" and "right-hand" tantrism and their respective attitudes toward human sexuality in ritual. 148 illustrations, 18 in color.

208 pages, paper $16.95

Arts, Art Therapy & Sandplay

BAYLES, D. & ORLAND, T.
Art & Fear: Observations on the Perils (& Rewards) of Artwork grapples with the daily problems and uncertainties of the artist in the real world. In exploring the way art gets made, a new understanding arises of the reasons it often doesn't get made, which can create an awareness of the artists' need to commit their future to their own hands.

122 pages, paper $10.95

CAMERON, JULIA
The Vein of Gold: A Journey to Your Creative Heart draws from extensive artistic and teaching experience to lead readers toward ever-widening creative horizons. The author includes material on the creative process and more than one-hundred imaginative, involving and energizing tasks leading to inner play.

304 pages, cloth $23.95

5

fingers above water, conversing and interacting with each other. Yet, under the surface of the water, they are really connected to the palm of the hand, and thus, to each other. Each person, Jung believed, has his own personal forgotten thoughts and experiences, but there is a collective unconscious mind that belongs to the entire race. Jung sometimes referred to the collective unconscious as the "psychic residue of human evolutionary development."

For Jung, the archetypes lie within the collective unconscious. An archetype, according to Jung, is a universal thought form or predisposition to perceive the world in certain ways. These archetypes appear to individuals in personified or symbolized pictorial form through dreams, myths, art, and ritual. He believed that they represented the total latent potentiality of the psyche. So when people get in touch with them, they go beyond developing their individual potentialities and become incorporated into the eternal cosmic process. Some of Jung's archetypes are birth, death, magic, the hero, God, the demon, and the earth mother. Notice that Jung's psychology reduces God to a mere archetypal image, a type of universal myth as opposed to the Bible's revelation of God as our Creator and Judge.

This concept is explained in a popular college textbook on psychology called *Personality Theories: An Introduction.*

> Whether or not God exists is not a question that Jung tried to answer. That which has no effect on us might as well not exist. Analytical psychology posits the existence of the archetypal God image—not God. Insofar as the archetype of God has a demonstrably clear effect on us, God is a psychic fact and a useful concept in our psychology. . . . Even more, attuning oneself to one's unconscious forces is a religious experience entailing acceptance of God. To be sure, the God that is accepted may not be the traditional deity of theism; rather, it is an indwelling god, a natural spirit within the universal psyche of man.[6]

Is it any wonder that so many young people go off to college and find their faith challenged, and often shattered, by this pseudo-academic atmosphere? In reality, modern psychology is a bankrupt "religion" with no real capacity for helping people. Under the guise of psychology, occult concepts have gained acceptance as being legitimate scientific principles. Hence, occultism is increasingly moving forward in the name of psychology and the human sciences.

Personality Theories, goes on to say:

> Jung's ideas have appealed to those who are discontent with western society and its modes of exploration and who seek to

expand their self-understanding by studying Eastern thought with its emphasis on introspection and experience. . . . His concept of God as revealing himself through the collective unconscious is particularly attractive to theologians who seek a more relevant articulation of traditional theistic concepts. . . . Jung's thinking compliments the recent interest in the East.[7]

In line with Eastern mysticism, Carl Jung believed that dreams were of great significance and based much of his teaching on the interpretation of his own dreams. Today, Jungian analysts train their students to keep dream journals and seek guidance for their lives from those dreams. God can certainly speak through spiritual dreams as He did when He told Joseph to take Mary as his wife. However, to believe that every dream is a form of spiritual guidance for one's life is to stand on shaky ground indeed.

Listen to the words of the prophet Jeremiah concerning false prophets and the relating of dreams: "I have heard what the prophets said, that prophesy lies in my name, saying, I have dreamed, I have dreamed. How long shall this be in the heart of the prophets that prophesy lies? yea, they are prophets of the deceit of their own heart. . . . Behold, I am against them that prophesy false dreams, saith the Lord, and do tell them, and cause my people to err by their lies, and by their lightness" (Jer. 23:25–26, 32a).

A friend of mine once sat in the sanctuary of a local Christian church, which displayed a beautiful banner saying "Worthy is the Lamb." Yet, there he heard the occult glorified, ESP explained in a favorable light, and demon possession passed off as only another form of spiritual guidance—representing someone's mind being taken over by an alien being. All of this was done by a specialist in Jungian psychology who was flown in from across the country for a special weekend seminar—with the full approval of the pastor.

Was Carl Jung a false prophet, and are his disciples being led astray into occult New Age thinking? The words of Jeremiah provide the answer. "For both prophet and priest are profane; yea, in my house have I found their wickedness, saith the Lord. . . . I have not sent these prophets, yet they ran: I have not spoken to them, yet they prophesied. But if they had stood in my counsel, and had caused my people to hear my words, then they should have turned them from their evil way, and from the evil of their doings" (Jer. 23:11, 21–22).

Pierre Teilhard de Chardin (1881–1955)

Another "thinker" who has been practically immortalized by New Age political and religious leaders is Pierre Teilhard de Chardin. His concepts and teachings run like a continuous thread through the tapestry of New Age spirituality. Everywhere we turn, we see the imprint of his thinking on the minds of individuals who have rejected the God of the Bible for a god who is nothing more than impersonal energy flowing through the universe. Amazingly, the circle of Chardin's influence has continued to expand, even after his death. Chardin wrote a number of widely read volumes; many of his disciples have written best-selling books as well.

An Obsession with Evolution

Pierre Teilhard de Chardin was born on May 1, 1881, in Sarcenat, France. He came from a traditional Catholic family, the fourth of eleven children. His father, Emmanuel, took pleasure in teaching his children how to understand and appreciate natural history. So it is easy to understand how Teilhard became interested in the study of geology at an early age.

While there is nothing wrong with studying geology, most writers of geology textbooks seem to be intent on promoting the theory of evolution. As one who studied geology in high school, I can personally attest to this fact. There has been no more successful strategy of Satan in preparing our world for the coming great delusion than establishing the concept of evolution in the minds of men.

Evolution became the passion of Teilhard's life. Because of his eventual far-reaching influence, a growing number of unprepared Christian leaders would conform and subjugate themselves to this supreme belief. As a Jesuit priest, Teilhard would always pursue his first love, which was the blending of the physical and spiritual worlds under the banner of evolution.

Chardin was a pantheist, despite his protests to the contrary. As mentioned earlier, a pantheist is one who sees the universe as the one and only reality and calls this God. According to this theology, the earth itself, as well as man, is divine. Many of Chardin's statements reflected this view of existence. He spoke about loving, adoring, and serving the earth in the same way many Christians would speak about loving God. He once said, "I want to love Christ with all my strength in the very act of loving the universe. . . . Besides communion with the earth, is there not also communion with God in and through the earth?"[8]

* * * * *

The following quotes from *The Making of a Mind* by Teilhard de Chardin demonstrate Chardin's futile attempts to blend pantheism and Christianity. They present his belief that man and nature are divine and together compose Christ (God).[9]

Sometimes I feel that my heart is full of things that should be said about "mighty Nature," about the meaning and the reality of her appeal and of her magic. . . . Meanwhile I am making notes and I am doing all I can to open up my mind to contact with God. (p. 91)

. . . when I have the chance to collect myself a little and think and pray I become aware of the growing light of this truth, so simple and yet so infinitely rich and fruitful, that God is all. (p. 84)

For me the real earth is that chosen part of the universe, still almost universally dispersed and in course of gradual segregation, but which is little by little taking on body and form in Christ. (p. 165)

. . . the incommunicable beauty and individual shade of every soul is not alien to Christ and is found again in perfection in Christ: for Christ is not only the supremely perfect individuality that has passed through our human society. He is also, in his mystical organism, the plenitude and form—fully worked out—of the *chosen* cosmos, so much so, that the beauties and individual gradations of souls acquire their *definitive significance* only as the traits and touches that make up the celestial visage of the great and unique reality. It is thus that we complete Christ. . . . One by one, through human effort aided by God, souls are distilled. . . . Each has its own exquisite value. In that lies the meaning of human work, of the desperate search to master the secrets and energies (good and bad) of the world: to perfect, to purify, psychic life. (pp. 180–181)

* * * * *

Unfortunately, the Christ Teilhard Chardin loved was not the Christ of the Gospels, but one of his own making. For him, Christ had to fit into the theory of evolution. He attempted to "pan-christify" the universe by stating that Christ and the universe formed a mysterious compound, which he named the Christ-Universal. To Teilhard, the world represented Christ's body and soul. In *The Future of Man* he says,

We cannot continue to love Christ without discovering Him more and more. The maturing of a collective consciousness accompanied by numerical expansion: these are two aspects inseparably linked in the historical unfolding of the Incarnation. . . . Without the process of biological evolution, which produced the human brain, there would be no sanctified souls; and similarly, without the evolution of collective thought, through which alone the plenitude of human consciousness can be attained on earth, how can there be a consummated Christ?"[10]

According to Teilhard's concept of evolution, in ages past God had not evolved enough to express himself through human consciousness. During the prehistoric period, for example, God could only express himself through animals. To put it differently, Chardin's process of evolution includes man becoming conscious of who he is— "God." And Christ, in this scheme of things, is incarnate in the entire universe.

> Christ is above all "the God of Evolution." He is its center, its Alpha and Omega, beginning and end. He is the Omega Point, the supreme summit of the evolutionary movement in which he is immersed and which super-animates. As "God the Evolver," he is the director, the leader, the cause and mover of evolution. Christ also is evolving into a Super-Christ. Humanity is the highest phase so far of evolution, but evolution is beginning to change into a Super-Humanity, which at its peak becomes the Omega Point.[11]

Teilhard Chardin's theology diverged so far from biblical teaching that in 1957 the Catholic Holy Office, in a surprise move, decreed that his works must be withdrawn from libraries, seminaries, and religious institutions. In 1962, the office issued a further warning to bishops, rectors of seminaries, and presidents of universities to protect the minds of the faithful against the heresies of Chardin's teachings. However, this did not put an end to the influence of this French priest-paleontologist-philosopher. Today, his pantheistic ideas on evolution have gained acceptance among many Catholic leaders, including Pope John Paul II. Chardin is being hailed in progressive Catholic circles as a great religious thinker and a scientific genius.

However, his influence goes far beyond Catholic circles as evidenced by the fact that he is the most widely read author in the New Age movement. In our local New Age bookstore, there is a display of bookmarks near the cash register with ten famous occult leaders pictured on them. Chardin is one of them. And in *The Aquarian Conspiracy*, arguably the most important and comprehensive modern work on the New Age movement written by a New Ager, there are at least sixteen different references to Pierre Teilhard de Chardin.

A Political Influence

Chardin has made his presence felt in American politics as well. Mario Cuomo, the former Democratic governor of New York, reads Chardin's works and gives copies of his books as gifts to interested friends. Cuomo was at one time considered to be a leading contender for the U.S. presidency and remains very active on the political scene.

Trilateralist Zbigniew Brzezinski is another admirer of Chardin. In his book, *Between Two Ages*, he quotes Chardin as saying, "Monstrous as it is, is not modern totalitarianism really the distortion of something magnificent, and thus quite near to the truth?"[12] Brzezinski served for many years as the National Security Adviser to President Jimmy Carter and continues to be a powerful voice in the pro-U.N./world government lobby.

Robert Muller, the New Age lawyer-economist and former U.N. assistant secretary-general, became a follower of Chardin through his associations at the United Nations. In his book, *New Genesis—Shaping a Global Spirituality*, he tells of his spiritual growth in a chapter entitled "My Five Teilhardian Enlightenments." In it he states, "Now after a third of a century of service with the U.N. I can say unequivocally that much of what I have observed in the world bears out the all-encompassing, global, forward-looking philosophy of Teilhard de Chardin."[13] Muller claims that Teilhard viewed the U.N. as the institutional embodiment of his vision.

Chardin has influenced U.S. Vice President Al Gore as well. In his popular book, *Earth in the Balance: Ecology and the Human Spirit*, Gore remarks,

> The religious ethic of stewardship is indeed harder to accept if one believes the world is in danger of being destroyed—by either God or humankind. This point was made by the Catholic theologian Teilhard de Chardin when he said, "The fate of mankind, as well as of religion, depends upon the emergence of a new faith in the future." Armed with such a faith, we might find it possible to resanctify the earth, identify it as God's creation, and accept our responsibility to protect and defend it.[14]

Although Gore is a professing Baptist, his beliefs draw heavily upon Chardinian philosophy and are more in line with pantheism than Christianity.

These are just a few of the powerful world figures who have been influenced by Chardin's teachings. He has had a profound impact on hundreds of politicians from Europe and the Third World.

Meanwhile, the United Nations has practically enshrined his beliefs, adopting many of them as its own.

Steeped in Pantheism

While Carl Jung conceived his ideas of the collective unconscious or "race mind" by going within to the underground caverns of his own psyche, Chardin looked to the outside world to formulate a similar theology. He looked at people, history, and the environment around him and discovered what he called the "noospere." This was his name for a vast global envelope of consciousness and shared thought that he believed surrounded the planet. According to Jung and Chardin, we are not unique individuals responsible for our own independent thoughts and choices, nor are we accountable to a personal God for those thoughts and choices. Rather, we are all part of a vast living, evolving organism—a global brain—that encompasses all of humanity and is God. This is the very essence of pantheistic religion.

Chardin stubbornly sought to merge his views of an evolving "Christ" with his ideas of a "sacred earth." Christian doctrine suffered greatly as a consequence. The author of Hebrews made it clear that Christ is not an evolving entity. Hebrews 13:8 proclaims that Jesus Christ is "the same yesterday, and to day, and for ever."

Regarding the concept of a sacred earth, there are many beautiful passages in the Bible that praise God for the wonders of His creation and the beauty of the earth. But these passages always direct our attention to God as the source of creative power. Chardin's reverence, on the other hand, was directed toward the earth itself. He turned created matter into an idol, and then worshipped that idol. His philosophy worships the created— not the Creator.

Interestingly, any study of witchcraft or magic (white or black) will show the connection of its occult practices to the worship of the "forces of nature." Witches, or Wiccans, believe they derive their spiritual powers from a mystical relationship with the earth. They live by the rhythms of the earth, moon, and planets. (Lucis Trust is just one of many organizations that promote full moon meditations.) The terms *Mother Earth* and *Mother Nature* are commonly used in these modern earth and goddess-worship circles.

These ideas have also become popular in the feminist movement. In fact, the National Organization of Women (NOW) has held conferences promoting such pagan/occult concepts. For example, at their twentieth annual conference held in Denver in June 1986, one of their workshops was entitled "Feminist Spirituality—The Goddess

Returns." These groups feel quite comfortable with many of the spiritual teachings of Teilhard Chardin.

A growing number of institutions are devoting their efforts to promoting these teachings of false hope. They include the Teilhard Center for the Future of Man, located in London; a special Teilhard Foundation in Boulder, Colorado; and a foundation in Paris dedicated to the study of Chardin's works.

Evolving Toward Omega Point

Teilhard Chardin saw every aspect of existence, from the earth itself to human beings, as moving in a purposeful forward motion to the Omega Point. For him, Christogenesis, the process by which the universe turns completely into Christ, is simply the last phase of evolution. He presented to the people of his day a new world religion he still considered Christian. But it was merely a vehicle for moving humanity into a new theological mindset, one that embraces a false view of a coming golden age. Man's own divine efforts, of course, would usher in this new age.

Teilhard believed he was giving the world a better Christianity, a religion that blended faith in God with faith in the world. As pointed out in an earlier statement by Al Gore, Chardin openly referred to this as the birth of a new faith. In an essay entitled "The Stuff of the Universe," he makes his view very clear.

> One could say that a hitherto unknown form of religion . . . is gradually germinating in the heart of modern man, in the furrow opened up by the idea of evolution. . . . Far from feeling my faith perturbed by such a profound change, it is with hope overflowing that I welcome the rise of this new mystique and foresee its inevitable triumph.[15]

Like the other three occult personalities we have studied thus far, the pantheistic concepts and beliefs of the East heavily influenced Chardin. While the others spent time in India, he spent time first in Egypt, and then many years in China. Because of this Eastern indoctrination, he came to believe that we are all in the process of experiencing a spiritually upward evolution and that at our Omega Point, we will become a united humanity in a spiritual sense. Some New Agers refer to this final step of evolution as "taking the quantum leap." Chardin states,

> A tendency towards unification is everywhere manifest, and especially in the different branches of religion. We are looking for something that will draw us together, below or above the level of that which divides. . . . Is the dilemma insoluble or

(as we would rather believe) only a temporary one, destined to vanish like so many others when we have reached a higher level of spiritual evolution?[16]

The fact is, Christianity is unique. True Christianity is diametrically opposed to every manmade religion on earth, all of which are based on humanity's futile efforts to attain divinity. When an attempt is made to blend the teachings of Jesus Christ with the religions of the world, Christianity suffers and ceases to be what God meant it to be. Chardin never presented sin, redemption, Christ's shed blood, and the nature of the Atonement in their proper perspective. Perhaps this failure to deal with the reality of sin and man's fallen nature is why his brand of spirituality has become so appealing to the human potential advocates of today. Second Timothy 4:3-4 warned of such a day: "For the time will come when they will not endure sound doctrine; but after their own lusts shall they heap to themselves teachers, having itching ears; and they shall turn away their ears from the truth, and shall be turned unto fables."

Pierre Teilhard de Chardin died on April 10, 1955, Easter Sunday, in New York City. After collapsing suddenly, he regained consciousness for a few moments. His last words were, "This time, I feel it's terrible."[17] A work entitled *My Litany* was found on his desk at the time of his death. The last lines of this litany indicated that Chardin stayed true to his hollow philosophy to the very end:

> Focus of ultimate and
> universal energy
> Centre of the cosmic
> sphere of cosmogenesis
> Heart of Jesus, heart of
> evolution, unite me to
> yourself.[18]

If Chardin were alive today, two things would immediately strike him: first, how incredibly popular his ideas have become; and second, how wrong his predictions of our golden future have been. Since his death in 1955, humanity has not been on an upward spiral, but on a downward slide. Our globe is experiencing at this moment more violations of human rights, spiritual and physical oppression, racial hatred, crime, and terrorism than ever before. The horrors of child pornography, drug abuse, abortion, the pandemic of AIDS and other sexually transmitted diseases, the breakdown of the family unit, and the overall escalation of immorality and violence hardly suggest an upward move of humanity.

The Bible tells us that man was originally created pure and was placed in a perfect environment. His rebellion against God, however, set him on a course of self-destruction, which in the last days would only accelerate. Jesus, as we have already seen, compared the time prior to His return to the condition of mankind in the days of Noah, which represented the most depraved period in human history. God has given the world His solution for our predicament, but many, like Chardin, through pride and pseudo-intellectualism, reject it as being too simplistic.

God's solution is to forgive us of our sins and to grant us eternal life in Heaven. However, in order to receive this pardon, we must accept the fact that Jesus paid the penalty for our sins by being punished in our place through His death on the cross. "God was in Christ, reconciling the world unto himself, not imputing their trespasses unto them. . . . For he hath made him to be sin for us, who knew no sin; that we might be made the righteousness of God in him" (2 Cor. 5:19, 21). "Whosoever therefore shall confess me before men, him will I confess also before my Father which is in heaven. But whosoever shall deny me before men, him will I also deny before my Father which is in heaven" (Matt. 10:32–33).

We will not reach the Omega Point in human history by being absorbed into a universal Christ (a myth). Rather, by kneeling in repentance at the feet of Him who said, "I am Alpha and Omega, the beginning and the end, the first and the last" (Rev. 22:13) we shall find forgiveness from our sins and we shall be united in worship to Jesus Christ forever.

Notes

1. Marilyn Ferguson, *The Aquarian Conspiracy* (Los Angeles: J.P. Tarcher, 1980), pp. 418–420.

2. Barbara Hannah, *Jung: His Life and Work* (New York: G.P. Putnam's Sons, 1976), p. 22.

3. Carl Jung, *Memories, Dreams, Reflections* (New York: Random House, 1961), p. 18.

4. Ibid., pp. 112–113.

5. Nevill Drury, *Dictionary of Mysticism and the Occult* (New York: Harper & Row, 1985), p. 137.

6. *Personality Theories: An Introduction* (Boston: Houghton Mifflin Company, textbook, 1979), p.112.

7. Ibid., pp. 112–113.

8. Leo S. Schumacher, *The Truth About Teilhard* (Twin Circle Publishing Company, booklet, 1968), p. 25.

9. Teilhard de Chardin, *The Making of a Mind: Letters from a Soldier Priest* (New York: Harper & Row, 1965). Page numbers are given in the main text.

10. Teilhard de Chardin, *The Future of Man* (San Francisco: Harper & Row, 1959), pp. 34–35, 23.

11. Schumacher, *The Truth About Teilhard*, pp. 30–31.

12. Zbigniew Brzezinski, *Between Two Ages* (New York: Viking Press, 1970), p. 73.

13. Robert Muller, *New Genesis–Shaping a Global Spirituality* (New York: Doubleday & Company, 1984), p. 160.

14. Al Gore, *Earth in the Balance: Ecology and the Human Spirit* (New York: Penguin Books, First Plume Printing, 1993), p. 263.

15. Teilhard de Chardin, *The Stuff of the Universe* (Paris: L'Activation de L'Energie, Editions de Seuil, 1963), p. 406.

16. Chardin, *The Future of Man*, pp. 196–197, 195.

17. Teilhard de Chardin, *The Divine Milieu* (San Francisco: Harper & Row, 1957), p. 33.

18. Teilhard de Chardin, *Christianity and Evolution* (Ft. Worth, TX: Harcourt Brace Jovanovich, 1969), p. 245.

4

Mysticism and Medicine

"The coming of the lawless one will be in accordance with the work of Satan displayed in all kinds of counterfeit miracles, signs and wonders, and in every sort of evil that deceives those who are perishing." 2 Thessalonians 2:9–10a (NIV)

As the twentieth century progressed, the occult philosophies of mystics such as Bailey, Jung, and Chardin continued to take hold in intellectual circles. With the quiet support and influence of the secret societies, it was not long before these ideas had penetrated virtually every major field of endeavor. By the 1950s and 1960s, Eastern practices such as Transcendental Meditation, yoga, hypnosis, and acupuncture had been introduced to the mainstream of Western society.

Although the foundations of biblical faith were being challenged on numerous fronts, nowhere would the erosion of Christian values be more apparent than in the area of medicine. The growing fascination with Eastern mysticism had sparked an interest in the so-called healing arts.

Amazingly, the figure most responsible for these developments in modern health died more than fifty years ago. Yet, his disciples, equipped with "special" esoteric knowledge, extensive literature, and an insatiable appetite for the occult, have successfully propagated his ideas to the point where they have become widely accepted. This "medical pioneer" is the American psychic Edgar Cayce.

Edgar Cayce (1877–1945)

Born in Hopkinsville, Kentucky, in 1877, Edgar Cayce was the only son in a family of five children. He considered his mother and grandmother to be his best friends. His father, it seemed, did not have much time for a small boy.[1]

Edgar didn't go to school until the age of seven, when a lady named Mrs. Ellison, who was temporarily boarding at his aunt's house, agreed to teach a class for small children. Mrs. Ellison was a Mormon who had come from the West, where, she claimed, she had been one of the wives of Brigham Young.[2] That same year Edgar recounted having his first experience playing with "spirit children."

Like his contemporaries Alice Bailey, Carl Jung, and Teilhard Chardin, Edgar Cayce was introduced to Christianity as a child. Like the others, he was also exposed to the occult, which, for whatever reason, would eventually gain the upper hand in his life. He attended Old Liberty Church, a Campbellite off-shoot of the Presbyterian denomination, and he received his first Bible in January 1887, at the age of ten. By the end of June that same year he had finished reading all of it. [3]

Edgar had heard one of the men in his church say he had "read the Bible through a dozen times." At that point Edgar decided to read the Bible once through each year of his life. In order to make up for all the years he had already lived, he read the Bible cover to cover repeatedly until he was caught up. Cayce biographer, Thomas Sugrue, elaborates:

> As soon as the idea entered his head he turned to Genesis and began the task. From then on he never went anyplace without his Bible, though he generally managed to conceal it so people didn't know he had it with him. He read at every possible moment, giving only the time that was absolutely necessary to his chores and paying almost no attention to his schoolwork.[4]

Since he was allegedly able to master his lessons simply by sleeping with his books beneath his pillow, his lack of effort in school didn't seem to matter much.[5]

Edgar had a special place in some nearby woods where he went to read his Bible. In the spring of his thirteenth year, Edgar, while sitting at his retreat reading, was met by an "angelic" woman who told him, "Your prayers have been heard. Tell me what you would like most of all, so that I may give it to you." He said he wished to help others, especially sick children.[6] This "wish" to be able to heal others would be realized later in his life.

The Association for Research and Enlightenment (A.R.E.), an organization devoted to spreading Cayce's philosophies, offers the following account of how he received his healing powers:

> At the age of twenty-one he developed a gradual throat paralysis which threatened the loss of his voice. When doctors were unable to find a cause for his condition, Cayce entered the same hypnotic sleep that had enabled him to learn his school lessons years before. In that state, he was able to recommend a cure which successfully repaired his throat muscles and restored his voice. It was soon discovered that he could do the same for others.[7]

Biographer Lytle Robinson, provides more details:

> About this time hypnotism was enjoying a fad throughout the country, and a friend suggested that he try it as a means of helping his condition. Cayce was willing to try anything that might cure his throat. A local hypnotist offered his services, and Edgar readily accepted. He insisted, however, that he put himself to sleep, with the friend making the suggestions after he was "under."

> The experiment proved to be more than successful. Cayce went into a deep trance and described the condition in his vocal cords, advising, strangely enough, what to do for it. The advice was followed by the hypnotist—that of suggesting the blood circulation increase to the affected area—and when Cayce awakened he had regained his normal speaking voice.[8]

In the following months, Edgar began doing clairvoyant/psychic readings for people with various diseases. These psychic readings involved diagnosing illnesses and prescribing treatment for physical problems. Robinson comments,

> He was uneducated and knew nothing of medicine or anatomy in his waking state. . . . For all Edgar knew he might prescribe something that would kill somebody! After all he had no idea what went on while he was asleep. . . . In most of the cases that developed over the years, the celebrated psychic never met the persons making the requests. They were received through the mail; the recipients of the readings were usually hundreds of miles away. All Cayce needed was the full name of the person, his address, and where he would be at the appointed time of the reading.[9]

Experts have made the following observations about Cayce's healing powers:

The participation of the patient in the experiment, by way of mental attitude, is a point which the readings themselves constantly stress. The person who desires help, and who seeks it humbly and prayerfully . . . will invariably get a better reading than the cynic who wants to be shown . . . those who have gotten the best results from their readings are those who have realized the spiritual implications of the experiment in which they have participated. These, for the most part, have entered into the philosophical side of the work, and gained mentally and spiritually, as well as physically. Those who have gotten least from their readings are those who have treated the phenomenon as a freak or a fad, and have haphazardly followed the instructions given them.[10]

Over the course of forty years, and without any medical training, Cayce gave a total of 14,246 psychic readings, all while in a trance. Although nearly 70 percent of his readings involved medical diagnosis and advice, other topics discussed in these self-induced hypnotic trances (altered states of consciousness) included reincarnation, aura charts, psychic phenomena, dreams and the interpretation of dreams, ancient civilizations—including Atlantis and prehistoric Egypt—spiritism, meditation, numerology, and the future of mankind and earth.

Cayce was noted for his predictions concerning future cataclysmic events. These included the catastrophic destruction of New York City, massive earthquakes that would devastate a large portion of America's coastal regions, and a major shift in the poles that would permanently alter the planet's weather patterns. Cayce believed that a New Age of global unity and prosperity would eventually emerge in the new millennium, following this widespread destruction.

Similarities with Nostradamus

Nostradamus, the mysterious occult prophet of the sixteenth century, also foretold a time of terrible destruction and terror that was to begin in the late 1990s and last through the first part of the new millennium. But the amazing similarities between Cayce and Nostradamus do not end here. Both men first became famous by using their mystical powers to diagnose illnesses and offer cures. Both were occult prophets, yet they operated in the name of Christ, as though they were Christians. And both became advisers to prominent world leaders and celebrities. (See Appendix C for a summary of Nostradamus' life and beliefs.)

Like Nostradamus, Cayce blended certain Christian ideas and terminology with the ancient religions of the occult. He tried to redefine Christ by turning Him into an occult figure who would fit all of the world's mystery religions—an impossible task. Summarizing Edgar's erroneous religious views, biographer Thomas Sugrue states,

> The system of metaphysical thought which emerges from the readings of Edgar Cayce is a Christianized version of the mystery religions of ancient Egypt, Chaldea, Persia, India, and Greece. It fits the figure of Christ into the tradition of one God for all people, and places Him in His proper place, at the apex of the philosophical structure; He is the capstone of the pyramid.[11]

In the realm of secret societies and the occult, the capstone of the pyramid—containing the eye of the pagan god Osiris or Baal, as pictured on the back of the U.S. dollar bill—is the symbol of Lucifer. Therefore, based on Sugrue's statement, Cayce knowingly or unknowingly presented Jesus Christ in the position of Lucifer. Although Jesus Christ is the cornerstone and capstone (author and perfecter) of the Christian faith, he is not the capstone of this present world system and should not be presented as such. Rather, the Bible identifies Satan as being the god, or prince, of this world (John 12:31; 16:11; Luke 4:5–7), while pointing out that Jesus' kingdom is not of this world (John 18:36).

From a biblical standpoint, both Cayce and Nostradamus should be exposed as false prophets for several reasons. First, they have been wrong in many of their predictions. Both men, while being accurate in some of their forecasts, have been off the mark a large percentage of the time. This is a fact rarely emphasized by the media tabloids that have tended to promote these men as genuine prophets. Unlike Cayce and Nostradamus, the prophets ordained by God and recorded in the Bible are 100 percent accurate.

Second, their predictions concerning the end of time differ drastically from what has been foretold in Scripture. Unlike the predictions of Cayce and Nostradamus, the Bible's prophecies clearly state that mankind would never usher in an era of true global peace. Rather, humanity would make a fatal mistake in the last days, giving its allegiance and power to the Beast (Rev. 13–14; 1 John 2; 2 Thess. 2). While this transfer of power might take place in the name of peace, Scripture reveals that it will eventually lead to a seven-year reign of terror. The Bible describes a ruthless system of world government and religion that will be so diabolical and powerful that it can only be destroyed by Jesus Christ Himself when He returns (2 Thess. 2; Rev. 4–22).

Third, both men, although professing Christianity, regularly went into occult trances in order to receive their messages from the spirit world. This is a satanic practice known as spiritism or divination and is strictly forbidden in Scripture (Deuteronomy 18:9–13). The "angelic" spirits who gave them their visions, including those on healing, were really demonic entities. Since one of man's chief concerns down through the ages has been his own health, it is only natural that the forces of deception would make their influence felt in this vital area.

The occult philosophies of Nostradamus and Edgar Cayce have far outlived both men, becoming even more popular and widespread after their deaths. The prophecies and teachings of Nostradamus, for instance, were carried forward largely by members of the European nobility, who had become convinced of the man's authenticity as a prophet. Although he died in 1566, his teachings would continue to influence world events, even into the twentieth century.

Cayce, on the other hand, gave "readings" on health and the paranormal for more than forty years. He died in 1945, but not until he had helped birth the holistic health movement. The Association for Research and Enlightenment, which continues to promote Cayce's work, comments:

> Cayce . . . saw total health as involving coordination among the physical, mental, and spiritual components of life. Any complete approach to health needed to consider an individual's entire being rather than simply illness. Because of this concept, it has been said that the beginnings of present day holistic health started from the readings of Edgar Cayce.[12]

Before we examine the Cayce-influenced holistic health movement, let's take a brief look at some of A.R.E.'s promotional literature to discover more about the man and his organization.

In the letter opposite, Dr. Charles Cayce, the grandson of Edgar Cayce, provides more details about his grandfather (sometimes referred to as the "Sleeping Prophet") and A.R.E., the organization he founded. Over the years A.R.E. has influenced thousands of individuals worldwide with its occult philosophies and psychic predictions. The organization's impact, through its large variety of programs and publications, continues to be extensive—particularly in the area of holistic health. A portion of A.R.E.'s membership brochure—describing some of its services—is displayed in Exhibit F-3.

A.R.E.®
Association for Research and Enlightenment, Inc.

67th Street and Atlantic Avenue, Virginia Beach, VA 23451 • 1-800-333-4499 • Fax: (757) 422-6921

. . . from the grandson of Edgar Cayce

Dear Friend:

We're glad you've expressed an interest in learning more about Edgar Cayce and his remarkable work.

The details of his life and psychic insights seem too incredible to be true . . .

How could a quiet, unassuming country boy put himself into a sleeplike state and answer with uncanny accuracy virtually any question put to him? What was the mysterious source of his information? How could people thousands of miles away be helped by this humble seer?

Numerous people, who were considered incurable by specialists, were healed of their ailments when they followed his unorthodox recommendations. The remedies he suggested at that time continue even today to help the sick and those seeking relief from disease.

Well, my grandfather was that man. And I feel certain that as you explore this material, you'll find it is more than just a fascinating story about a psychic who lived until 1945. You'll discover an organization that is active and vital – continuing to help more people around the world in one year than Edgar Cayce himself was able to reach in the forty-three years that he gave psychic readings.

When Edgar Cayce founded the A.R.E. in 1931, he intended to share the hopeful suggestions covered in his readings on such topics as holistic healing, spiritual growth, dream interpretation, ESP, reincarnation, psychic development, ancient civilizations, meditation, the purpose of life, and much more.

At his death, a legacy remained: thousands of case histories that science is still at a loss to explain completely. That is part of the work that the A.R.E. is doing today. From its small beginnings with a handful of dedicated people, it has grown steadily to become a highly respected center for parapsychological study.

The Edgar Cayce discourses themselves—some 14,000 of them—are on file in our library here in Virginia Beach. They can be studied by any interested person . . . and they are endlessly fascinating.

As mentioned earlier, not all of the discourses were on health issues. For example, Edgar Cayce accurately predicted World War II (giving precise dates), the death of two presidents while in office, and racial strife in America. A number of prophetic events—some yet to come—were covered in his readings:

- Events concerning Russia, China, Israel, and the United States.
- The discovery of evidence that the lost continent of Atlantis actually existed.
- Changes in the earth due to volcanic eruptions, earthquakes, and tidal waves.
- A Hall of Records being uncovered in the area of the Sphinx in Egypt.
- New methods of healing incurable diseases.

Exhibit F-1

I doubt that he ever imagined, however, the worldwide impact that his material would have on tens of thousands of people. Across the globe, the A.R.E. continues to serve many seeking guidance on the multitude of concerns affecting their lives today. Through year-round educational seminars, local fellowship study groups, and membership publications, individuals study and apply his timeless wisdom and practical suggestions for experiencing a better life.

If this interests you, why not join us in exploring the greatest frontier of all—the frontier of the human spirit! I hope you will consider becoming a part of this adventure where, in the convenience of your own home, you can delve into subjects that some call paranormal, mystical, or mysterious. A.R.E.'s membership program offers a wonderful way for individuals to examine these fascinating subjects on their own or with others of like mind.

Each month our membership materials present a number of intriguing topics from the Edgar Cayce readings. Some will be so fascinating and practical that you'll want to try them in your own life. Each person takes whatever he or she finds useful from the extraordinary resource of knowledge left by Edgar Cayce.

To start you on your exploration, we are going to send you two months of our membership materials. There is no cost or obligation. At the end of two months you'll have the opportunity to continue your membership for the year, or ignore the renewal and discontinue receiving materials. You'll receive our membership publications: *Venture Inward* magazine and *The New Millennium* journal. I am certain that once you have examined them you'll want to continue receiving them by becoming an A.R.E. member.

Special Introductory Membership Offer:
1 Year Sponsoring membership, $53.00; or 1 Year Associate membership, $33.00

Whether or not you become a member, we'd like you to know that many A.R.E. activities are open to the general public. For instance, we conduct lectures each year in major cities. There is also our worldwide Study Group program in which small groups of people—affiliated with the A.R.E., but not necessarily members—meet on a regular basis in private homes to study spiritual subjects, to share and grow together. There may even be such a group in your own neighborhood.

I think it is safe to say that the Edgar Cayce discourses offer hope for virtually every human problem. Literally thousands of people have been helped by his work. Here in Virginia Beach, we are privileged to receive firsthand reports from those whose lives have been transformed. Our chief concern is to make that miracle available to all who seek.

We ask that you consider being an A.R.E. member. In every age, there have been people who stand out from the rest . . . people who have the backbone to go against tradition . . . who look for alternative approaches to finding a more harmonious, fulfilling life. I think you might be that type of person.

Join in our research of the Cayce material and consider the opportunities for a better life for yourself.

Sincerely,

Charles Thomas Cayce, Ph.D.
President, Edgar Cayce Foundation

MN-129

Exhibit F-2

┌─────────────── **Benefits for All Members** ───────────────┐

The New Millennium Journal

Each issue of this bimonthly journal explores a major holistic concept from a variety of perspectives, all aimed at assisting in creating a closer relationship with the Divine. Knowledgeable and well-known writers and lecturers provide thought-provoking articles and essays that unite the principles in the Edgar Cayce readings with other compatible spiritual philosophies.

A.R.E. Conferences and Seminars

You will receive regular notices about programs held at A.R.E. headquarters in Virginia Beach and special seminars and retreats presented in your area.

Venture Inward Magazine

A year's subscription to A.R.E.'s bimonthly magazine, *Venture Inward.* This publication will keep you abreast of the latest research on dreams, meditation, and many other topics covered in the Edgar Cayce readings. You will also enjoy these regular features:

◆ Interviews ... of widely known experts in such fields as ESP and parapsychology.

◆ Articles/columns ... timely information on holistic health, dreams, spiritual development.

◆ Book reviews ... thoughtful examinations of recently published books on psychical research.

Study Groups

Members and friends have the opportunity to join one of the hundreds of groups worldwide who meet regularly to discuss and apply in greater depth the material in the Edgar Cayce readings. This is one of the best ways to become part of the A.R.E. community and meet like-minded friends.

Prayer Services

A.R.E. maintains an extensive worldwide prayer network. You may take part in this group or add your name to our prayer list.

Circulating Files of Cayce Readings

Over 400 files, available to you by mail, these compilations contain actual texts from the Cayce readings on a variety of topics. They include both medical and metaphysical subjects such as: "Arthritis," "Psoriasis," "Reincarnation," and "Psychic Development."

A.R.E. Camp

Members may enjoy vacations for their entire families or for their children at A.R.E. Camp in the foothills of Virginia's Appalachian Range. Outdoor activities, spiritual renewal, and a healthful diet are offered in this unique experience of holistic living.

Harold J. Reilly School of Massotherapy

While in Virginia Beach, you may enjoy a discount on a variety of reasonably priced massage and hydrotherapy services given by graduates of our exclusive school. The school also offers a 600-hour diploma program in massage therapy. It is the only massage school which incorporates the Cayce holistic approach to health.

Atlantic University

The university founded by Edgar Cayce offers a master's degree in transpersonal studies. Courses compare concepts from the Cayce readings with ideas in psychology, parapsychology, religious traditions, science, and other spiritual philosophies. Independent study/correspondence courses are also available.

A.R.E. Books by Mail

The A.R.E. Press offers books on such diverse topics as holistic health, earth changes, psychology and self-help, parapsychology, and comparative religion—all of which are available by mail.

Exhibit F-3

Your Planets and Stars

Edgar Cayce, as well as many others, including Carl Jung, see astrology as a beneficial tool in understanding oneself, one's life, and one's relationships with others. Here are some quotes from Jung and Cayce:

The fact that it is possible to reconstruct a person's character fairly accurately from his birth data shows the relative validity of astrology. Carl Jung

I do not hesitate to take the synchronistic phenomena that underlie astrology seriously. Carl Jung

❶ Birth Profile

... the position of the planets give the tendencies in a given life ... 3744-4

"I thought the entire analysis of me and my life was extremely accurate. It was also helpful to confirm how I feel and to emphasize what I need to improve. I truly salute your work."
–R.M., New York

Horoscope and Interpretation $24.95

❷ Astral Forecast

As in all influences, there are those indications of signs, omens; which is the first law as He gave, that the sun, the moon, the stars, the planets in their course were given to man as signs, as omens, as indications that the way may be clear to those who seek. 2326-1

"This astrology forecast is finely tuned, most accurate. I will recommend you to others. Many thanks for a most helpful tool in the task of understanding oneself."
–P.R., Texas

12-Month Map of the Heavens and Comprehensive Report $24.95

❸ Relationship Profile

... astrological conditions do influence, a KNOWLEDGE of same certainly gives an individual a foresight into relationships with individuals. 311-3

"Amazing. My wife and I never thought so much could be known about our relationship by looking at the stars."—J.D., California

Dual Horoscope and Comprehensive Comparison $24.95

❹ Past-Life Profile

The inclinations of man are ruled by the planets under which he is born, for the destiny of man lies within the sphere or scope of the planets. 3744-4

"It was right on; helped me tremendously."–B.H., Ohio

Horoscope and Past-Life Profile $24.95

Edgar Cayce Readings © 1971, 1993, 1994, 1995, 1996 by the Edgar Cayce Foundation. All rights reserved.

Call toll-free with your credit card order, or fill out the order form and mail it today. We'll turn your order around in two to three weeks. Use an extra sheet of paper if you wish more charts than our order form provides. Thank you. Your satisfaction is guaranteed.

Exhibit F-4

Exhibit F-4 represents another page from one of A.R.E.'s many brochures. This particular flier offers telling statements by Carl Jung and Edgar Cayce on the subject of astrology. As you can see, both men were strong believers in this occultic practice and actively promoted its use. Their statements not only demonstrate the compatibility of their mystical philosophies, but reveal the true origin of at least some of their beliefs. Few people outside of New Age circles recognize the fact that many of the underlying ideas and practices of holistic health had their beginnings in astrology.

Holistic Health

Today's fast-paced, stressful way of life has produced a nation of fast-food consumers with incredibly poor and lazy health habits. The recent emphasis on preventative medicine, personal health responsibility, exercise, and less reliance on drugs are welcome and badly needed changes. Unfortunately, holistic health concepts do not stop there.

Holistic health—sometimes referred to as the new medicine, alternative medicine, or simply, the healing arts—is now influencing millions of lives with "Cayce-styled" New Age practices and ideas. These inroads are possible because of a redefined concept of "energy." In the past, we have thought of human energy as meaning that which results from proper sleep, good nutrition, and an absence of sickness or disease. Today's definition in holistic circles, however, involves much more than that. It includes one's entire concept of spiritual truth.

Redefining Energy

As explained earlier, New Age spirituality maintains that God is the sum total of all life, the "life force" that flows through all living things. New Agers believe that this life force flows through our bodies and determines our state of health. Many promoters of holistic health see most of our problems as the result of the misalignment of this latent energy within the body. Supposedly, by manipulating this force in a prescribed fashion, one can restore alignment, and therefore, health. This mysterious energy appears to be a "spiritual" force that can only be explained through a pantheistic/occult belief system and, interestingly enough, only seems to "work for" those who have faith in, or submit themselves to, this system.

To restore good health, millions of people in Western society are now submitting themselves to practices based upon this Eastern view of the nature of God, which maintains that "all is one and connected" through a mystical divine energy. The implication is that man is not separated from God and, therefore, is not in need of salvation. Dr. Harold Bloomfield, a promoter of transcendental meditation, while addressing the 1978 Holistic Health Conference in San Diego, stated, "In your essential nature you are divine and that's a major focus of our holistic health movement."[13] In line with this, the Association of Holistic Health defines itself as "becoming aware of higher levels of consciousness."[14] In this system of thought, there is no creature-Creator distinction. All manifestations of power are godly, and the mind is divine and potentially omnipotent. What a perfect cover for the activity of demonic power in these last days! Notice how these beliefs of today's holistic leaders parallel the teachings of Edgar Cayce. (See the Cayce quotes section below.)

Quotes by Cayce

Cayce had much to say about God, energy, evolution, astrology, reincarnation, and the oneness of the universe. The distinct similarities between his ideas and the pantheistic views of Nostradamus, Carl Jung, and Teilhard Chardin are difficult to ignore. Cayce's spiritual world view is reflected in his following statements:

Philosophy of God

The mind of God embraces the one total life energy with its universally evolved portion called mind, in all its forms, all its states of development, and all of its self-conscious, individual viewpoints, including ourselves. Yet while in the physical form we possess not the Creator's kind of mind, but rather the kind that mind becomes in materiality. (Case # 792-Ca)

Source: Lytle Robinson, *Edgar Cayce's Story of the Origin and Destiny of Man*, (Berkley Publishing Group, New York, NY, Copyright by The Edgar Cayce Foundation, 1972), p. 33.

Q. Are souls perfect, as created by God in the beginning? If so, where is there any need for development?

A. The answer to this may only be found in the evolution of life, in such a way as to be understood by the finite mind. In the First Cause or Principle, all is perfect. That portion of the whole (manifest in the creation of souls) may become a living soul and equal with the Creator. To reach that position, when separated from Him, it must pass through all stages of development in order that it may be one with the Creator. (Case # 900-10)

Source: Lytle Robinson, *Edgar Cayce's Story of the Origin and Destiny of Man*, (Berkley Publishing Group, New York, NY, Copyright by The Edgar Cayce Foundation, 1972), p. 45.

Know that thyself, in its physical state, is a part of the plan of salvation, or righteousness, of truth, of the Creative Forces, or God, in the earth. . . . Each person is a corpuscle in the body of that force called God.

Source: Thomas Sugrue, *The Story of Edgar Cayce: There Is A River*, (A.R.E. Press Publication 1997, Association For Research and Enlightenment, Virginia beach, Virginia, Original copyright 1942), p. 320.

Cayce on Reincarnation

Reincarnation offers man the false hope of many lives after death, insulating him against any fear of judgement. This belief is fast becoming part of America's "new religion." According to a *U.S.A. Today* poll conducted the week prior to the airing of Shirley MacLaine's television mini-series, *Out On A Limb*, in 1987, twenty-three percent of Americans believed in reincarnation.[15] This was more than a decade ago. The percentage would be significantly higher today, given the growing number of people involved in the New Age movement.

Not surprisingly, the acclaimed actress formulated much of her theology, including her beliefs on reincarnation, through the teachings of Edgar Cayce, as presented by The Association for Research and Enlightenment. (See Appendix D.) The following statements from A.R.E. summarize Cayce's views on the subject.

> From Cayce's perspective, we are not simply physical bodies or even physical bodies with souls, but are instead spiritual beings who are currently having a material experience. As souls, we have manifested in the earth in order to learn lessons that will enable us to return to our former state of spiritual awareness. At the same time, one purpose we all have in common is to bring the spirituality of the Creator back into the earth.
>
> A soul can choose to be born into either a male or female body in any given lifetime or, as Cayce called it, an "incarnation." A soul selects that environment (parents and family, location, personal obstacles, etc.) which will best allow for the learning of lessons it needs for completeness.
>
> One frequently misunderstood concept regarding reincarnation has to do with karma. From the standpoint of the Cayce material, karma is not destiny, it is only memory. . . . Karma provides us with the potential to learn a lesson we need in order to grow at a soul level . . .
>
> Source: Association For Research and Enlightenment Inc., Edgar Cayce Foundation—*Reincarnation: Have We Lived Before?* [web page], (Copyright 1995/1996 by A.R.E.; http://www.are-cayce.com/reincar.htm) [Accessed January 13, 1997]

The chakra centers of yoga and the meridians of acupuncture are an excellent example of this energy flow concept. The energy flow of acupuncture is referred to as "chi" and involves the interplay of yin and yang. These are the supposed opposite forces of nature that produce day-night, summer-winter, sun-moon, male-female polarities. According to this theory, yin and yang circulate in the body from organ to organ along invisible meridians. It is believed that disease results when the body's energy flow becomes unbalanced or blocked. By inserting long, very fine needles into specific spots, this energy flow is allegedly influenced and balanced.

The underlying philosophy of this practice is spiritual, not physiological. The question Christians should be asking themselves is not "Does this seem to work?" but rather, "What are the long-term, spiritual consequences of these practices?"

This basic idea of a mystical, nonphysical energy that somehow unites man with the cosmos is central not only to acupuncture and yoga, but also to polarity therapy, applied kinesiology, homeopathy, Reichian therapy, reflexology, and iridology. The fact that we can never quite explain how these nontraditional therapies work always comes back to the fact that they are so closely connected to this elusive "spiritual" energy force. Let's take iridology as an example.

Iridology

Iridology has become one of the most popular techniques used in holistic circles. There are well over twelve thousand practitioners of iridology in the United States today. This form of eye diagnosis originated in China and can be traced back to astrology.

Iridology involves diagnosing the state of the physical body through the condition of the iris. It seems to offer a combination of pseudo-science and the occult, depending upon the practitioner's religious world view. A person doesn't necessarily have to be involved in the occult to believe in certain aspects of iridology. For example, a small percentage of practitioners, some who I personally know, are convinced that certain diseases can be detected by the reactions they produce in the iris; which, they believe, can be identified by a trained eye. This belief in the medical validity of iridology may explain why iridology has gained some acceptance in Christian circles. Nevertheless, many people are becoming involved in this practice without examining the philosophy behind it.

During the last three decades a growing number of conventional physicians, particularly those with metaphysical leanings, have been attracted to this form of diagnosis. However, results from the first scientific study on this subject, presented in the September 28, 1979 issue of the *Journal of the American Medical Association*, proved to be less than favorable. Dr. Bernard Jensen, a Los Angeles naturopath/chiropractor—considered to be the leading authority on iridology—

was one of three iridologists who participated in this study involving the detection of kidney disease. In this experiment, one iridologist correctly identified only 26 percent of the patients undergoing dialysis as having the disease.

The biggest problem with iridology—along with the fact that it is inaccurate a high percentage of the time—is that many practitioners use it "mediumistically" rather than medically. When used in this fashion, the eye serves as a point of contact, in much the same way as the hand does to a fortune-teller. Ironically, in cases where this occultic method is used, eye diagnosis can be somewhat successful. In fact, some mystics with practically no medical training have diagnosed illnesses with amazing accuracy while claiming to use this technique.

Counterfeit Miracles

It is most unwise to accept some new technique simply because it appears to work. We must always look at the philosophy behind the technique and remember that the attraction of the occult is that it sometimes does work, at least temporarily. Our tendency is to underestimate the power of Satan, including his ability to perform miracles. We forget that when Moses stood before Pharaoh, Pharaoh's magicians were able to duplicate, in succession, each of the miracles that God performed through Moses—up to a point. While some of these duplications may have been nothing more than illusions, others were quite possibly real miracles performed with the assistance of demonic power.

Scripture tells us that in the last days Satan will display "all kinds of counterfeit miracles, signs and wonders" (2 Thess. 2:9). The word "counterfeit" in this passage is often misunderstood to mean something which is not real but only appears to be real to the naked eye, such as an act of illusion. However, the term "counterfeit" in the above context does not imply an illusion; it refers instead to a miracle of demonic origin whose source is evil. Such miracles, although very real, did not originate with God and in this respect are considered spiritually counterfeit.

God performs miracles for the good of His people, to uphold truth and to bring glory to His name. Satan, on the other hand, performs miracles to deceive and enslave those who refuse to accept the Bible's truth. He always has ulterior motives which prompt his actions—motives that are aimed at lifting himself above God. Discernment is needed to distinguish between God's miracles and Satan's counterfeit miracles.

God's miracles, including the healing of illnesses, usually occur in response to our heartfelt prayers, accompanied by a simple faith—our belief that God truly hears us when we pray in the name of Jesus Christ. It is God's own omnipotent supernatural power that heals us according to His will. Satan's miracles, on the other hand, are usually the result of people going into altered states or trying to manipulate "energy." This has the effect of summoning demonic entities, giving them a license to come through and perform a counterfeit healing. Such "healings" are usually temporary and serve only to establish the victim's confidence in the occult.

I am convinced most practitioners of the occult are unaware of the fact that the so-called life force or energy they rely on is nothing more than the manifested power of demonic spirits. Many people involved in the occult would probably cease their practices if they really understood this fact. However, the belief in a mysterious force of nature that can somehow be tapped and ultilized is a much more pleasant and acceptable explanation for the existence of this "energy."

Occult-based Medicine

A close look at the thousands of holistic health centers around the United States reveals that they teach a variety of energy related occult practices. These include past-life regression, astrology, sensory isolation, altered states of consciousness, Native American shamanism (another name for witch-doctoring), hypnosis, and various forms of divination.

An excellent example is Boulder College in Boulder, Colorado—a school which offers credit courses in the healing arts. Courses include: Jung and the Evolution of Mythology, Tarot, Fundamentals of Holistic Health, Iridology, Transpersonal Astrology, Oriental Herbology, Symbolic Aspects of *I Ching*, Nutritional Biochemistry, and Stress Management. This hodgepodge curriculum of health and occultism boasts a faculty of twelve master's degrees and seven Ph.D.s, one with a Ph.D. in biomedical engineering from the Massachusetts Institute of Technology.

Another example of this marriage of the occult to holistic health practices is found in a program guide to the Whole Life Expo, a conference that was held in Boston in 1986. Workshops offered at this convention included: Pioneering a New Planetary Perspective, Health Forces: The Art and Cultivation of Human Energy, Love Is Power: Gaining Self-Awareness through the Insight of a Trance Medium, Rebirthing and Therapeutic Touch, and Ecstasy in Marriage: A Spiritual Technology Deeply and Directly into Your Higher Self. The conference also abounded with workshops on acupuncture, iridology, astrology, meditation techniques, and trans-channeling.

Whole Life Expo featured programs with doctors from Harvard Medical School and Johns Hopkins University. Obviously, occult-based medicine is no longer on the fringes but has made major strides in blending with traditional medical practices. This trend in the medical community picked up momentum in the 1980s, when Eastern thinking and medicine first began influencing the public in a major way. Additional examples of developments from that decade follow.

Gaining Acceptance

The Catholic Health Association of the United States 1986 Achievement Citation went to St. Mary's Hospital and Health Center in Tucson, Arizona. The award was presented to the hospital for their "integration of Traditional Indian Medicine into today's health system." A subsequent conference emphasizing the spiritual focus of the healing process was offered at the hospital in January 1987. Their brochure states, "Participants learn from Traditional Medicine people, increasing their awareness and expansion of consciousness through experiential learning to develop a sensitive, spiritual approach to the healing process."[16]

The word "spiritual" is very popular in New Age circles. People need to be aware of the vast difference between the New Age concept of spiritual and the biblical meaning of this word. The contrast is evident in an article by Lawrence Le Shan, Ph.D. in *Science of Mind*. In describing holistic medicine, he states,

> Interestingly enough, holistic medicine has come to a very clear and practical definition of "spiritual". . . . It means such very hard disciplines as prayer and meditation, that bring you to those moments where you really know 'I am one with the cosmos.' You know that we are all parts of the universe, that we stand on the bedrock of the universe, and that our isolation, loneliness and alienation are in large part illusion.[17]

Dr. Le Shan has also taught classes at the Oasis Center (Chicago), a New Age awareness mecca. Another center of this type is the Stress Reduction and Learning Center in my home state of Indiana. This facility, located in Ft. Wayne, features a New Age bookstore and sensory isolation tanks which are designed to take the brain to the trance-inducing alpha level. It also conducts classes in the Energies of Ancient Music, Folklore, Herbs and Magic, and Energy Transfer: A Therapeutic Touch Process. This last class has been taught by Myra

Till, a locally popular registered nurse. A description of this class informs potential students,

> The main goal of the course is for you to become aware of your own energies, the energy that is both within and beyond the boundaries of your skin. You will learn to direct these energies to another person in aiding them to move into profound states of relaxation and pain management.[18] We will explore the process of energy transfer with one's hands, eyes, voice, and presence.[19]

Myra Till lectures throughout the state and writes articles for *Beginnings: A Newsletter of the American Holistic Nursing Association*. Not surprisingly, she was presented the Indiana Nurse of the Year Award in 1986. She was also director of all school nurses for Ft. Wayne Community schools and worked with a former governor of Indiana in setting up guidelines for school nurses throughout the state. Our children might be getting more than conventional medical treatment when they report to the office because of an upset stomach.

Even the Girl Scout program is not exempt from these influences. In the *Girl Scout Badges and Signs* book, the yin/yang symbol of Eastern mysticism is used to represent the "World in My Community" proficiency badge. In the *Junior Girl Scout Handbook*, yoga exercises are explained. The theme for their 1987 program was "The Year of Magic." We are past the day when one had to join a cult or seek out a "guru" to be influenced by these unorthodox spiritual practices. Instead, our problem now is trying to avoid them.

In addition to those already mentioned, there are currently hundreds of other New Age/holistic organizations located throughout the United States, many of which are connected. A study center in Big Sur, California, known as Esalen, is one of the best known New Age retreats in the country. In a section of the New Age book, *Aquarian Conspiracy* entitled "California and the Aquarian Conspiracy," Marilyn Ferguson stated,

> In the 1950s and 1960s, Aldous Huxley was among those who encouraged Michael Murphy and Richard Price in their 1961 decision to open Esalen, the residential center in California's Big Sur area that helped mid-wife much of what came to be known as the human-potential movement . . . a human potential movement would help break down the barriers between mind and body, between Eastern wisdom and Western action, between individuals and society, and thus between the limited self and the potential self.[20]

Seminar leaders at Esalen have included the famous psychologists Carl Rogers, Abraham Maslow and Rollo May, author Carlos Castaneda, Zen enthusiast Allen Watts (formerly an Episcopal priest), futurist B. F. Skinner, and popular New Agers such as Jean Houston and the late Norman Cousins.

In *Psychic Healing*, an excellent book exposing the occult influence on holistic health, Christian authors John Weldon and Zola Levitt tell of a similar center also located in California.

> The famous authority on death and dying, Dr. Elizabeth Kubler-Ross, is another example of how even professionals can become occulticly involved. A psychic-healing advocate, she currently has about five spirit-guides ("Salem" is her favorite) . . . at her Shantih Nilaya retreat center in California (where psychic healing and spiritism work hand in hand).[21]

Today, California, the Pacific Northwest, New York City, Virginia Beach, Kansas City, and the Denver/Boulder area are among the main centers of New Age activity in the United States. From these areas, the latest occult trends seem to spread to the rest of the country, with pockets of concentrated activity often located in each state.

A Spiritual Battle

If we think that by hard work we can make the New Age movement go away, we will quickly lose heart. The nature of the spiritual battle in which we find ourselves is evident in statements made by Donald Keys, president of Planetary Citizens, in his New Age book, *Earth at Omega*.

> The world needs large numbers of constructive social-change persons who can stand strongly as the old order crashes down about them causing dismay and pessimism in the minds and lives of those who lack vision and who do not understand the nature of the transition. . . . Transformative infiltration is proving valuable notably within the medical profession.[22]

Keys' comments concerning the spiritual infiltration of the medical community are disturbing, but true. Many hospitals now offer "Body, Mind, and Spirit" recovery programs. With few exceptions, the spiritual principles advocated in these sessions are more in line with New Age theology than biblical Christianity. If the current Administration had its way, some of these practices would, more than likely, become part of our national health plan. Edgar Cayce would be pleased with the "progress" being made!

Occultists have always sought to avoid the ultimate spiritual results of man's fall into sin by trying to gain control over life and death. The forces of darkness are only too willing to accommodate such efforts, often leading people to believe that they are "in charge" when they are not. This is one reason Scripture forbids involvement in the occult.

God, the great physician, has already given us His plan for good health. Proverbs 4:20–22 says, "My son, attend to my words; incline thine ear unto my sayings. Let them not depart from thine eyes; keep them in the midst of thine heart. For they are life unto those that find them, and health to all their flesh." We must heed this advice if we are to lead a physically and spiritually healthy life as Christians.

For those times when we do become ill, God wants us to bring our needs to Him in prayer.

> Is any one of you sick? He should call the elders of the church to pray over him and anoint him with oil in the name of the Lord. And the prayer offered in faith will make the sick person well; the Lord will raise him up. If he has sinned, he will be forgiven. Therefore confess your sins to each other and pray for each other so that you may be healed. The prayer of a righteous man is powerful and effective. James 5:14–16 (NIV)

God can also work through competent physicians to alleviate pain and restore health. The fact that Luke—one of the authors of the New Testament—was a doctor demonstrates that God approves of sound medical practices. At times God allows sickness to occur in order to draw us closer and keep us dependent upon Him. Paul, for example, had a "thorn in the flesh," which may very well have been a physical ailment. In spite of his repeated pleas, God did not deliver him of the problem. There is also sickness unto death in which case God will not heal us because He has determined that our time on this earth is completed.

Whatever our physical condition may be, it is important that our actions stay in line with God's Word. As our Creator, God knows what is best for us. Pursuing occult remedies is not one of His options.

Notes

1. Thomas Sugrue, *The Story of Edgar Cayce: There Is a River* (Virginia Beach, VA: A.R.E. Press, 1997), p. 40.

2. Ibid., pp. 40–41.

3. Ibid., pp. 42–43.

4. Ibid., p. 43.

5. Association for Research and Enlightenment/Edgar Cayce Foundation: Edgar Cayce (Web page http://www.are-cayce.com/ edgar.htm [accessed January 13, 1997], copyright 1995/1996 by A.R.E.).

6. Sugrue, *The Story of Edgar Cayce*, p. 45.

7. A.R.E./Edgar Cayce Foundation: Edgar Cayce (Web page).

8. Lytle Robinson, *Edgar Cayce's Story of the Origin and Destiny of Man* (New York: The Berkley Publishing Group, 1972), p. 211.

9. Ibid., pp. 211–212.

10. Sugrue, *The Story of Edgar Cayce*, p. 323.

11. Ibid., p. 305.

12. Association for Research and Enlightenment/Edgar Cayce Foundation: Health, Healing, and Wellness (Web page http:// www.are-cayce.com/wellness.htm [accessed January 13, 1997], copyright 1995/1996 by A.R.E.).

13. Wilson and Weldon, *Occult Shock and Psychic Forces* (Colorado Springs, CO: Master Books, 1980), p. 155.

14. Ibid., p. 157.

15. Monica Collins, "Not Some Spaced-Out California Concept," *USA TODAY,* January 16, 1987, p. 2A.

16. *Traditional Indian Medicine in Today's Health System* (Tucson, AZ: St. Mary's Hospital and Health Center, January 1987, report).

17. Dr. Lawrence Le Shan, *Science of Mind* (New York: Collier Books, November 1983), pp. 12–13.

18. *Stress Reduction Newsletter,* Current Seminars, January 1986.

19. *Stress Reduction Newsletter,* January 1987.

20. Marilyn Ferguson, *The Aquarian Conspiracy* (Los Angeles: J.P. Tarcher, 1980), pp. 137–139.

21. John Weldon and Zola Levitt, *Psychic Healing* (Chicago: Moody Press, 1982), p. 20.

22. Donald Keys, *Earth at Omega* (Bronx, NY: Branden Publishing, 1982), pp. 129, 127.

5

Toward World Unity

"Thus saith the Lord of hosts, Hearken not unto the words of the prophets that prophesy unto you: they make you vain: they speak a vision of their own heart, and not out of the mouth of the Lord." Jeremiah 23:16

"These have one mind, and shall give their power and strength unto the beast." Revelation 17:13

If the occult dream of a new world order was ever to be realized, New Agers would eventually have to present their case to the public. They would have to convince mankind that the old world order—based on an ancient system of sovereign nations and influenced to some extent by biblical principles—had failed and that a new order was essential for the continued survival of the planet. This would not be an easy task.

While the conditioning process for this deception had been underway for decades in the fields of medicine, psychology, and academia in general, a creative mass appeal was necessary to get people to consciously support such drastic changes. Occultists would have to wage an unprecedented public relations campaign including the writing of books and the production of films. They would have to inform everyone about the merits of this "noble" cause. The need for global unity would somehow have to be ingrained in every person's mind.

Although New Age organizations such as the World Constitution and Parliament Association had begun networking for global unity (world government) in the 1960s, their campaign did not gain broad acceptance until the 1980s. During that time, New Age ideas went from being "far out" to being fashionable. With the end of the Cold War in sight, an unprecedented wave of unity events began to sweep the world. Behind this wave an enormous amount of occult collaboration occurred, although it went largely unnoticed by the public. An unusual book called *The Planetary Commission* was responsible for spawning much of this activity.

Written in 1984, *The Planetary Commission* charted the course for humanity to achieve the "quantum leap" into the Aquarian Age—the Omega Point of human evolution alluded to by Alice Bailey, Teilhard Chardin, and other occult visionaries of the past. In order to launch this "move toward immortality," the author—instructed by his spirit guide—presented a plan for the largest human unity endeavor since the Tower of Babel. This massive worldwide event was called World Healing Day and took place on December 31, 1986. Portrayed as a gathering together of humanity to promote world peace, the event would actually serve to consolidate the efforts of New Agers worldwide, creating the momentum necessary to usher in their new occult order.

More than twelve years have come and gone since World Healing Day, but its effects continue to be felt. It helped inspire other milestone unity events, such as the Rio de Janeiro Earth Summit in 1992, and the Parliament of World Religions Conference in 1993—meetings organized by some of the same people. Because of the international success of World Healing Day and the events it set in motion, the author of *The Planetary Commission* has become recognized in occult circles as a special prophet on a spiritual mission. The name of this so-called "prophet" is John Randolph Price.

John Randolph Price (1932–)

John R. Price began his metaphysical quest in 1967 out of a sense of spiritual restlessness and lack of fulfillment. He had enjoyed great success in the field of advertising and public relations serving as executive vice president of a Chicago agency and president of a Houston-based firm. But he experienced a spiritual void and was searching for answers. Unfortunately, he looked in all the wrong places.

Price's desire to discover the meaning of life led him deeply into New Age mysticism. He began researching the philosophic mysteries of "Ancient Wisdom," integrating those teachings with "spiritual" psychology and metaphysics. His knowledge in this area would eventually make him a featured speaker on the Unity Church and New Thought circuits.

Price's theology emphasizes man's supernatural "God-like" qualities and presents the idea that man is quite capable of achieving heaven on earth—that is, if he allows the "universal energy" to direct his life. His philosophy is typical of New Age spiritual leaders. In his 1981 book, *The Super Beings,* he theorizes,

> It has been said that behind all fiction is a basis of fact. Does this mean that there is a grain of truth in the fictional Superman? What did the original creator of this comic strip and movie character have in mind when he first conceived the idea? Did he intuitively believe that man may someday evolve into a super-human creature with "out of this world" powers? If so, he was right.[1]

He goes on to surmise,

> Modern Science reports that the entire universe is made up of energy. The Illumined Ones tell us that this Energy is in reality the One Presence and Power of the universe—all Knowing, all-Loving, everywhere present, and that this pure Mind Energy is individualized in man, as man.[2]

Notice how quickly Price jumps from a fact of science to a speculative statement from the "Illumined Ones." Such presumptions are evident throughout Price's books. They demonstrate that his writings and plans for World Healing Day were spiritually directed.

John and Jan Price: A Biographical Summary

John Randolph Price and his wife, Jan, are the co-founders of the Quartus Foundation. Described by them as "a spiritual research and communications organization," the foundation was formed in 1981 and is headquartered in Boerne, Texas, near San Antonio.

Their Biographical Sketch states,

> The Prices have devoted more than 25 years to researching the philosophic mysteries of Ancient Wisdom and integrating those teachings with psychology and spiritual metaphysics. In recognition of their work, they were presented the *Light of God Expressing Award* by the Association of Unity Churches in 1986. John was named the recipient of the 1992 Humanitarian Award presented by the Arizona District of the International New Thought Alliance, and in 1984 he was presented the INTA's Joseph Murphy Award "in recognition

and appreciation of his distinguished service and leadership provided to the New Thought movement throughout the world."

John is a prominent New Age writer, having authored twelve books, including the national best-seller *The Angels within Us* (Fawcett Columbine), and its sequel, *Angel Energy: How to Harness the Power of Angels in Your Everyday Life.* Other popular titles by John include *Practical Spirituality,* "a book dealing with the practical application of metaphysical principles, including the benefits of meditation, establishing a bridge between mind and heart, and the 12 initiations required for mastery"; *A Spiritual Philosophy for the New World; The Superbeings;* and *The Planetary Commission,* which introduced World Healing Day, "a mind-link for peace" that began in 1986 and has continued each year on the same date.

His wife, Jan Price, has enjoyed success as well. She is a nationally known lecturer on the dynamics of positive living and the author of *The Other Side of Death* (Fawcett Columbine), "a book based on her near-death experience and visit beyond the veil in 1993. She also writes a column on practical spirituality for *Whole Health Magazine.*" Together the Prices have become a powerful duo in the New Age movement.[3]

The following exhibits offer a glimpse into the spiritual world of John and Jan Price.
Exhibit G-1 describes the "Spirit School," an annual New Age seminar hosted by the Prices. Exhibits G-2 and G-3, on the other hand, are from an advertisement promoting John's book, Angel Energy.
An examination of this material leads one to conclude that the Prices have been influenced by prominent occultists from the past. They seem to have integrated Edgar Cayce's mystical views on healing with the occult psychology/philosophy of Carl Jung and Teilhard Chardin; while simultaneously drawing from Alice Bailey's teachings on ageless wisdom, energy, pure light, and higher consciousness.
Occult topics frequently covered in Quartus publications include: healing, meditation, communicating with angels, and secrets of the ancient mystery religions. The Price's also promote the concept of self-divinity and have developed their own twisted account of creation in which humans are all part of "I AM" (God). They quote scripture out of context throughout their writings, yet have started their own "prayer network," creating the appearance of a legitimate religious organization. (For more information on The Quartus Foundation and its publications see Appendix E.)

Announcing

SPIRIT SCHOOL

March 5-8, 1998

An Intensive on

THE LIFE, WORLD, AND PURPOSE OF THE DIVINE *I*-SELF

presented by John and Jan Price

In order to enter the Inner World of Spirit, we must have a greater understanding and knowledge of what meditation is, and how to be lifted from the realm of effects into the pure Light of our true nature. We will do that.

From there we will take the journey inward--into new dimensions and realities--to attain a new awareness of why we've incarnated at this time, our Self's purpose for this lifetime, and to see through the Higher Vision to realize there are not two worlds...only the perfect expression and manifestation of Will-For-Good.

Our goal is to literally experience life from the highest frequency, and then, when we return to this world, to witness what was there all the time: the Ideal Body, Ideal Abundance, Ideal Success, Ideal Relationships, and the Ideal Life. In essence, we have to leave this plane for a time, so that when we return we can see with new eyes the glory that is already ours, already manifest in the physical world.

The Intensive will be held again at the Tapatio Springs Resort & Country Club in Boerne, Texas--truly an escape to peace and tranquility. The accommodations are luxurious with very affordable rates, and the large dining room offers a variety of delicious food for your eating pleasure. For sport and recreation there's golf, tennis, swimming, jacuzzi, and fully equipped exercise facilities with separate saunas for men and women.

Exhibit G-1

Take an extraordinary journey into the inner world of the Shining Ones

In *ANGEL ENERGY*, John Randolph Price—award winning author of more than a dozen books on the power within and the dynamics of creative living—reinforces your understanding of the Truth of Being, shows you how to free the awesome power of the angels—and with over 80 true life angel experiences, reveals what has happened in the lives of others who have discovered these indwelling Living Energies.

You will read about the mighty hands of the angels, inner guidance from the angels—and the angels and right livelihood, prosperity, physical healing, and relationships—also angel appearances and other strange events, what an angel sees for the future, and more.

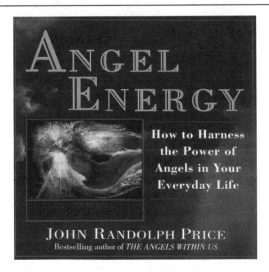

Exhibit G-2

> *The natural expression of the angels is* Truth. *If we deny the truth, we repress the energy of the angels. But when we fully accept the eternal verities of life, the angels go to work to bring everything up to the divine standard.* . . .
>
> Within each one of us dwell the twenty-two angels, centers of Living Energy that provide us with all we need to sustain us on our journey through life. They await only our readiness.
>
> However, the angels require our assistance to manifest changes in our lives. They are able to free us from disease and death, loneliness and unfulfillment, lack and limitation only when we free them. And so the author of the bestselling *The Angels Within Us* has written this book to help us set free the positive vibrations of these inner archetypes and their "nothing-is-impossible" energy.
>
> Through meditations, affirmations, exercises, dialogues with the twenty-two angels, and true stories of the miracles and transformations wrought by them, he helps us liberate the power of the Divine within so that we can:
>
> ❖ **Awaken our higher consciousness**
> ❖ **Heal the past**
> ❖ **Communicate with angels awake and dreaming**
> ❖ **Find our right livelihood**
> ❖ **Enjoy prosperity**
> ❖ **Open ourselves to physical healing**
> ❖ **Find fulfillment in our relationships**
> ❖ **Surrender to unconditional love**
> ❖ **And much more**
>
> Our angels are the very law of our being. This remarkable book helps us to connect and flow with their universal rhythm of wholeness, to become who and what we really are.

Exhibit G-3

Achieving Critical Mass

According to Price, his spirit guide, Asher, had communicated to him about the destructiveness of "negative thought patterns" and the significant role the year 1987 would play in reversing this trend. Based on his theology, which emphasizes "mind power," we, as collective humanity, have the negative thought power to cause wars, famines, tornadoes, and even violent crime. When enough people think negative "black thoughts," it affects the entire planet and adversely influences the actions of other people. This belief is referred to in New Age circles as the Hundredth Monkey concept.

The analogy goes something like this: There were ninety-nine monkeys on a certain tropical island. One day a monkey learned to wash his sweet potato before eating it. Soon he taught another monkey to do the same, and eventually all ninety-nine monkeys on this particular island were washing their sweet potatoes. Simultaneously, on the next island, without any personal contact, the hundredth monkey began washing his sweet potato on his own. The monkeys had taken an evolutionary "quantum leap" into a higher state of consciousness, establishing this new pattern in the "race mind" of monkeys. Price explains, "Because we are all related and connected on the subjective level, every single impulse in consciousness is impressed and registered in the collective consciousness of mankind—the universal energy field referred to as the race mind."[4]

This concept, based on the Jungian and Chardinian teachings of the collective unconscious and the global brain, holds that the mass of dark energy in the race mind has been "sub-critical" thus far in human history. In other words, the chain reaction of negative consequences has not been self-sustaining. Occultists generally believe that the world has not yet self-destructed because enough "positive light" has been released in the past through the appearance of various Spiritual Masters. These Masters, they claim, penetrated the darkness, thereby preventing mankind from destroying himself. Jesus, they would have us believe, was one of many such great masters.

In order to hold back any future manifestations of dark energy, John Price, following the instructions of his spirit guide, called for a worldwide, mass meditation (World Healing Day). This meditation, he asserted, would permanently reverse the polarity of the force field, supposedly achieving a critical mass of positive energy. Price believed that if fifty million people would meditate simultaneously, releasing their energies into the earth's magnetic field, the entire vibration of the planet would begin to change. That is why this event was designed to occur simultaneously throughout the world. A timetable given on page 155 of *The Planetary Commission* revealed that the event was coordinated to take place at noon, Greenwich time. If you live in Moscow, you would have meditated at 3 P.M.; Tokyo, 9 P.M.; Honolulu, 2 A.M.; Denver, 5 A.M.; and so on around the world.

Price was also hoping for five hundred million people to give their "mental consent" for the healing of the planet through this process. This would "not only maintain the negative energy mass in a sub-critical state, but will also begin to break up the severe intensity of the 'dark pockets'—thus preparing the collective consciousness for the massive penetration of Light on the final day of 1986." Price believed that if this endeavor was successful, "This world can be transformed into a heaven—right now."[5] If all of this sounds more like a weird science-fiction movie than an actual event designed to change the world, you can be certain that Price and his accomplices were—and still are—dead serious. (See Exhibits G-4 and G-5.)

WORLD
INSTANT
OF
COOPERATION

On December 31, 1986, humanity will be presented with an extraordinary opportunity. A planetary healing meditation, the WORLD INSTANT OF COOPERATION will be held throughout the world at noon Greenwich time (5:00 a.m. Mountain Time). The world's spiritual leaders will be asked to jointly assemble their believers in a moment of spiritual harmony and cooperation to heal our planet. 50,000,000 people will gather simultaneously to pray, meditate, and contemplate the harmony and oneness of all life on earth. Another 500,000,000 people will be asked to endorse this moment of harmonious resonance.

At this moment, at least 10% of the earth's population will be asked to suspend, for one hour, all thoughts of separation, conflict, and fear that exist *within each of us*. A positive, unified force field will be created by this moment of cooperation. A sufficient mass of people focusing for a sufficient period of time on an image of global peace and harmony *can* change the consciousness of our planet for the benefit of all living things.

In Denver, we plan to fill McNichols Arena for this momentous event. We ask everyone, regardless of their faith or belief, to help create the local manifestation of what is being created globally. Join with your brothers and sisters from throughout the metropolitan area as we hold this dream in our thoughts and prayers for one hour.

We invite you to participate in whatever way you feel is appropriate for you, to make this event a reality. Sign or circulate a petition consenting to the healing of the planet. Attend the event at McNichols Arena. Contribute your own special expertise to the preparations for the gathering, or contribute financially. Urge your friends and groups you are involved in to participate. And, most importantly, help it all happen by creating within yourself the peace, harmony, and sense of oneness that you desire for the planet.

You *can* make a difference. If you wish to participate in any way, or desire more information, please call or write: WORLD INSTANT OF COOPERATION, 1107 Cedar Avenue, Boulder, Colorado 80302, (303) 449-7188.

1107 Cedar Avenue
Boulder, CO 80302 U.S.A.
303 449-7188

Exhibit G-4

THE SEEDS OF PEACE WERE SOWN ON DECEMBER 31, 1986

At noon Greenwich time, December 31, 1986, men, women and children around the world participated in the most comprehensive prayer activity in history — a planetary affirmation of peace, love, forgiveness and understanding involving millions of people in a simultaneous global mind-link. It was called World Healing Day, the World Instant of Cooperation, and World Peace Day. Whatever the term or label, it was a New Beginning in restoring this world to sanity.

The majority of individuals and organizations participating in this activity were operating under the umbrella of the Planetary Commission, a worldwide non-denominational, non-political organization without a headquarters, structure or staff. The Commission was, and is, simply a grass roots cooperative effort to unite people in a common bond of love and bring our planet back into balance.

Perhaps the best summary of the 1986 Event was found in the *Los Angeles Times*: "It was billed as the biggest participatory event in history. The grass roots World Peace Event on Wednesday called upon peace activists to band together for a common cause: to spend an hour praying for world peace.

"And that's what millions of them did between 4 and 5 a.m. PST, an hour when it was New Year's Eve in all the world's time zones.

"They gathered in ashrams and town squares in India, at mountaintop ski resorts in Colorado, in churches and temples in San Diego and in the privacy of their own homes...to ring in what they hope will be the beginning of a new era of world harmony.

"In New York City, public radio station WBAI carried a satellite hookup with the Soviet Union to celebrate the World Peace Event. The four-hour special featured entertainment provided by artists from the East and West, and included greetings of peace and the reading of a Soviet child's letter to President Reagan about the need to eliminate nuclear arms.

"Event organizers based the estimate of the large response — 150 million to 400 million — on a computer analysis of information from sources worldwide — religious leaders and private citizens who have organized large gatherings in their own nations." (Excerpted from articles written by *Los Angeles Times* staff writers Maria L. La Ganga and Dennis McLellan)

The Commission did not disband after December 31, 1986. Between 500 million and 800 million of the world's citizens came together on the annual World Healing Days of 1987 and 1988, and the activity has expanded and gathered strength each year since. Have we seen any results? An earlier report from the Stockholm International Peace Research Institute provided encouraging news. Walter Stuetzle, the Institute's director and a former West German undersecretary of defense, said that "1988 has seen remarkable progress

toward a potentially more peaceful world...there was a clear break in the pattern of a constant increase in the number of major conflicts with which the world had grown accustomed during the 1980s."

Rather than "media events," the 1991 celebrations around the world focused on family, neighborhood, and community gatherings — as shown by this letter:

"World Healing Day is going strong here in Greenwood Lake, New York, on the edge of Sterling Forest. We had very enthusiastic people, including our singers all the way from Brooklyn and Jersey City, a priest, Monsignor, and a Lutheran pastor. And we were given permission to present the program from the main altar steps of the Holy Rosary Church. At the end we were given a standing ovation. Some folks just popped in on their way to work, and the cops came at their change of shift. Other folks tuned in at home. Monsignor calls us 'the Dawn Patrol'."

With continued dedication to Peace, this world can be totally transformed — and we ask you to participate in three ways:

1. Make a dedicated effort to practice and express Peace on a daily basis, realizing that Peace must begin within the heart and mind of each individual.

2. Reserve one hour on the last day of each month to meditate on Peace. This need not take place at noon Greenwich — any one-hour period that is most convenient for you will be satisfactory.

3. Meet again in spirit for the **Annual Global Mind-Link** at noon Greenwich time, December 31st — *and continue it at the same time on the last day of every year until the last one comes into the Light!*

Exhibit G-5

Exhibit G-4 represents just one of thousands of advertisements which were used to promote World Healing Day, also known as the World Instant of Cooperation. Exhibit G-5 depicts a follow-up promotional sent out by Price's group five years after World Healing Day, reviewing their success and urging followers to keep the momentum going.

Planning for the Event

Massive plans were made to ensure the success of World Healing Day. To help publicize the event, the Quartus Foundation put out monthly updates highlighting their activities in major cities across the planet. In one of these reports Price stressed,

> Millions more must be reached and influenced. Journalists must write about the Commission for the mass media. Those in broadcasting and film production must spread the word. Every counselor, seminar leader, healer, minister, practitioner, author, publisher, educator, teacher, and writer must speak and write of the Commission. Every spiritual group must rise above competitive attitudes and join together in a spirit of cooperation for world healing. . . . No conflict of philosophies should keep us from supporting one another in this endeavor.[6]

Any true Christian should have had a serious conflict of interest participating in the events of World Healing Day, since the motives and theology of the organizers ran diametrically opposed to the teachings of the Bible. Consider the following arrogant remarks by Price.

> It should be pretty obvious that there is no outer god who is about to yell, "Whoa boys, you've gone far enough; I'm coming down to earth to take over and establish peace among men and nations!" The God who is to save mankind, if it is to be saved, is the divine potential within humanity itself, the celestial spark within each individual. . . . There isn't much doubt any longer that this Universe is designed as a dwelling place for a race of gods.[7]

Statements such as these appear throughout Price's writings.

In the May 1, 1986 *Report from the Planetary Commission*, Price boasted of his carefully laid plans and listed the organizations "In Active Support of the Planetary Commission and World Healing Day." The list included: The National Association of Metaphysics, Emissaries of Divine Light, The Elisabeth Kubler-Ross Center, Findhorn, The International New Thought Alliance, The Association of Unity Ministers, and Prison Fellowship.

According to reports published by Quartus, major sports facilities rented for World Healing Day included the Houston Astrodome, McNichols Arena in Denver (with the late John Denver performing), the Omni Coliseum in Atlanta, the Metrodome in

Minneapolis, the San Diego Stadium, and the University of New Mexico Sports Arena in Albuquerque.

Other gatherings were planned for most of America's largest cities. A New Ager in Kansas City announced his intentions for that community: "We want to bring forth the creativity of Kansas City through music, visual arts, dance and drama with everything keyed off Teilhard de Chardin's line—'The future of the world is in our hands.'"[8]

In Alaska, one woman contacted several hundred churches by telephone, "reassuring" pastors that World Healing Day crossed all religious and political lines. She hoped, therefore, that everyone would participate. *The Methodist Peace with Justice Task Force* got the word out to all their Methodist churches in the same state. A Lutheran minister carried the idea back to her seminary in the fall of 1986, while the president of Alaska Pacific University made the information available to students there. Developments in Alaska were typical of those in other states.

Meanwhile, international plans were moving forward as scheduled. The August 1986 report from Quartus revealed that eighteen African nations would participate, and that the entire population of Sri Lanka—fifteen million people—would be involved. A New Age couple in Israel organized an outreach group with the objective of uniting their entire country behind this event. The New Age Communications Network of Australia announced that they were producing a fifty-minute television special called *Stop the Clock*, which was to help achieve the "critical mass of positive energy." And the occult Light Center of Findhorn, Scotland, drew international attention to the Planetary Commission through its New Age publication *One Earth*.

The Results

Fortunately, World Healing Day attracted fewer numbers than expected in the United States. This may have been due in part to a number of Christian ministries throughout America who exposed the occult nature of the event. This dark side had come to light through some of the event's publicity materials.

While results in the U.S. may have been less than hoped for, the media certainly did its part to promote and cover the event. The *Seattle News Times* reported, "7000 Meditate on Peace In Seattle Kingdome"; *Peoria Journal Star*, "Peorians Light City in Instant of Cooperation Peace Vigil"; *Los Angeles Times*, "Hands Joined in Prayer All Around the Globe."[9] The January 1987 update from the Quartus Foundation claimed that twenty-three hundred people in Santa Cruz participated in a five-hour program, while twenty-five hundred in Kansas City heard U.N. Assistant Secretary-General Robert Muller reflect on the power of World Healing Day. Price's event had successfully made the headlines in almost every major city. This free publicity alone made the meditation worthwhile in the eyes of New Agers.

Price enjoyed more success overseas, reporting that a total of 77 countries and 524 organizations participated in promoting the event. Encouraged by the response, his foundation immediately announced its plans for a "Second Annual Global Mind Link." His wife, Jan, declared, "See you on December 31, 1987, noon Greenwich time— and on and on until everyone on Earth joins in and the last one comes into the Light."[10]

It is important to remember that the outcome of these events is ultimately in God's hands and that Satan's plans will only proceed until God intervenes. Psalm 2:1–4 reminds us that the Lord is in control and will have the final say.

> Why do the heathen rage, and the people imagine a vain thing? The kings of the earth set themselves, and the rulers take counsel together, against the Lord, and against his anointed, saying, Let us break their bands asunder, and cast away their cords from us. He that sitteth in the heavens shall laugh: the Lord shall have them in derision.

Mankind has the tendency of seeking a human or occult-based answer to his problem of sin—anything but God's solution, or so it seems. In 1 Samuel, Chapter 8, the Israelites pleaded with God to give them an earthly king so that they could be like the other nations around them. God reluctantly gave them a king, proclaiming, "They have rejected me, that I should not reign over them" (1 Samuel 8:7b). Saul, the first king of Israel, became involved in the occult, seeking out the witch of Endor rather than God's counsel. The results were disastrous, and he soon lost his life in the battle against Israel's enemies.

The Bible reveals that destruction and devastation always occur when man rejects God's perfect ways in favor of Satan's empty promises. This still holds true today. First Thessalonians 5:3 warns, "For when they shall say, Peace and safety; then sudden destruction cometh upon them, as travail upon a woman with child; and they shall not escape."

On December 31, 1986, and several times since, millions of people gathering "in the name of peace" have tried to manipulate world events through "magic vibrations," in effect summoning demonic spirits via occult meditation, instead of interceding to the Prince of Peace through prayer. Unless the inhabitants of earth repent of their occult activities, Satan will soon be fully empowered to carry out his destructive plans.

On page 157 of *The Planetary Commission*, John Price gave the World Healing Meditation, which he hoped everyone would use during this "transforming" planetary hour. I share just a part of it here.

> Now is the time of the new beginning. I am a co-creator with God, and it is a new Heaven that comes as the Good Will of God is expressed on Earth through me. . . . I begin with me. I am a living Soul and the Spirit of God dwells in me, as me. I and the Father are one, and all that the Father has is mine. In truth, I am the Christ of God. . . . There is total Oneness, and in this Oneness we speak the Word. Let the sense of separation be dissolved. Let mankind be returned to God-kind.

This is nothing short of blasphemy. In the 1960s and '70s, various cult leaders claimed to be "the Christ" or the "new messiah." Most people dismissed their claims as nonsense. Today we are witnessing millions of people at the same moment saying, "In truth, I am the Christ of God." Jesus warned of such a blasphemous time in Luke 21:8, "Take heed that ye be not deceived: for many shall come in my name, saying, I am Christ; and the time draweth near: go ye not therefore after them." We are the generation witnessing the fulfillment of this prophecy!

Pressing Toward Their Goal

In *The Super Beings*, Price boasts that the movement towards a global society and a world religion is rapidly progressing.

> The revolution has begun. It started more than one hundred years ago, but now the pace is quickening. Throughout the world, men and women are joining in the uprising and are coming forward to be counted as part of a new race that will someday rule the universe.[11]

To achieve their Luciferic goal to establish a new world religion and global government, occult elitists are integrating their ideas into our culture in subtle, yet powerful ways. "We Are the World," for example, is not just a popular song; it has become a New Age theology. Human unity events promoted by top New Age performers are now the popular trend. We have had U.S.A. for Africa, Live Aid,

Farm Aid, the Goodwill Games, the First Earth Run, and Hands Across America, to name just a few. These enormous consciousness-raising events have been invaluable in promoting the idea of this planet as a single living organism, an interdependent "global village."

Live Aid alone was allegedly seen by 1.5 billion people in 160 countries. That represents almost one in every four people in the world. These events have shown how easy it is to get massive numbers of people to support major causes if they are well promoted. Price's organizers had every reason to expect World Healing Day to be the biggest in this series of global events.

Big name entertainers appeared at these functions to ensure large crowds. Some of them were practicing New Agers. Willie Nelson, for example, was the featured performer on July 4, 1986, at the Farm Aid Concert at the Houston Astrodome. In a newspaper published by the group New Age Activists, he shared his strong belief in reincarnation.[12]

Harry Belafonte, on the other hand, was the musician responsible for organizing the "We Are the World" concert and album. This event was purportedly designed to alleviate world hunger. However, in a later interview in *Billboard* magazine, Belafonte pointed out that it really was another part of the campaign to overthrow the present nation-state system and set up a U.N.-run world government.[13]

Media-mogul Ted Turner did his part by sponsoring the Goodwill Games. At one of his conferences, he stated that America must elect a "New Age" president if it wanted to survive through the year 2000. (He got his wish, but America may not survive as a result!) Turner also announced his conclusion that America is the greatest problem in the world.[14] It seems that his "good will" does not extend to his own country, whose free enterprise system has enabled him to become one of the world's wealthiest people. Instead, he is helping to build his New Age dream of global government by sharing his wealth with the United Nations.

Billions to Be "Cleansed"

John Price claims that the New Age has already begun, but that humanity now has the responsibility of creating the civilization to go with it. This "Aquarian Civilization," once in place, will undoubtedly open its arms of welcome to all who embrace its new theology. However, those who take Jesus at his narrow words—"I am the way, the truth, and the life: no man cometh unto the Father, but by me" (John 14:6)—may need to experience a "cleansing" because of their "self-centered, separatist" ideas.

New Agers consider Christians to be selfish or self-centered because they accept the biblical teaching that each person began his or her existence in time at the moment of conception as a creature separate from the all-powerful Creator. To be separatist, therefore, according to New Age theology, is to reject the pantheistic belief that all is God. Those separatists who reject the teachings of pantheism and who do not believe that all the world's religions can be melded into one religious system are in the way and must be dealt with.

In *Practical Spirituality*, Price expresses his hope that the building process of the Planetary Commission can be done in peace and harmony, with its activities resulting in a dramatic change for the good of all mankind. However, his spirit guide, Asher, seems to see things a bit differently.

Asher explained his concept of the "cleansing process" in some detail to Price:

> This fusing of energies, which will reach a peak on December 31, 1986, will remove the threat of global war but will not eliminate all local hostilities. It will also cause dramatic advances in scientific discoveries, revamp the concept of established "religion and church," and serve as a ring of protection for more than three billion people. . . . Nature will soon enter her cleansing cycle. Those who reject the earth's changes with an attitude of "it can't happen here" will experience the greatest emotion of fear and panic, followed by rage and violent action. These individuals with their lower vibratory rates, will be removed during the next two decades.

Price responded to his guide, "I know that one of the most serious problems we have today is overpopulation, but wiping more than 2 billion people off the face of the earth is a little drastic, don't you think?"

Asher replied, "Who are we to say that these people did not volunteer to be a part of the destruction and regeneration—for the purpose of soul growth?"[15]

Adolf Hitler was responsible for the deaths of as many as 50 million people worldwide through the terrible world war and persecution he precipitated. Yet, Asher is calling for the elimination of more than 2 billion people to accomplish his New Age goal. Incredibly, this is being proposed in the name of world peace and unity! Despite this satanic threat to destroy billions of lives there is virtually no criticism from New Age leaders against this monstrous genocidal plan.

Adding insult to injury, Price received comprehensive coverage of his event from the international media—virtually all of it favorable. It is difficult to imagine that all of the media members covering World Healing Day were ignorant of the event's real purpose. Did none of them take the time to research Price's occult background? If they did, why didn't they warn us? Could it be that some in the media support his New Age agenda?

And what about our political leaders in Washington? How much do they know? Most of them have remained strangely silent when it comes to exposing the New Age movement and its deadly plans against Christians and God-fearing Jews.

Price once again alluded to Asher's sinister plans for planet Earth in a report promoting World Healing Day:

> Through the efforts of millions of men and women with purity of motive and a consciousness reaching for Christhood, the world of illusion will separate into islands of Light and Darkness. Those attracted to the Light will gather as one . . . and they shall be taken into the Light and they will become the Light. And the light shall spread to the island of darkness *and it will cease to exist.*[16] (italics added)

Statements such as these remind one of *The Screwtape Letters*, by C. S. Lewis. Everything is backwards. Individuals involved in these misleading occult activities would do well to heed the warning of the prophet Isaiah, "Woe unto them that call evil good, and good evil; that put darkness for light, and light for darkness; that put bitter for sweet, and sweet for bitter! . . . So their root shall be as rottenness, and their blossom shall go up as dust: because they have cast away the law of the Lord of hosts" (Isa. 5:20, 24b).

Thus far, we have examined the influence of one man and his demon spirit guide on World Healing Day. Lest we believe that Price's theology was unique among those promoting this massive New Age meditation, let us consider another key individual who devoted much time and energy toward making this event a success.

Barbara Marx Hubbard (1929–)

Barbara Marx Hubbard is a pleasant-looking, gray-haired grandmother with an infectious smile and a great enthusiasm for solving the world's problems. Unfortunately, regardless of how well intentioned she may appear to be, she has been blinded by the great deceiver and is leading thousands of unsuspecting followers down the path of spiritual darkness.

Barbara grew up in a privileged home as the daughter of the late toy manufacturer Louis Marx. Her list of credentials and scope of influence reads like a *Who's Who In America*. She graduated cum laude in political science from Bryn Mawr College, and in 1970 co-founded the Committee for the Future with John Whiteside. She also helped found the World Future Society in 1966 and continues to serve on its board of directors. It has since grown into an international organization with more than 30,000 members in 80 countries. The society operates local chapters in over 120 cities. Its influence reaches all the way to the White House and Congress. (See Exhibits H-1 and H-2.)

Hubbard leads a very active political life. She is a former member of the Presidential Committee on National [Education] Curriculum and was a Democratic Party nominee for the vice presidency of the United States in 1984. (That was the year Walter Mondale ran for President and Governor Mario Cuomo addressed the Democratic National Convention.) She is also the founder of the New World Center in Washington, D.C., and has been an advisor to such organizations as the Federal Energy Administration, the House of Representatives, and the Senate.

Barbara has also produced a radio program called "New News from the Peace Room," which, according to her, is an "international radio outreach for 'IT'—the whole field of people who contain within them the planetary DNA—the next step in evolution."[17] She currently directs an organization called the Center for Conscious Evolution, which promotes her occult ideas.

The World Future Society's far-reaching influence is demonstrated by the political dignitaries who speak at its functions. According to the society, Al Gore spoke on the environment and population at their annual conference in 1989, while Newt Gingrich shared his ideas for "reinventing Congress" at their 1993 meeting. The organization also helped create the Congressional Clearinghouse on the Future which involves 100 members of Congress.

Exhibit H-1 (overleaf) displays the back page of one of the society's promotionals, providing an overview of the organization's notable accomplishments. Notice some of the leading statesmen and "thinkers" who have attended their meetings on the future. With powerful globalists such as Robert McNamara, Maurice Strong, and Glenn Seaborg on its board of directors, it is easy to understand how The World Future Society influences the world's elite to support the cause of global government.

In the 1980s, the society sponsored Worldview '84—the first in a series of world government planning forums. This conference served as a platform for the World Constitution and Parliament Association, of which Glenn Seaborg has been a member.

Exhibit H-2 is from another page of the same brochure. It describes the society's main publication, The Futurist, *and names some of the individuals who have written for it. The list includes New Agers Alvin Toffler, Buckminster Fuller, Marilyn Ferguson, John Naisbitt, and Matthew Huxley, to name just a few.*

THE WORLD FUTURE SOCIETY

Founded in 1966, the World Future Society is chartered as a nonprofit organization in Washington, D.C. Through the years the Society has had a number of significant accomplishments.

- Helped establish the Congressional Clearinghouse on the Future, which now has over 100 members of the United States Congress.
- Prepared a report for the National Science Foundation and the Library of Congress entitled "Resources Guide for America's Third Century."
- Helped establish the study of the future as a scientific discipline. (Future studies are now taught in over 200 universities and many more schools.)
- Briefed President Reagan on the future, along with Vice President Bush, Donald Regan, and other White House staff. This White House luncheon was attended by the WFS president along with a group of distinguished futurists.
- Now publishes three periodicals: THE FUTURIST: A Journal of Forecasts, Trends, and Ideas About the Future; FUTURES RESEARCH QUARTERLY: a scholarly journal emphasizing methods and techniques for studying the future; and FUTURE SURVEY: A Monthly Abstract of Books, Articles, and Reports on Forecasts, Trends, and Ideas About the Future.
- Held major worldwide conferences attracting leading statesmen, thinkers, and others, including Gerald R. Ford, Buckminster Fuller, Arthur C. Clarke, Alvin Toffler, John Naisbitt, Isaac Asimov, B.F. Skinner, Albert Gore, Newt Gingrich, Ted Kennedy, Bertrand de Jouvenel, Herman Kahn, Harvey Cox, Harrison Brown, Gary Hart, Barbara Mikulski, Julian Simon, John Anderson, Betty Friedan, Gene Roddenberry, Hazel Henderson, Robert Jungk, Amitai Etzioni, Elise Boulding, Claiborne Pell and other prominent statesmen, authors, scientists, researchers, and others from all over the world.
- Published over 20 books including: *Communications Tomorrow; The Computerized Society; Careers Tomorrow; Future Survey Annual; The Study of the Future; The Futures Research Directory; Habitats Tomorrow; Global Solutions; The Great Transformation; and The Global Economy: Today, Tomorrow, and the Transition.*
- Operates the Futurist Bookstore, the world's only store devoted solely to books dealing with the future. (Located at the Society's headquarters in Bethesda, Maryland.)

DIRECTORS

Clement Bezold, executive director, Institute for Alternative Futures

Harlan Cleveland, president, World Academy of Art and Science

Hugues de Jouvenel, executive director, Association International Futuribles, Paris, France

Victor Ferkiss, professor of government emeritus, Georgetown University

Orville Freeman, attorney; former U.S. Secretary of Agriculture

John W. Gardner, author and philosopher; founder, Common Cause

William E. Halal, professor of management science, The George Washington University

Barbara Marx Hubbard, president, Foundation for Conscious Evolution

Sol M. Linowitz, attorney, former U.S. ambassador to the Organization of American States

Eleonora B. Masini, chair, executive council, World Futures Studies Federation, Rome, Italy

Robert S. McNamara, former president, World Bank; former U.S. Secretary of Defense

Michael Michaelis, president, Partners In Enterprise, Inc.

Sandra Postel, senior fellow, Worldwatch Institute

Glenn T. Seaborg, Nobel Prize-winning chemist; former Chairman, U.S. Atomic Energy Commission

Irving S. Shapiro, attorney; former chairman, E.I. du Pont de Nemours & Co.

Maurice F. Strong, secretary general, U.N. Conference on Environment and Development

Rowan A. Wakefield, former senior editor, *The American Family*

OFFICERS

Edward Cornish, president

Graham T.T. Molitor, vice president and legal counsel

Kenneth W. Hunter, treasurer

WORLD FUTURE SOCIETY
7910 Woodmont Avenue, Suite 450, Bethesda, MD 20814

Exhibit H-1

Now You Can Learn About Tomorrow... Today

Benefits of

THE FUTURIST

A JOURNAL OF FORECASTS, TRENDS, AND IDEAS ABOUT THE FUTURE.

This exciting bimonthly magazine brings important updates of new technologies, forecasts, and scenarios that may affect peoples' lives in the years ahead. Articles by leading experts provide a fascinating glimpse of the world that is yet to come. Contributors have included author Alvin Toffler, Vice President Al Gore, Speaker of the House Newt Gingrich, MIT Media Lab Founder Nicholas Negroponte, comprehensive designer Buckminster Fuller, computer theorist John Diebold, anthropologist Margaret Mead, sociologist Amitai Etzioni, author Stuart Chase, theologian Harvey Cox, careers expert Richard Bolles public opinion expert Daniel Yankelovich, physicist Fritjof Capra, political scientist Bertrand de Jouvenel, science-fiction writer Frederik Pohl, author Marilyn Ferguson, Nobel Prize-winning chemist Glenn T. Seaborg, space scientist Gerard K. O'Neill, forecaster Marvin Cetron, economist Jay Forrester, Wall Street forecaster David Bostian, former Czech President Vaclav Havel, publisher and health authority Robert Rodale, as well as interviews with John Naisbitt, author of *Megatrends*, and Matthew Huxley, author and son of Aldous Huxley, among many others.

THE FUTURIST BOOKSTORE CATALOG

AND DISCOUNTS ON OVER 300 BOOKS

The World Future Society operates the world's only "Bookstore of the Future" carrying over 300 hard-to-find books, scores of tapes, and other products. Members get special discounts on almost everything.

"Futurism is no longer at the service of mere curiosity. No longer does it serve the simple wish to be entertained and astonished. It has become an indispensable adjunct to business and government."

— Isaac Asimov

Exhibit H-2

113

A Major Organizer

Hubbard's chief passion is bringing about global unity through a restructuring of the world's governments. As a result of her influence, the Human Unity Conference established a subgroup of forty people to make contact with the heads of all religious groups in the world to encourage their support of World Healing Day.

Barbara also spread the word through her many workshops, lectures, and international travels. In the spring of 1986, for example, she made a special trip to the Soviet Union with eighty other American "citizen diplomats" to engage in dialogue with their counterparts on the theme "In Search of a Positive Future." While there, she discovered that Joseph Goldin, a Moscow writer who supposedly had never heard of the Planetary Commission, was working on an event for New Year's Eve 1986, which was nearly identical to the World Healing Day envisioned by Price and herself.

Joseph Goldin shared his own vision:

> Who would write a script for a global New Year's Party involving two billion people participants? After the success of the global Live Aid Concert on 13 July 1985, which brought together a phenomenal worldwide audience to match the importance of the event, a global New Year's Party with a focal point in Moscow is not so wild a dream. Still, how does one go about writing a script for such a mega-vision? People on different continents will be thrilled by experiencing a sense of distant proximity and might gladly go along with lighting candles. As a result, two billion people across the globe will see one another via space bridges.[18]

Needless to say, Barbara Hubbard and Joseph Goldin began working together.

Goldin received help for his international communications from Yevgeny Velikhou, vice president of the Soviet Academy of Sciences. Velikhou was involved with Mikhail Gorbachev's drive to widen the use of computers in the U.S.S.R. The U.S. Department of Commerce had reportedly already given the go-ahead for computer links to Goldin's U.S. contacts. In fact, Ted Turner and a "Moscow faith healer" had talked on the linked system.

It appears that Joseph Goldin targeted the December 31st Peace Event as a major focus for his electronic exchanges. Arrangements were made with MTV (Music Television) to set up a seven-continent global television linkup, similar to the one organized for Live Aid.

In addition to networking with Goldin on World Healing Day, Hubbard sponsored numerous one-world dialogues with the

Russians. Of her experiences, she states: "I will never forget the Soviet-American Citizen Summits we organized in the early Gorbachev years. It was a demonstration of synergy unlike any I'd ever previously experienced. We invited Soviets and Americans to meet in task forces to develop joint projects and social innovations for the Third Millennium."[19]

Reinterpreting the Bible

Barbara Hubbard viewed December 31, 1986, as a "Planetary Pentecost," where participants would have the powers of Christ to heal, resurrect the dead, and even transform their physical bodies as Christ transformed His. Hubbard teaches that we are all cells of the global brain. By holding, connecting, and sharing the global brain, we will unlock the key to the planetary shift in consciousness, taking the "quantum leap" in spiritual evolution toward reaching our own godhood.

Her New Age explanation of what happened on the day of Pentecost in the Upper Room to the 120 followers of Jesus is most interesting. It twists biblical spiritual reality into a New Age occult experience.

> I believe a magnetic field of consciousness was created which activated the dormant powers, which exist in each of us. They became fearless and were transfigured by resonance, unconditional love, which provided a field in which to experience Spirit collectively. A Planetary Pentecost would be a mass transfiguration and empowerment of millions at once . . . a "second coming" through lifting our own consciousness to Christ-centered consciousness.[20]

This concept dovetails with John Price's New Age explanation of the second coming of Christ, which in reality describes the emergence of the coming Antichrist and his world system. The "return of Christ," according to this occult view, is a reference to a phenomenon in which a new energy field will seed human consciousness, causing it to become the "Christ" individualized. Who will experience this kind of second coming? Obviously, not true Christians. Mrs. Hubbard tells us that we cannot reach the "Tree of Life" (the Tree of Immortality) in a state of self-centered consciousness, laboring under the illusion that we are separate. The power humans will inherit is too great for a "self-centered" species.

To facilitate her goals, Barbara has composed her own version of the Book of Revelation called *Manual for Co-Creators of the Quantum Leap*. In her book *The Evolutionary Journey*, she explains what led to the writing of this material. She tells us, "All my life I have been a seeker for meaning. Born of a Jewish agnostic, affluent background in 1929, I received no spiritual training." Her "seeking" led her down many paths until eventually she read *The Phenomenon of Man* by Teilhard Chardin. She explains,

> It was an epiphany for me. There is a continuing, evolving pattern in the process of nature that leads to greater whole systems, higher consciousness and freedom . . . and it's going on NOW. It's unfinished. The world is evolving, not just the individual. Not only do I have unused growth potential . . . so does the world . . . so does our species . . . and so does the universe! Something new is coming. The magnetic attraction was right. I could trust my intuition.[21]

After studying Chardin's writings, Barbara sought out people around the world who were working on aspects of humanity's next step forward and who, like her, felt the attraction that Chardin described. Chardin's teachings on quantum transformation, spiritual evolution, and everything being globally connected appealed to her and drew her into the heart of his theology.

The main problem, from Barbara's perspective, was that humanity was still self-centered and was suffering from the illusion of separation from God. Remember, according to New Age theology, to be self-centered and separatist is to believe that you are a sinful creature in need of the grace and forgiveness of a personal God. In truth, that describes a God-centered, not a self-centered, person. New Agers turn everything upside down. It is they who are self-centered by seeking their own personal empowerment and liberation from a personal God rather than seeking to serve and love him as the Creator of all life.

Hearing from the Other Side

In a state of frustration, Hubbard rented a house in Santa Barbara in January 1980 to write a book on her evolutionary perspective. Near a monastery, she claimed to hear the voice of Jesus telling her, "My resurrection was a signal for all of yours." At this point, Barbara made the mistake of her life: She listened to the words of a false Christ (a fallen angel) and became a channel for what is untrue. Here is what this voice of deception had to say:

> The communion ceremony is to become the union ceremony. . . . As each person has a higher, wiser self, so does the species-as-a-whole. . . . Be members of a more mature species. You HAVE THE POWERS OF A NATURAL CHRIST.

This is what I came to Earth to reveal. . . . Yours are the powers. Yours the glory. You—all of you who are desirous and ready—are the way. Be a beacon of light unto yourselves. This tiny band, this brave congregation of souls attracted to the future of the world are my avant-garde, my new order of the future. They are self-selected souls who have come to earth to carry the miracle of the resurrection into action as the transformation of Homo sapiens to Homo universalist.[22]

Barbara shares some of her reactions and thoughts as these "revelations" were given to her:

The floodgates of my mind had opened. It was as if an unseen hand was activating the memory bank of my brain. I organized nothing. I "thought" of nothing. I simply recorded the stream of ideas. . . . Sometimes a voice that called itself "Jesus" interpreted authoritatively. . . . In other passages it seemed as though the voices were those of our elder brothers and sisters who have gone before and already know the way. I feel that "I"—my normal waking, conscious personality, who has been a seeker—virtually co-created the text with a hierarchy of other, higher selves. . . . Other sections seemed to come from a collective species consciousness.[23]

Destruction of the Old Order

With her mind opened to the spirit realm, Hubbard began to see the New Testament in a different light. The New Testament to her became a book of instructions for the final countdown to birth, the selection of the "God-centered" from the "self-centered." Her experiences led her to conclude that the Book of Revelation was a terminal warning to earth-bound, self-centered people, revealing details of the tribulation to come and a glimpse of the New Jerusalem that "enlightened" humanity is to build.

Hubbard's "voices" proceeded to give their interpretation of the sixth chapter of Revelation. She expects us to believe that this was a divine revelation and that she—a woman with practically no previous Bible training and no personal relationship with the Creator—was the chosen vessel. The explanation Hubbard gave for why she "heard from on high" was that she had been confused and was seeking answers. What follows sounds very much like another letter to Wormwood from Uncle Screwtape, C. S. Lewis' fictitious demon character. Of Revelation 6:4, Hubbard's voices say:

Humanity will not be able to make the transition from Earth-only to universal life until the chaff has been separated from the wheat. The great reaper must reap before we can take the quantum leap to the next phase of evolution. No worldly peace can prevail until the self-centered members of the planetary body either change or die. That is the choice. The red horse is the destruction during the birth process of those who refuse to be born into God-centered, universal life. . . . This act is as horrible as killing a cancer cell. It must be done for the sake of the future of the whole. So be it: be prepared for the selection process which is now beginning. The second seal revealed a red horse ridden by one with the power to take peace from the Earth. It stands for the necessity of the selection process which shall rip apart the old order and destroy those who choose to remain self-centered remnants of the past.[24]

Barbara's voices have repeatedly tried to intimidate Christians who are spreading the truth of Jesus Christ: "The modern moralists who preach the irremediable degradation of human beings as sinners are assassinating the witnesses to hope. . . . But even now my legions are growing." The pointed message to Christians is clear.

The Apostle John tells us that Jesus alone can release us from our sins by his blood (Revelation 1:5). However, Barbara Hubbard listens to voices telling her a different gospel. She mocks and counters true Christians, saying, "Evangelists are proclaiming that the kingdom of God is at hand. They are urging repentance and acceptance of Jesus as your personal savior. . . . It is your work to envision the New Jerusalem as a society of full humanity wherein each person is a natural Christ. Dearly beloveds, you are my New Order for the future."[25]

My Bible paints a very different picture of the New Jerusalem. "And the city had no need of the sun, either of the moon, to shine in it: for the glory of God did lighten it, and the Lamb is the light thereof" (Revelation 21:23). This same Lamb is the one who is in full control of all the events described in the sixth chapter of Revelation. He is the one who breaks the seals in verses 1, 3, 5, 7, 9, and 12. He also later breaks the seventh seal of silence, environmental catastrophe, and darkness in Revelation 8:1. Who is this Lamb? John the Baptist identifies him as being Jesus Christ (John 1:29).

Hubbard's demon voices continue their anti-Christ version of the Great Tribulation:

We, the elders, have been patiently waiting until the very last moment before the quantum transformation, to take action to cut out this corrupted and corrupting element in the body of humanity. It is like watching a cancer grow; something must be done before the whole body is destroyed . . . the self-centered members must be destroyed. There is no alternative. Only the God-centered can evolve. Fortunately you, dearly beloveds, are not responsible for this act. We are. We are in charge of God's selection process for planet Earth. He selects, we destroy. We are the riders of the pale horse, Death. We will use whatever means we must to make this act of destruction as quick and painless as possible to the one-half of the world who are capable of evolving. . . . Now everything is global and connected. Each person is about to inherit the power of destruction and co-creation. The inner voice, the higher self, each person's own connection to God–independent of priest, text, church or mentor–must be heard directly. . . . Those of you who know what is happening—the one-fourth who are now listening to the higher self—are to be guides for the rest who will be panicked and confused.[26]

Notice that "the elders"—the most powerful demons—want to make this destruction painless, not for those who are to be destroyed, but for "the co-creators" (their human helpers) who will have to witness the destruction. This material goes on for pages, but the preceding paragraphs sufficiently demonstrate the dangerous mind-set of Mrs. Hubbard and the voices guiding her.

Nearly two thousand years ago the Apostle Paul warned against listening to anyone who twists the Words of God. "But even though we, or an angel from heaven should preach to you a gospel contrary to that which we have preached to you, let him be accursed. . . . And no wonder, for even Satan disguises himself as an angel of light" (Gal. 1:8; 2 Cor. 11:14, NASB). Barbara Hubbard obviously has not taken this warning seriously. She has repeatedly demonstrated a willingness to accept false explanations that invert or alter biblical truth.

Revelation 21:5 states, "And he that sat upon the throne said, Behold, I make all things new. And he said unto me, Write: for these words are true and faithful." Barbara, however, has reinterpreted this passage as follows: "And he who sat upon the throne said to me, 'Behold I am writing anew, through scribes on earth who are willing to listen to me.'"[27] She has knowingly rewritten Scripture based upon what "her voices" have told her.

There is a strong warning in the Book of Revelation, which, if heeded, would have prevented Barbara from beginning her odyssey into distortion.

For I testify unto every man that heareth the words of the prophecy of this book, If any man shall add unto these things, God shall add unto him the plagues that are written in this book: And if any man shall take away from the words of the book of this prophecy, God shall take away his part out of the book of life, and out of the holy city, and from the things, which are written in this book. (Rev. 22:18–19)

What the Lord said two thousand years ago still applies today.

Other "Unity" Events of the Eighties

World Healing Day, as it turned out, was merely the climax to a series of esoteric events that took place throughout 1986, which had been designated by the United Nations as the International Year of Peace. These events were designed to cumulatively shift human consciousness into viewing the world as one interdependent whole. Some of the more significant endeavors from that year are summarized below.

Million Minutes of Peace

One of the events leading up to World Healing Day was called The Million Minutes of Peace. I first learned about this undertaking through a mailing from Lucis Trust, the organization founded by Alice Bailey.

Million Minutes of Peace puts out a monthly newsletter called *Minute by Minute*. In the first issue of this newsletter they proclaimed, "What started out as a project for the United Nations International Year of Peace in Australia has mushroomed into a global initiative with over 40 countries taking part." Their other publication, called *Your Thoughts Count*, explained that their aim was to collect pledges not of money, but of thoughts of peace. These "Million Minutes"—consisting of "thoughts of peace"—ran from September 16 to October 16, 1986.

Promoters stressed the fact that people were linking with others in thought, regardless of belief, tradition, or political differences. On page 2 of their first issue, they talked about the "hundredth monkey" concept and went on to say, "There are two prerequisites: First, pure thought must be sustained over a relatively long period. Second, a critical number of people must think thoughts of peace in order for the thought pattern to become common awareness." This appeal for global unity was launched in the foyer of the United Nations. The U.N. chapel was open from noon to five o'clock for people to donate their minutes of peace.

The list of groups and individuals, which either endorsed this event or actively worked for its success, included Lucis Trust, Eileen Caddy (co-founder of Findhorn), "His Holiness" the Dalai Lama, Institute of Noetic Sciences (Willis Harman's group), Friends of the Earth, Planetary Citizens, Brahma Kumanis World Spiritual Organization, author Sydney Sheldon, Rt. Hon. Bishop Desmond Tutu, author/lecturer Marilyn Ferguson, Sen. Edward Kennedy, the president of the World Council of Churches, the Church of Religious Science, Unity-in-Diversity Council, and the Human Unity Institute, to name just a few.

The Appeal climaxed at a Peace Concert that was held at St. John the Divine Cathedral in Manhattan. An estimated ten thousand people watched as the final count of the minutes donated worldwide was presented to Dr. James O. C. Jonah, assistant Secretary General of the United Nations. A candle lighting ceremony symbolized the minds' pledges of peaceful thought.[28]

This same church—St. John the Divine Cathedral—displays a female Christ on the cross, complete with shapely hips and full breasts. The "Very Reverend" James Parks Morton, dean of the cathedral, states that the response to the crucifix has been very positive. One wonders how far blasphemy can go. Developments such as these remind one of ancient Israel's spiritual corruption and the resulting consequences. Zephaniah declared, "Her prophets are light and treacherous persons: her priests have polluted the sanctuary, they have done violence to the law" (Zeph 3:4).

Join us for the Launching
on September 16, 1986
at 12 noon at the 'Chapel'
Church Center for the U.N.
U.N. Plaza & 44th Street

CUT ALONG DOTTED LINE AND MAIL THIS CARD

AFFIX
14¢
STAMP
HERE

The Million Minutes of Peace Appeal
P.O. Box 2492
New York, N.Y. 10163

"A Minute of peace is a truth that the hands can touch."
—Ben Kingsley (Actor)

"With peace there can be continuing life. And life can be wonderful."
—Irving Wallace (Author)

"The cause of peace is, of course, the most important issue facing all people of the world."
—Lawrence R. Klein
(Benjamin Franklin Professor of Economics)

"May I take this opportunity to congratulate you and your associates on this beautiful initiative and to assure you of our collaboration and our prayers for peace."
—Archbishop Giovanni Cheli
(Permanent Observer of The Holy See to the U.N.)

"All of the obstacles are human-made, and hence can be dissolved by human choice. We only need to be willing to pay the price. The price is a total change of mind."
—Willis Harman
(President, Institute of Noetic Sciences)

"In peace we thrive. I have seen war in Vietnam. I pray with all my heart for peace on earth. And love between men."
—Oliver Stone, Film-maker

"A world of peace——not pieces."
—Sidney Sheldon (Author)

Remember to be there October 22 at the Cathedral of St. John the Divine for a spectacular international event!

Your Thoughts...
...Count!

The Million
Minutes
of Peace

An International Appeal

LUCIS TRUST
113 University Place
11th Floor
New York, N. Y. 10003
RETURN POSTAGE GUARANTEED

**International Year
of Peace 1986**

Exhibit I-1

"I shall pray much for the success of this event. Specially that it may lead people to prayful silence, for the fruit of prayer is faith, the fruit of faith is love, the fruit of love is service."

— Mother Teresa

The Million Minutes of Peace
An International Appeal

AIMS

The Million Minutes of Peace International Appeal is a unique, worldwide people's program that will be held in 42 countries from September 16 to October 16, 1986.

This global initiative is currently capturing the imagination of people all over the world, because it is designed with the sole purpose of bringing together people from diverse ethnic, political and religious backgrounds in a program to espouse and support peace.

The unifying and symbolic component of the program is that individuals, families and community groups will essentially donate to The Appeal minutes of peace, through positive thoughts, meditation or prayer.

The Appeal will climax on October 16 at large public programs in major cities of the world. A spectacular international celebration will be held in New York City on October 22 at the Cathedral of St. John the Divine. This event will be followed by a thematic international presentation of Multi-Million Minutes of Peace to the Secretary General of the U.N. on United Nations Day, October 24, 1986.

What Can You Do To Support The Appeal?

To make The Million Minutes of Peace a resounding success in the U.S., individuals, families and community groups can make donations to The Appeal in the following ways:

■ Sending in pledge forms to the local Million Minutes of Peace office giving the number of minutes donated to The Appeal through positive thoughts, prayer or meditation.

■ Attending at least one of the community programs organized in their cities/towns to celebrate The Million Minutes of Peace between September 16 and October 16.

■ Organizing family/group/community events to celebrate The Appeal between September 16 and October 16.

■ Encouraging other individuals, families and groups to participate in The Appeal, and distributing pledge forms to these persons to donate minutes.

Organizers

To make The Appeal a truly international event, National Appeal Advisory Committees of prominent persons have been formed to oversee the coordination of The Appeal in each country.

A National Appeal Advisory Committee has been formed in the U.S., with local Appeal Committees in 25 cities/towns. There are also four co-sponsors of The Appeal — Brahma Kumaris World Spiritual Organization, The Child Development Foundation, Human Unity Institute and Planetary Citizens.

Supporting Organizations:

The Experiment in International Living
OXFAM-America
Christian Peace Conference
Universal Children's Gardens
The Christophers

To find out how you can actively participate in The Million Minutes of Peace International Appeal, write or call:

The Million Minutes of Peace Appeal
P.O. Box 2492
New York, N.Y. 10163

Telephone: (212) 557-6251 or
(718) 424-3091
(9 a.m. to 8 p.m. daily)

CUT ALONG DOTTED LINE AND MAIL THIS CARD

PLEDGE DONATION CARD

I / We hereby pledge or donate:
☐ Positive Thoughts ☐ Meditation ☐ Prayer (Please check appropriate box)
_____ minutes per day for _____ days, in

NAME _____ (Person or Organization)

ADDRESS _____

CITY _____ STATE _____ ZIP _____

TELEPHONE # _____ (PLEASE DO NOT SEND ANY MONEY)

Exhibit I-2

LUCIS TRUST

3 Whitehall Court
Suite 54
London
England SW1A 2EF

113 University Place
11th Floor
New York, N.Y. 10003
Tel: (212) 982-8770

1 Rue de Varembé (3e)
Case Postale 31
1211 Geneva 20
Switzerland

Three Spiritual Festivals, 1986

Dear Friend,

Each year at this time we become aware of an augmentation of energies available to humanity for use in lifting human consciousness and preparing for the reappearance of the Christ. These additional energies are the Forces of Restoration, the Forces of Enlightenment and the Forces of Reconstruction and they add in succession their potencies to the energies available at the time of the full moons of Aries, Taurus and Gemini. This three month period constitutes the higher interlude, or the high point, of the spiritual year and provides us with inspiration and direction for our work in the nine months that follow.

We invite you and your friends, therefore, to celebrate the three major spiritual Festivals this year:

Easter Festival	March 25 –	Aries full moon
Wesak Festival	April 23 –	Taurus full moon
Christ's Festival and World Invocation Day	May 23 –	Gemini full moon

By working with these Festivals and distributing the energies available through prayer and meditation, and especially through the use of the Great Invocation, we are cooperating in a world service of vital importance at this critical time.

We have in 1986 an unusual convergence of the time cycles of the new group of world servers with which we customarily align our work. The activities of the new group follow a rhythmic pattern based upon three time cycles: a three year cycle; a nine year cycle; and a twenty-seven year cycle. This year these cycles converge in "emergence and impact on public consciousness." So it is an appropriate time to consider the meaning of peace and the fact that a world at peace is a requisite before the Christ can return. The emergence of Hierarchy is already underway and the energy of the will-to-good is evoking the energy of goodwill in human hearts and minds and leading to right human relations on an ever wider scale. This year, then, is one where public opinion will be unusually receptive to the ideals of a new and just world order. It is an opportunity to "strike a spiritual blow upon the consciousness of humanity."

There is another reason why 1986 calls for our special efforts. Significantly this year has been designated by the United Nations as the International Year of Peace and millions of people are being encouraged to think deeply about peace and about the way it can be achieved. A powerful thought-form of peace is being built around the planet.

The United Nations has three objectives for the Year of Peace: 1. To stimulate concerted and effective action by the United Nations, governments, groups and organisations for the promotion of peace on the basis

The Lucis Trust is a non-profit tax-exempt educational corporation founded in 1922.

Exhibit I-3

Exhibits I-1 and I-2 display a flier sent out by Lucis Trust promoting The Million Minutes of Peace. Exhibits I-3 and I-4, also from Lucis Trust, present a letter highlighting some of the organization's "spiritual" activities for 1986.

of the Charter of the United Nations; 2. To strengthen the United Nations as the principal international system devoted to the promotion and maintenance of peace. To urge Member States to implement the principles of the Charter. To enhance the effectiveness of the Security Council in the maintenance of international peace and security. To increase public awareness and support for the activities of the United Nations; and 3. To focus attention and encourage reflection on the basic requirements of peace in the contemporary world.

Numerous projects in many nations and among non-governmental organisations are already underway in cooperation with the Year of Peace and a number of the Lucis Trust publications and activities throughout the year will be related to this global theme of peace. A special flyer blending the objectives of the Year of Peace and World Invocation Day is enclosed and we welcome your help in distributing it as a contribution to this special year. Please indicate your needs on the enclosed reply slip.

The challenge to explore what we mean by peace and how best to attain it will be taken up in the Arcane School Conference in New York, Geneva and London. We can all help in the work of defining what 'peace' really is so that the subjective realities will emerge and whatever conflict still exists will be kept on the mental plane. It was the failure to maintain this spiritual tension that resulted in the World Wars and is still a major concern as we look about us. This has been clearly recognised in the constitution of UNESCO which states, "Since wars begin in the minds of men, it is in the minds of men that the defenses of peace must be constructed."

Peace is often taken to mean a static state of tranquility with no worries or no challenges. For an increasing number of people of goodwill, however, it means something much deeper and has its origin in the mind and heart. It is a subjective state within ourselves that can be externalised and can bring about a peace based on goodwill and the will-to-good that will be lasting and universal. A direct line or thread of divine will reaches from the highest place of being to the lowest point. The will-to-good of the spiritual Source can become the goodwill of the Kingdom of God and be transformed into right human relations by intelligent humanity. It is on the foundation of right human relations that a world at peace will be built and it is to a world at peace that the Christ will come. The symposium in New York and the meetings in Geneva and London are designed to clarify our thinking about the ingredients of true peace. A notice of the New York event is enclosed.

We look forward to seeing those who can arrange to join us for the Festivals and Arcane School Conference meetings both here and abroad and to linking up subjectively with those who cannot. One of the joys of this work is that we can participate in spite of distance and time. We can also work wherever we are to create a nucleus of love and light and power that will help lift the consciousness of those around us to an understanding of the part goodwill and the will-to-good can play in the development of lasting peace.

Our keynote for the year is: "The will-to-good of the world knowers is the magnetic seed of the future and the urge to goodwill in humanity is the key to right human relations and peace."

We welcome your cooperation.

                                        Your companions in service,

                                        LUCIS TRUST

The Arcane School Conference will be held in
            New York on   April 26 & 27, 1986
            Geneva   on   May 17 & 18, 1986
            London   on   May 24 & 25, 1986

Exhibit I-4

Peace the 21st

In another mailing from Lucis Trust I learned about Peace the 21st. Since 1986, this outreach has taken place on the twenty-first day of those months representing the change of seasons: March, June, September, and December. A member of the Love of Peace Alliance stated that since the goal was to transform the planet, it made sense to meet on the days when the earth undergoes natural changes.

Participants believe that the collective thought of the human race is the most powerful force in the world. Therefore, guided meditations are conducted at their meetings. As a result of their organized action, by 1987 over one hundred peace poles had been erected around the country, the stated purpose being to cause people to think and meditate on peace. The phrase "May Peace Prevail on Earth" are written in four different languages on the poles.

A toll-free number was given for those who wanted more information about Peace the 21st. Not surprisingly, when a friend called the number listed, the operator who answered was taking pledges for Hands Across America. It appeared that these two groups were working together. (Not only that, but the U.S.A. for Africa Foundation—the sponsor of Hands Across America—also happened to sponsor We Are the World.) Hands Across America would join approximately six million people, allegedly to solve one of the world's greatest problems: hunger.

It is not my intent to undermine legitimate efforts to alleviate hunger. I am aware of many organizations, particularly Christian ones, who have been at the forefront of helping those in need. I have supported some of them. My concern is with the massive New Age unity events and the motivation behind them. No matter how benevolent they appear to be on the surface, their main purpose is to lead us subtly toward a one-world political, economic, and religious system.

The First Earth Run

In 1986, we also experienced the First Earth Run. The purpose of this event was supposedly to unite people all around the world, igniting a global sense of hope for the future. A contribution of five hundred dollars entitled one to carry the torch for one kilometer along the planned around-the-world path. UNICEF was to be the beneficiary of any excess proceeds from the project.

The torch left the United Nations on September 16 (the launch date for Million Minutes of Peace) and was passed to thousands of runners before returning. The torch originally was to be delivered to the United Nations on New Year's Eve, but because of supposed financial difficulties, it was returned somewhat sooner. This demonstrated that most of the world's people had not yet "caught the vision."

The Vatican Interfaith Conference of 1986

During the last week of October 1986, Pope John Paul II did his part to promote global unity, inviting over one hundred leaders from major non-Christian religions to join him in fasting and praying for peace. Among those present were Buddhists, Hindus, Zoroastrians, Native Americans, African animists, and snake worshipers. The Basilica of Santa Maria degli Angeli in Assisi, Italy, was a wild array of colors— robes of crimson, black, red, and blue; gold crucifixes; feathered headdresses; and ceremonial African beads were worn throughout the audience. The Dalai Lama of Tibet, a close personal friend of the Pope, was also present. (New Agers consider the Dalai Lama to be one of the leading occult masters in the world.)

Peter Hebblethwaite, Vatican affairs writer for the *National Catholic Reporter*, summarized, "[The pope] has—modestly but implicitly—made himself a spokesman for all the world religions. His words shaped the meaning of this event":

> While we have walked in silence, we have reflected on the path our human family treads: either in hostility, if we fail to accept one another in love, or as a common journey to our lofty destiny, if we realize that other peoples are our brothers and sisters. . . . Either we learn to walk together in peace and harmony, or we drift apart and ruin ourselves and others.[29]

I am not suggesting that Christians should not support efforts promoting peace that could stop the senseless suffering of thousands of people caused by wars and revolutions. I am in favor of any serious effort to bring warring parties together to discuss differences. However, I do not see how I could overcome the spiritual differences I have with a Buddhist or a snake worshipper. I can't imagine men like Peter, James, Paul, and others in that first-century Jerusalem Council, meeting with people from satanically inspired religions for any purpose except to tell them about the saving grace of the Lord Jesus Christ. Uniting true Christianity with pagan religions is impossible to do.

Interestingly, one organization in support of the Vatican Interfaith Conference was Lucis Trust. Their newsletter stated, "Another heartening initiative was the Pope's invitation to the leaders of various world religions to come together in Assisi, Italy, in the spirit of St. Francis, to pray for peace. No one formula or ritual of worship was imposed and this we understand will characterize the *new world religion"* [italics added].[30]

How strange that an organization, originally founded under the name Lucifer Publishing Company, would endorse and applaud a Christian leader's initiative. And how strange that the Pope was selected the 1994 Man of the Year by *Time* magazine, a publication that has consistently promoted globalism and non-Christian values.

The Harmonic Convergence

Building on the momentum of World Healing Day, the World Congress on Illumination held a meeting of twenty-five hundred "light workers" in Honolulu, Hawaii, on August 16–22, 1987. The meeting, which was intended to keep the theme of unity and oneness with nature alive, was held in conjunction with the Harmonic Convergence celebrations taking place globally the same week. Patricia Diane Cota-Robles, president of the New Age Study of Humanity's Purpose, stated in her March 4, 1987 newsletter,

> There are many indications from ancient calendars and present day inner guidance that August 17, 1987 is a day of utmost significance. We have been guided from within to organize a global activity at that time that will serve as a vehicle through which Light Workers from all over the world can come together to meet each other and form a unified cup. This activity will be held with the force-field of Peace and Harmony that pulsates at Diamond Head in Hawaii.[31]

An afternoon workshop at this conference was entitled "Workshop and Guided Visualization to Energize our Unified Chalice of Service." These words remind one of God's description of the false religion of the last days. Revelation 17:4 declares: "And the woman was arrayed in purple and scarlet colour, and decked with gold and precious stones and pearls, having a golden cup in her hand full of abominations and filthiness of her fornication."

An organization in Boulder, Colorado, named Harmonic Convergence had this to say about the event:

> Harmonic Convergence is a conscious bonding of people to support an evolutionary shift from separation to unity and from fear to love. At the core, 144,000 people will gather at sunrise on August 16 at sacred sites around the globe. They will join at these Earth "acupuncture points" to create a resonating link between Universal Energies and the Earth.[32]

Here we see a blending of New Age ideas (an evolutionary shift in consciousness) with Oriental beliefs in the earth's energy (expressed in acupuncture). This pattern is consistent with the pantheistic mindset of occultists, who see "Mother Earth," or "Gaia," as being sacred. The organizers' desire to "express unity with all life," and their emphasis on sites of pagan worship around the world, reveal their occult inclinations.

Like Barbara Hubbard, the people who sponsored this event are familiar with the Book of Revelation but have distorted its meaning and are trying to make it conform with their own theology. Their choosing of 144,000 people (Revelation 7:4) and their reference to a unified "cup" (Revelation 17:4) leave little doubt of their intent.

Gaining Momentum

Together, all of these efforts from the 1980s fanned the flames of the one-world movement in an unprecedented fashion, prompting New Age events to become more numerous and focused. In the years since, the plans of Aquarian engineers such as John Price and Barbara Hubbard have gained considerable momentum, with occultists becoming more outspoken and militant against Christians who stand in their way.

Dick Sutphen, the founder of New Age Activists, reveals the hostile and deceptive nature of this end-time battle. Sutphen boasts,

> One of the biggest advantages we have as New Agers is, once the occult, metaphysical and New Age terminology is removed, we have concepts and techniques that are very acceptable to the general public. So we can change the names and demonstrate the power. In so doing, we open the New Age door to millions who normally would not be receptive. On the other hand, the born-again Christians, our most vocal antagonists, relate everything back to the blood of Christ and to the Bible. . . . But our momentum will become so great that the combined efforts of all antagonists can't stop us unless they do so politically. Laws are the only way to block the New Age movement from growing within the consciousness of our population. . . . New Age Activists encourage you as an individual to network with your family, friends, and associates, and to infuse New Age concepts and awareness into every area of your personal world, from the office to the bridge club, from the schoolroom to the Little League.[33]

Clearly, New Agers have an agenda. They intend to infiltrate and permeate every segment of society with their occult beliefs, and they are not planning to go away. They will continue their pursuit until their goal of a new world order has been achieved—and the "problem" of Christianity has been eliminated.

Fortunately, they will only succeed for a short time. As we will see, God has his own plan for unity, and it is not the one presented by Asher. God's unity is based on truth, not deception. His plan is perfect and will last throughout eternity.

Notes

1. John Randolph Price, *The Super Beings* (Austin, TX: The Quartus Foundation for Spiritual Research, 1981), p. ix.

2. Ibid., p. x.

3. *Biographical Sketch of Jan and John Randolph Price* (Boerne, TX: The Quartus Foundation, 1998).

4. John Randolph Price, *The Planetary Commission* (Austin, TX: The Quartus Foundation for Spiritual Research, 1984), p. 21.

5. Ibid., pp. 27–28.

6. John Randolph Price, *Report from the Planetary Commission* (Austin, TX: The Quartus Foundation for Spiritual Research, May 1986), p. 6.

7. *The Quartus Report* (Austin, TX: The Quartus Foundation for Spiritual Research, 1986), vol. V, no. 8, pp. 8–9.

8. Ibid., p. 1.

9. *Commission Update* (Austin, TX: The Quartus Foundation for Spiritual Research, January 1987, newsletter), p. 1.

10. Ibid., p. 3.

11. Price, *The Super Beings*, p. 1.

12. "Reincarnation TV Special," *What Is* (Agoura Hills, CA: New Age Activists/Reincarnationists, Inc., Summer 1986), p. 5.

13. Peter and Patti Lalonde, "We Are The World," *The Omega Letter*, September 1986, p. 6.

14. Samantha Smith, "Half-Billion Asked to 'Harmonize'," *The FORUM*, August-September 1986, p. 13.

15. John Randolph Price, *Practical Spirituality* (Austin, TX: The Quartus Foundation for Spiritual Research, 1985), pp. 18–19.

16. *The Quartus Report*, p. 12.

17. Price, *Report From The Planetary Commission*, p. 4.

18. Ibid., p. 4.

19. Barbara Marx Hubbard, *The Revelation, A Message of Hope for the New Millennium* (Mill Valley, CA: Nataraj Publishing, 1995), p. 322.

20. Barbara Marx Hubbard, *Manual for Co-Creators of the Quantum*

Leap, pp. 10–11. A similar quote by Hubbard appears on page 34 of her book, *The Revelation, A Message of Hope for the New Millennium.*

21. Barbara Marx Hubbard, *The Book of Co-Creation, Evolutionary Interpretation of the New Testament* (Centreville, VA: New Visions, 1980, unpublished manuscript), p. viii.

22. Ibid., p. xi.

23. Ibid., pp. xiii, xiv.

24. Hubbard, *Manual for Co-Creators,* pp. 55–57.

25. Ibid., pp. 101, 95.

26. Ibid., pp. 60–61.

27. Hubbard, *The Revelation, A Message of Hope for the New Millennium,* p.265.

28. *Your Thoughts Count,* Issue 1 (New York: The Million Minutes of Peace Appeal, newsletter), p. 1.

29. Peter Hebblethwaite, "Pope Wins Gamble as Religions Pray in Assisi for Peace," *National Catholic Reporter,* vol. 23, no. 3, November 7, 1986, pp. 1, 8.

30. *Lucis Trust Newsletter* (New York: Lucis Trust, April 1987).

31. Patricia Diane Cota-Robles, *New Age Study of Humanity's Purpose,* March 4, 1987, newsletter.

32. *Harmonic Convergence* (Boulder, CO: mailing of 25 March 1987).

33. Dick Sutphen, "Share, Alert and Network: Infiltrating the New Age into Society," *What Is* (Agoura Hills, CA: New Age Activists/ Reincarnationists, Inc., Summer 1986), pp. 14–15.

6

The Environmental Agenda

"They exchanged the truth of God for a lie, and worshipped and served created things rather than the Creator—who is forever praised. Amen." Romans 1:25 (NIV)

During the 1990s, the efforts of New Age activists have continued to intensify, with occultists increasingly pushing their agenda for global unity under the banner of environmental reform. In fact, many of the "successful" one-world meetings during the last ten years have convened for the alleged purpose of solving the environmental crisis. This chapter will look at a few of these notable gatherings, including the 1992 Rio Earth Summit. A review of these events and the people behind them will help the reader understand the real purpose and nature of the New Age environmental movement.

Among those at the forefront of this movement, there is one individual who stands out more than any other. Believed by many to have fallen from the political scene with the collapse of the Soviet Union, he currently wields more power and influence in shaping the future of the world than perhaps any diplomat of our generation. Yet strangely, most of us are not even aware of his influence, let alone that he has risen to the top of the one-world movement. His keen sense of timing and political prowess have enabled him to forge alliances where others before him have failed. His friends include many of the world's most adept politicians, financial power brokers, and religious leaders. The person of whom I am speaking is Mikhail Gorbachev.

Mikhail Sergeyevich Gorbachev (1931–)

Born on March 2, 1931, in the southern Russian village of Privolnoje, Mikhail Gorbachev grew up in a home of peasant farmers. Although his family was Russian Orthodox, Mikhail rejected Christianity at the age of twenty-one, when he joined the Communist Party (CPSU).[1] Three years later, after graduating in law from Moscow State University, he began his political career in the city of Stavropol. There he served as first secretary of the Komsomol (Communist Youth League) City Committee from 1955 to 1958. He rose through the ranks and in 1970 was elevated to the most powerful Communist position in the Stavropol region. Partly as a result of his reputation and experience in Stavropol politics, he was elected to the Communist Party Central Committee in 1971. During the next twenty years, Mikhail held virtually every major position in the Party, steadily climbing the ladder of power and influence.

Mikhail was personally chosen and groomed for leadership by his close friend Yuri Andropov, long-time KGB head and Soviet president from 1983–1984.[2] It is no secret that untold millions were persecuted and put to death at the hands of Russian leaders during the Andropov years, both inside and outside the Soviet Union, especially in Afghanistan. His regime was ruthless.

In 1985, following Andropov's death and Konstantin Chernenko's brief term in office, Gorbachev advanced to the position of general secretary of the powerful Politburo. After several years of holding this top political post in the Central Committee (CPSU), he became president of the Soviet Union, a position he held from 1990–1991. During his six years at the helm of Soviet politics, he wrote his most famous books including, *A Time for Peace* (1985) and *Perestroika: New Thinking for Our Country and the World* (1987). It was this latter book that introduced Gorbachev's concepts of glasnost (a new policy of openness in the media) and perestroika (economic and political restructuring or reform). These Gorbachev initiatives were to bring permanent democratic reforms to Soviet government and society.

Did Gorbachev really abandon Communism in pursuit of world peace, or were his writings and the accompanying publicity a mere front? Some of his statements from that period provide a clue.

In his book *Perestroika* Gorbachev wrote:

> The essence of perestroika lies in the fact that *it unites socialism with democracy* and revives the Leninist concept of socialist construction both in theory and in practice. Such is the essence of perestroika, which accounts for its genuine revolutionary spirit and its all-embracing scope. . . . In

politics and ideology we are seeking to revive the living spirit of Leninism. (italics in original)[3]

In 1987, the same year he launched perestroika, Gorbachev unabashedly proclaimed, "In October 1917, we parted with the Old World, rejecting it once for all. We are moving toward a new world, the world of Communism. We shall never turn off that road."[4]

In 1989, the year that the Berlin Wall came down, he announced, "I am a convinced Communist. For some that may be a fantasy. But for me it is my main goal." And in 1990, when he was being hailed in the Western media as the man who ended Communism, he emphatically stated, "I am now, just as I've always been, a convinced Communist."[5]

His most stunning remark, however, came during a speech before the Politburo in 1987:

Gentlemen, comrades, do not be concerned about all you hear about glasnost and perestroika and democracy in the coming years. These are primarily for outward consumption. There will be no significant internal change within the Soviet Union, other than for cosmetic purposes. Our purpose is to disarm the Americans and let them fall asleep.[6]

In spite of admissions such as these, Mikhail Gorbachev won the Nobel Peace Prize in 1990 for his work in breaking up Communism. With a feather in his hat and his international popularity secure, Mikhail focused his aim more directly on America and the West. In 1992, he came to the United States to establish the International Foundation for Socio-Economic and Political Studies, better known as The Gorbachev Foundation.

The Gorbachev Foundation

Ironically, this important policy-making think tank is located at a former U.S. military base—the Presidio in San Francisco. From his headquarters at the Presidio, Gorbachev is systematically unveiling his blueprint for a world government in the twenty-first century. This blueprint, as we shall see, involves manipulating the earth's inhabitants into accepting a new world order in the name of saving the planet from environmental catastrophe.

In order to accomplish his goal, Gorbachev is calling for a global perestroika, a complete restructuring of our world and lives—including our economy, political system, and religious views. He has already begun using his organization to lobby for global taxation and major "international military" reforms that will be necessary to fund and enforce this massive undertaking. His proposals to scale back America's armed forces while increasing the presence of foreign troops on American soil have been followed almost to the tee. The recent round of U.S. military base closings were due in part to Gorbachev's initiatives.

In 1994 we received our first look at his plans when he presented his new Global Security Programme in a speech before the Council on Foreign Relations. (See Exhibits J-1 and J-2.) After being introduced by David Rockefeller, Gorbachev proceeded to share the highlights of his agenda, which include a tax to be levied on conventional arms production. If approved by Congress, this tax would empower the United Nations by funding the creation of several new U.N.-based agencies and authorities, all of which would be part of the emerging world system. Eventually, this tax and others yet to be introduced would be shouldered by taxpayers throughout the world.

Since unveiling his plans, Gorbachev has steadily gained endorsements from world political and spiritual leaders. Among those who support his agenda are former U.S. Secretary of State George Schultz, chairman of the board of advisors for the Gorbachev Foundation; Senator Alan Cranston of California, chairman of the board of directors; and James Garrison of the new age Esalen Institute, president of the Gorbachev Foundation. Also listed on Gorbachev's board of advisors are John Naisbitt, author of *Megatrends*; and Father Theodore Hesburgh, former President of Notre Dame University and considered by many to be the leading Catholic educator in America. (See Exhibit J-3.)

Former U.S. President, Richard Nixon, sized up Gorbachev's popularity after observing him at a political function:

> Gorbachev's neatly tailored suits, refined manners, beautiful wife, and smooth touch with reporters have made him a star with the press and the diplomatic corps. An American official who met him was impressed by the startling fact that he had "good eye contact, a firm handshake and a deep, melodious voice." A British politician even remarked that Gorbachev was the man he most admired in the world. A disarmament activist took this a step further, saying, "Gorbachev is like Jesus. He just keeps giving out good things like arms control proposals and getting nothing but rejections."[7]

Nixon took special note of the affection which American politicians lavished on Gorbachev:

> When he applied his public-relations talents at the superpower summit in December 1987, the city of Washington lost its collective senses. He had conservative senators eating out of his hand. He dazzled and charmed the Washington social

set. The usually aggressive star reporters of American adversary journalism became pussycats in his presence. Business leaders and media moguls, when they met him in a private audience, did not question some of his obviously outlandish statements. . . . No democratic leader—not Churchill, not de Gaulle, not Adenauer—ever enjoyed the kind of fawning, sycophantic treatment Gorbachev did.[8]

GORBACHEV FOUNDATION USA

Box 29434 – The Presidio
San Francisco, CA 94129
Tel: 415-771-4567
Fax: 415-771-4443

THE GLOBAL
SECURITY
PROJECT

Mikhail Gorbachev
Honorary Chair

Senator Alan Cranston
Chair, Board of Directors

Secretary George Shultz
Chair, Board of Advisors

James Garrison
President

Participants
Dr. Cecilia Albin
Dr. Kadyr Alimov
Dr. Anatoly Antonov
Mani Shankar Ayer
Dr. Yuri Baturin
Dr. Abram Chayes
Sen. Alan Cranston
Amb. Jonathan Dean
Prof. Sidney Drell
Dr. Daniel Ellsberg
Prof. Richard Falk
Randall Forsberg
Peter Gladkov
Najma Heptulla
Amb. Abid Hussain
Irina Isakova
Amb. Kassa Kebede
Victor Klimenko
Chandresh Kumari
Alexander Konovolov
Andrei Kortunov
Prof. Saul Mendlovitz
Joseph Montville
Rep. David Nagle
Dr. Gwyn Prins
V. Ramachandran
M.K. Rasgotra
Dr. Barbara Seiders
Georgi Shaknazarov
Dr. Jeremy Stone
Dr. Vamik Volkan

EMBARGO: October 19, 1994
12:00pm
Contact: John Balbach
(415) 771-4567

Mikhail Gorbachev
unveils new
Global Security Programme

Speech hosted by the New York Council on Foreign Relations
highlights final report of the Global Security Project

San Francisco -- In a major policy speech delivered today at the Council on Foreign Relations of New York, Mikhail Gorbachev unveiled the final report of the Global Security Project, an eighteen month collaborative effort undertaken by the Gorbachev Foundation/USA, the Gorbachev Foundation Moscow and the Rajiv Gandhi Foundation of New Delhi to provide a comprehensive approach to global security crises in the post cold war world.

Entitled the "The Global Security Programme", the report represents a hard won and practical consensual agreement between security experts from Russia, India and the United States, and is a major step forward in confidence building measures between the North and South. The report makes step-by-step recommendations to governments and citizens worldwide to move multilateral and bilateral efforts from the cold war stage of arms control to genuine disarmament and effective peacekeeping.

The report covers:

1.) Measures to move from existing nuclear arms control agreements (START) which allow owner states to retain control and storage of nuclear weapons to genuine disarmament, including specific recommendations for the five declared nuclear states, as well as the nuclear threshold states;

2.) New security and peacekeeping arrangements designed to reduce perceived needs to rely on nuclear weapons, including measures to strengthen the authority of the United Nations and regional security institutions; and

3.) A new approach to conflict prevention and conflict resolution.

-more-

Exhibit J-1

-2-

Mikhail Gorbachev, President of the Gorbachev Foundation Moscow and Chair of the Global Security Project, presented the final report of the ground-breaking project to 300 distinguished members of the New York Council on Foreign Relations. David Rockefeller, Sr., founder of the Council, introduced Mr. Gorbachev.

The initiative was undertaken to take advantage of real post cold war opportunities in these critical areas and in recognition of the limitations of the existing global security structures, all designed during the bi-polar superpower era. The Carnegie Corporation of New York, among others, was a strong supporter of the effort.

Alan Cranston, head of the U.S. delegation for the Global Security Project and Chairman of the Board of the Gorbachev Foundation USA, stated at the unveiling of the report: "This initiative represents a major step forward in building consensus for the emerging global security system for the coming century, an era where cooperation among nations and peoples must replace our outmoded and dangerous aggressive brinkmanship. We have undertaken to build upon the historic efforts for world disarmament unveiled at Reykjavik and clearly articulated through the Global Security Project process."

Highlights of the report include:

• *". . . drastic cuts in nuclear weapons of the five nuclear weapons states to the level of 100 nuclear warheads, to be achieved within ten years, by 2005 A.D. All these reductions must be made irreversible through dismantling reduced warheads and missiles and the transfer of the fissile material. . . to internationally controlled and monitored storage. Further, the remaining nuclear weapons of all nuclear weapon states should be neutralized by separating warheads from delivery systems and placing both under international monitoring in the owner state territory."*

• *"Effective measures are essential for restricting transfers, stockpiling and production of conventional arms through the establishment of an international authority and the imposition of a tax on their production and sale. The proceeds of the tax should go to the UN and, where appropriate, to regional security organizations for their peace-keeping operations."*

• *"For effective prevention and resolution of conflicts the UN's capacity to keep watch on areas of potential strife should be enhanced by the establishment of a UN General Assembly Commission for the Avoidance of Conflict supported by a UN Observer Corps and an Institute for Conflict Resolution."*

Complete copies of the report or additional information on the Global Security Project can be obtained by contacting:

John Balbach
Voice: (415) 771-4567
Fax: (415) 771-4443

# # #

Exhibit J-2

The Gorbachev Foundation/USA

Revisioning Global Priorities

**GORBACHEV
FOUNDATION
USA**

Box 29434 – The Presidio
San Francisco, CA 94129
Tel: 415-771-4567
Fax: 415-771-4443

• Fostering international debate and cooperation on the vital contemporary issues confronting humanity.

• Providing humanitarian assistance to those adversely affected by political and social turbulence in the former Soviet Bloc.

• Redefining global security in a rapidly changing world.

• Promoting sustainable uses of the world's resources, and mitigating devastating human impact on our fragile environment.

THE GLOBAL
SECURITY
PROJECT

THE STATE OF
THE WORLD
FORUM

HUMANITARIAN
ASSISTANCE TO
EMERGING NATIONS

THE PRESIDIO
DIALOGUES

Mikhail Gorbachev
Honorary Chair

Secretary George Shultz
Chair, Board of Advisors

Senator Alan Cranston
Chair, Board of Directors

James Garrison
President

John Balbach
Vice President

Amy Vossbrinck
Administrative Director

Board of Advisors
Dwayne Andreas
Senator Dick Clark
Sidney Drell
Senator Gary Hart
Theodore Hesburgh
Rep. Mel Levine
Senator Charles Mathias
Thomas Miner
James Miscoll
Rep. David Nagle
John Naisbitt
Walter Shorenstein

In January of 1992, Mr. Gorbachev established the International Foundation for Socio-Economic and Political Studies in Moscow, known as the Gorbachev Foundation. The Gorbachev Foundation/USA was established concurrently in San Francisco to articulate and address the challenges of the post Cold War world through *Revisioning Global Priorities*. The Foundation strives to both clarify the fundamental crises facing the human community, and creatively address those crises through the convening of the world's most innovative thinkers in consensus building processes.

The Gorbachev Foundation/USA (GF/USA) is a tax exempt, non-profit institute dedicated to social, political and geostrategic change in the post cold war era. Our current areas of activity include:

STATE OF THE WORLD FORUM: As the world enters an era of increasing uncertainty, the State of the World Forum will bring together world leaders and those preeminent individuals whose experience, wisdom and knowledge can collectively serve to articulate a clear vision for the road ahead. The State of the World Forum will serve not only to present a series of respected and highly visible recommendations for a new generation of leaders entering the 21st Century, but also help set the stage for more in-depth discussions regarding the future of human development. The event will be held September 27 through October 1, 1995, in San Francisco.

REDEFINING GLOBAL SECURITY: Working in conjunction with Mikhail Gorbachev and his Moscow staff and the Rajiv Gandhi Foundation in India, GF/USA is bringing together the world's leading experts to both discuss and recommend to the international community means by which our institutions, structures, and understandings of security can adapt to the new challenges facing humanity in the areas of nuclear proliferation, the architecture of global security, and conflict resolution.

Exhibit J-3

State of the World Forum

To officially launch his program, Gorbachev convened a special meeting called the State of the World Forum in 1995. Held in San Francisco from September 27 to October 1, the event was nothing less than a world government planning session with Gorbachev at the helm. Due to the summit's overwhelming success, Gorbachev decided to make it an annual event.

Held in the fall of each year, the State of the World Forum brings together a who's who of the one-world movement. Samantha Smith, journalist and author of *Goddess Earth*, attended the first Forum in 1995. She shared with me her disbelief over the blatant nature of the conference and the fact that it received virtually no coverage from the media. This lack of coverage was due in part to the fact that many of the roundtables were closed to the press, including deliberations on human overpopulation, environmental reform, and the redistribution of the world's wealth.

Samantha shared her experience in our Fall 1995 newsletter:

> More than 500 elder statesmen, business leaders, religious figures and scientists (paying $5,000 each) enjoyed their gourmet meals prepared by the city's most celebrated chefs, while Gorbachev drove home the issues of world hunger, poverty, social upheaval, spiritual crisis, overpopulation, environmental degradation and the need for a world government. Although Gorbachev speaks fluent English, he spoke to the crowd in Russian, with a translator. He said, "We must reinvent the world together. We need unity in diversity."

> His "diversity" referred to broad variations—like rich and poor, cultural differences and selected religious beliefs—with total compliance by all to new international law.

> Throughout the conference, we heard the words "New World Order," "World Government," "Global Governance," and "Global Government." Zbigniew Brzezinski (Jimmy Carter's National Security Advisor) said in a speech, "Finally, I have no illusions about World Government emerging in our lifetime . . . we cannot leap into world government through one quick step . . . a consensual global system is not just a matter of good wishes or good will, but it requires a process . . . the precondition for eventual and genuine globalization is progressive regionalization."[9]

Samantha continued:

Gorbachev harped on the importance of having "consensus" for Global Governance—where nations under world government will lose sovereignty, giving way to international laws that will dictate common beliefs, values, standards, and behavior, and conform to the consensus of a chosen group of leaders. The former head of Russia's Communist Party has selected 100 elite "innovative thinkers," called the "Global Brain Trust," or the "Council of the Wise," who will meet annually at the Presidio in San Francisco, to guide global issues during the transition into the next century.[10]

Samantha Smith described the conference as "a coming-out party for New Age elitists." Among those present were Shirley MacLaine, Dennis Weaver, John Denver, John Naisbitt, Carl Sagan, Ted Turner and Jane Fonda, Barbara Marx Hubbard, Maurice Strong, Robert Muller, Dr. Deepak Chopra, Matthew Fox, Alan Jones, Michael Murphy, and James Garrison. Some spoke in workshops, while others simply attended.[11]

Smith noticed the spiritual theme that was woven throughout the conference. One of the sessions was called "The Global Crisis of Spirit and the Search for Meaning." She reported: "Attendees were told they have a god-shaped vacuum in their hearts that needs to be filled. Religious panelists eagerly offered a number of different 'gods' and Eastern Philosophies from which to choose."[12]

Gorbachev's fascination with Eastern mysticism and the occult was evident in his choice of "spiritual" leaders invited to the forum. The list included Isabel Allende, author, *House of Spirits*; Richard Baker, abbott, Crestone Mountain Zen Center; Akio Matsumura, founder, Global Forum of Spiritual and Parliamentary Leaders; and Sonia Gandhi, founder, Rajiv Gandhi Foundation. Gorbachev's endorsement of Eastern mysticism was further reflected in the fact that the Gandhi Foundation (a Hindu organization) co-sponsored his activity.

In addition, Gorbachev selected Thich Nhat Hanh, a renowned Vietnamese monk, to lead a special half-day Buddhist meditation at the forum. This popular Zen Buddhist is the author of the occult book *Living Buddha, Living Christ*.[13] Hanh has devoted his life to merging Buddhism with Christianity, believing such a synthetic religion would be ideal for the emerging world order. In an interview printed in the *San Francisco Chronicle* on October 1, 1995, Hanh revealed that "he has Christ on his altar alongside the Buddha."

Like Hanh, Gorbachev is calling for the unity of Buddhism and Christianity. In an interview with the *Los Angeles Times* he stated,

In this new synthesis, we need democratic, Christian and Buddhist values as well, which affirm such moral principles as social responsibility and the sense of oneness with nature and each other. The future should be built with these moral building blocks that are centuries old.[14]

Mirroring this quest for a new spirituality, Gorbachev's Web site opens with the following words. "We need a new system of values, a system of the organic unity between mankind and nature and the ethic of global responsibility."[15] This statement has become Gorbachev's campaign slogan and appears on many of his reports, invitations, and promotionals.

As strange as it may seem, the words and actions of Mikhail Gorbachev classify him as a New Age Leninist. He is literally seeking to replace Christianity with a new religious order in which humanism (the central teaching of Communism) and pantheism (the basis for Eastern mysticism) are combined. To make this new religion more acceptable, he is lacing it with Christian terminology. In using this tactic, he is simply following the lead of Chardin, Jung, Hanh, and other mystics who have done the same. In reality, Gorbachev's religion is anti-Christian to the core.

Throughout the forum, Gorbachev shared glimpses of his vision for uniting the planet. He clearly stated his intentions of using humanity's concern over the environment to strategically further his world government agenda. Revealing his motivation, he declared, "The environmental crisis is the cornerstone for the New World Order."[16]

One reason why the environment has taken center stage in Gorbachev's campaign for world government is that by its very nature it is an "international" issue that evokes strong feelings. This makes it especially easy to manipulate. To globalists like Gorbachev, it is the perfect issue behind which they can rally a naive and easily misled public.

Another reason why the environment is such an important issue to Gorbachev is that it will enable him to introduce and ratify comprehensive international treaties granting unprecedented power to seize government and private property, all in the name of protecting the environment. In fact, Gorbachev's mandate for the future includes the imposition of stringent global environmental laws that would regulate every area of life. Toward this end he has been supporting the creation of an all-encompassing planetary document called *The Earth Charter*. Samantha Smith confirms these developments: "At this conference, we were told that an Earth Charter, a Bill of Rights for the Planet, would be presented to the General Assembly of the United Nations for ratification, then hopefully adopted by the year 2000."[17]

According to Smith, Maurice Strong, the U.N.'s top environmental activist, referred to *The Charter* as "a Magna Carta for Earth."[18] Gorbachev goes even further, describing *The Charter* as a new set of rules to guide humanity.[19] He states, "My hope is that this charter will be a kind of Ten Commandments, a 'Sermon on the Mount,' that provides a guide for human behavior toward the environment in the next century and beyond."[20]

The United Nations currently administers nearly three hundred environmental treaties. The conventions on Biodiversity, Climate Change, Ozone Depleting Substances, Desertification, Endangered Species, Wetlands and World Heritage Sites, have already given the U.N. extensive authority over the "global commons." Gorbachev and the U.N. are simply waiting for the proper moment to implement any final agreements in order to begin full enforcement of their programs. Together with other major environmental legislation already drafted, *The Charter*, if accepted, will govern life in the twenty-first century.

Campaigning in the Heartland

On October 8, 1996, I had the opportunity of hearing Gorbachev speak on this subject in Indianapolis, Indiana. I listened as he carefully built his case for environmental reform, calling for a global restructuring to deal with this immense "crisis." A few of his statements follow:

> We need a new paradigm of development in which the environment will be a priority. . . . World civilization as we know it will soon end. . . . We have very little time and we must act. . . . If we can address the environment problem, we have hope . . . but it will have to be done within a new system, a new paradigm. . . . We have to change our mindset—the way humankind views the world.

Gorbachev wasted no time in presenting *The Earth Charter* as the only solution to the global environmental crisis, asserting that *The Charter* would "be the basis for changing current values." In order to make this transition into a new global society, people everywhere would have to be educated. He stated that he was already working with UNESCO (The United Nations Educational, Scientific and Cultural Organization) to introduce new education curriculums in all countries. He also indicated that he was working through his special environmental organization, Green Cross International, to bring about these changes, revealing that chapters of Green Cross were already active in seventeen countries with a dozen more countries to be added soon. (His affiliate in the United States is Global Green.) He purported that government organizations throughout the world were already "seeking the involvement of Green Cross International to help solve these problems."

Considered by some to be the most elite of the environmental action groups, Green Cross is at the forefront of working for the ratification and implementation of *The Earth Charter*. For this reason, *The Charter* has been dubbed "Gorbachev's baby," even though Maurice Strong initially introduced the document and continues to play a critical role. While Gorbachev commended his colleagues from the Club of Rome, Green Peace, and the World Wildlife Fund for their efforts in trying to get *The Charter* ratified, his highest praises were reserved for Maurice Strong and Vice President Al Gore, his closest allies in North America. Researchers on this subject frequently refer to Gorbachev, Strong, and Gore as the "Three Musketeers" of the environmental movement, with the understanding that former U.N. Assistant Secretary-General Robert Muller, Prince Philip, and Prince Charles also play important roles in advancing this agenda.*

Strong, who founded the influential Earth Council has worked closely with Gorbachev in overseeing the development and progress of *The Earth Charter*. Gorbachev confirmed this relationship during his talk, stating, "Since environmental problems are of a global nature, we have joined forces with the Earth Council, headed by Maurice Strong." He went on to discuss their joint cooperation with the United Nations, indicating they intended to launch their all out push for *The Charter's* ratification in 1998, presenting the final draft of *The Earth Charter* for implementation no later than the year 2002. In giving these dates, Gorbachev also revealed his timetable for the start of global government (sometime between 1998 and 2002), since *The Charter* is slated to be part of that government.

After reprimanding the United States for some of its "isolationist" policies and for not taking a strong enough stand on the environment, he closed by stressing that "the main work is still ahead

---

* Prince Philip, Duke of Edinburgh, has been an outspoken environmentalist for most of his life. In 1961 he became the first president of The World Wildlife Fund (U.K.), serving in that capacity until 1982. From 1981 to 1996 he served as the organization's International President and still acts as President Emeritus. Prince Charles has continued in his father's footsteps. Viewed by many as Europe's most powerful environmental advocate, he is the patron or president of some 200 organizations, covering a wide range of interests, including the environment. In 1990, Charles produced a television special on environmental issues for the British Broadcasting Corporation called The Earth in Balance. (Source: web page http://www.royal.gov.uk/family.htm)

of us," but that together with him "the U.S. can play an important role in helping to establish the New International Order." Gorbachev had mesmerized the crowd. Upon delivering his final words, the audience, consisting of more than three thousand local dignitaries, erupted in a loud standing ovation as if they agreed with everything he just said. His agenda appeared to be an "easy sell."

Environmental Events of the Nineties

Considered by New Agers to be the most serious document on global unity to date, *The Earth Charter* is the product of years of U.N. summits and international meetings spearheaded by Gorbachev, Strong, and their closest allies. Along with the private forums organized by the Gorbachev Foundation, other environmental conferences, receiving more widespread media coverage, have been held to build public support for *The Charter* and the accompanying United Nations programs. Maurice Strong has taken the lead in organizing many of these special U.N.-sponsored events. The ulterior political and religious motives behind this agenda will become more evident as you review the following summaries of these environmental gatherings and examine the resulting document.

Rio Earth Summit 1992

In June 1992, the largest gathering of world leaders since the end of the Cold War took place in Rio de Janeiro, Brazil. The "Earth Summit," officially known as the United Nations Conference on Environment and Development, or UNCED, brought together thousands of the world's top politicians, economists, and New Age scientists for the purpose of developing global environmental laws— laws deemed by them as necessary to save the planet from ecological disaster. The media hype surrounding this event was unprecedented. It received virtually all favorable coverage throughout its duration.

At the conference, a series of important U.N. documents were introduced, including the now infamous *Convention on Biodiversity* and its comprehensive counterpart, *Agenda 21*. These documents will facilitate the enforcement of *The Earth Charter*.

The *Convention on Biodiversity* created the framework for nations to develop strategies and make international commitments for conserving biological diversity. Though this sounds benign, the implementation of this treaty will enable international groups and national government agencies to elevate environmental protection to draconian levels. *Agenda 21*, on the other hand, has been expanded to contain everything needed to internationally regulate life—from agriculture to transportation, from our children to reproductive rights.

Vice President Al Gore, who led the U.S. delegation to the Earth Summit, expressed his support for such radical changes. In his book, *Earth in the Balance: Ecology and the Human Spirit*, he writes:

> Adopting a central organizing principle—one agreed to voluntarily—means embarking on an all-out effort to use every policy and program, every law and institution, every treaty and alliance, every tactic and strategy, every plan and course of action—to use, in short, every means to halt the destruction of the environment and to preserve and nurture our ecological system.[21]

By introducing these environmental documents, the Rio Earth Summit provided a great boost to the global government movement. According to the International Institute for Sustainable Development (IISD), influenced by Maurice Strong (UNCED's secretary-general), the Rio Earth Summit was part of a larger picture of "world cooperation." Its explanation is quite revealing:

> UNCED also holds a broader significance. The environment issue was set up as a global issue in need for global action. There were demands to strengthen international law, which could make nations tow the line. Non government organizations (NGOs) had been forming global networks and were working on global campaigns. These efforts at the global level directly contributed to building a sense of global identity, or global citizenship which would be the first step towards global governance. Such global governance would further distance power from the people while giving unlimited access to governments and multinationals.[22]

Continuing on, the institute makes another provocative statement: "Development continues to be the process of internationalization of another's culture and history. The push towards globalization and global government is in motion. . . . There is no running away from the realities of today's world."[23]

The Rio documents reflected Gorbachev's mandate, going beyond the political into the spiritual realm. In his final address to the conference, then United Nations secretary-general Boutros Boutros-Ghali revealed the significance of the event:

> I should like to conclude by saying that the spirit of Rio must create a new form of good citizenship. After loving his neighbour as the Bible required him to, post-Rio man must

also love the world, including the flowers, birds and trees—every part of that natural environment that we are constantly destroying.

Over and above the moral contract with God, over and above the social contract concluded with men, we must now conclude an ethical and political contract with nature, with this Earth to which we owe our very existence and which gives us life.

To the ancients, the Nile was a god to be venerated, as was the Rhine, an infinite source of European myths, or the Amazonian forest, the mother of forests. Throughout the world, nature was the abode of the divinities that gave the forest, the desert or the mountains a personality which commanded worship and respect. The Earth had a soul. To find that soul again, to give it new life, that is the essence of Rio.[24]

The president of Brazil, Fernando Collor, in his closing speech at the summit, outlined a concept of unity in line with Boutros-Ghali:

The Rio Conference does not end in Rio. The spirit that guided its debates and deliberations—what Secretary-General Boutros-Ghali called the "spirit of Rio"—must linger on and guide us into the future, much beyond 1992. The Commission on Sustainable Development must be the faithful expression of that spirit. Our aim is to forge unity.[25]

Most of the countries that participated in the Summit ended up supporting its global initiatives. Even nations of lesser influence agreed to conform in major ways. Mario Soares, president of Portugal proudly shared in his address that his country was "creating the civilization of the 'universal' of which Teilhard de Chardin spoke."[26]

The Rio Earth Summit was the largest environmental conference of its kind ever held. It played a major role in solidifying the global unity movement, while keeping the movement's true agenda hidden from the public. The results were sweeping.

A Hidden Agenda

During October 17-20, 1990, a little known meeting called the World Environment Energy and Economic Conference was held in Winnipeg, Manitoba. Over 3000 global environmental leaders attended this meeting to discuss plans for the future. Its theme was "Sustainable Development Strategies for the New World Order."

The Manitoba Provincial Government, which hosted this event, produced a detailed report entitled *Sustainable Development For A New World Agenda*. The report was introduced by Manitoba's Premier, Gary Filmon, and contained a preface from Colin N. Powers, UNESCO's Assistant Director-General. The document, which outlined the conference's main points, dedicated an entire chapter to the concept of a "Global Green Constitution." On page 15, the report speculated about the sweeping powers of a future world government which would enforce such a constitution:

> The issues are not about *if* a global politics is necessary. The question is *how* do we achieve binding agreements in Law complete with effective programs for applying sanctions against non-compliance that would oblige each nation, regardless of size, to abide by a set of principles that are required to guarantee the survival of life on this earth. Perhaps we will find that there is no other alternative to a system of rigid controls that some would equate to a police state.

> Unfortunately, in order to save the planet from biocide, there have to be very powerful constraints from doing the 'wrong' things. The constraints must transcend national boundaries, be world-around and enforceable. . . .

> Enforcement agencies would need the power to act without being invited by the offending nation. Therefore, there needs to be an agency that is acceptable to all nation states on the planet. We can probably accept the fact that there will always be one or more nations that will not go along but there must be effective sanctions in place. If sanctions do not work, then physical occupation and the installation of a World Trusteeship would be imposed upon the offending nations.

This bold statement conveys the radical agenda of the global environmental movement, whose goals were advanced through the Rio Earth Summit (For more revealing statements by global environmental leaders, see Appendix F.)

Global Forum '92

During the convening of the Earth Summit, another convention known as Global Forum '92 was underway in the same city. This event, which received less attention than the summit, brought together twenty thousand members of various non-governmental organizations (NGOs). The supposed purpose of Global Forum was to act as a voice for "the common people of earth," impacting government officials who were attending UNCED.

NGOs are "international" groups of "concerned" citizens, or, simply put, global special-interest groups. Over the past few years, NGOs have become extremely useful to the world-government movement. They exist by design. Pretending to represent a cross section of humanity, they oppose nationalism, promoting globalization instead. Thus they create the misleading impression that a majority of the public supports the world-government agenda.

According to Marek Hagmajer, the secretary-general of the World Federation of U.N. Associations, the NGO accreditation process for the Summit was a sham. He described it as "the biggest manipulation ever."[27] Elaine Dewar, author of *Cloak of Green*, said, "As far as I could tell, those organizations accredited as NGOs to Rio were not exactly democratic or representative."[28]

NGOs for the Earth Summit were created and accredited for a specific purpose—to show support for the globalization plans of UNCED leaders. Even "phantom" NGOs appeared on the roster, adding to the size and scope of this "grassroots" influence.[29] The IISD, in one of their publications, openly explained the reason for this NGO setup.

> The co-operation of NGOs also plays a role in global governance. In order to appear democratic, the illusion of a strong opposition allowed to voice its grievances is essential. By selecting and allowing a certain opposition to function, all other opposition is easily painted as radical and extremists.[30]

This blatant manipulation of the public should have been exposed by the mass media, but it wasn't.

Global Forum '92 created a massive set of NGO *Alternative Treaties*. These "alternative treaties" addressed issues of population, youth, agriculture, consumption, right "Earth relations," and a host of other concerns. In essence, NGOs created "a peoples' alternative" to *Agenda 21*—UNCED's "human management" document. However, these alternative treaties demanded even more stringent controls under an ever deepening web of occult spirituality. In other words, to the attending NGOs, the Rio Earth Summit didn't go far enough in protecting "Mother Earth" and promoting a global spiritual union.

The Forum had a more visible spiritual agenda than the Earth Summit. In fact, the Dalai Lama, Buddhism's leading master, opened the meeting. To ensure the meeting's success, Maurice Strong's wife, Hanne, held a three-week vigil with Wisdomkeepers, a group of "global transformationalists." This group held the "energy pattern" through round-the-clock sacred fire, drumbeat, and meditation for the duration of the summit.[31] Lucis Trust also contributed to the spiritual energy of this conference. Their *Great Invocation* was recited by the audience on two separate occasions.

Global Forum '92 was described by some as a circus. ASA News summed up the event accordingly: "The Global Forum was part soap-opera, part new-age carnival, part human zoo."[32] Weirdness aside, Global Forum '92 had a greater influence on eco-spirituality and world unity than many would have thought. The convention, for example, was instrumental in the development of the "new scripture" for the next century, creating the appearance that *The Earth Charter* is truly a peoples' document.

Rio+5 and The Earth Charter

From March 13 to 19, 1997, world leaders would gather again in Rio to review the advancement of the '92 Earth Summit's initiatives over the previous five years. Aptly titled Rio+5, this gathering, hosted by the Earth Council and Green Cross International, would be a time for celebrating progress while fine-tuning UNCED's strategy for global government.[33]

The first day's topic was "Assessing Past Performance and Future Prospects for a Sustainable Planet." This session analyzed the complete process of globalization, from United Nations programs and developments in financial institutions to the role of education and philanthropy. Speakers that day included Christopher Flavin from the Worldwatch Institute; Bella Abzug, a key player at the U.N. World Conference on Women in Beijing; and Wally N'Dow of the U.N. Centre on Human Settlements.[34]

After a weekend of more meetings and consultations, Tuesday, March 18th, was entirely devoted to the subject of "Global Governance." Considered to be the high-point of the conference, this was a special time to address the on-going task of advancing spiritual, political, and ecological unity on a macro level. Speakers included James Wolfensohn of the World Bank; James Gustave Speth of the United Nations Development Program; and Lincoln Chen of the Rockefeller Foundation. Of course, Maurice Strong, Mikhail Gorbachev, and other influential world figures addressed the conference as well.[35]

The most celebrated outcome of the Rio+5 meetings was the presentation of *The Earth Charter*. During his speech at the conference, Gorbachev again explained its significance:

> We have to set directions and act on planetary, national and individual levels. The main goal of the Earth Charter, the

draft of which we adopted 18 March, 1997, is formation of a new outlook; a new set of values. . . .

I admit that this document is far from being ideal. It is far from those 10 or 15 Commandments which we all know about and which have played their role for 2000 years. But here is the document which can be considered as an important step toward those famous testaments. . . .

In its essence the Earth Charter shifts the focus to people on the Earth, their responsibilities, their morals and spirituality, their way of consumption. To save humankind and all future generations, we must save the Earth. By saving the Earth, humankind saves himself; it is that easy to understand![36]

He continued:

Both the Earth Council, Maurice Strong and we in the Green Cross feel the difficulties which we encounter, trying to implement ideas of radical changes in our everyday life, thus answering the challenge of the biosphere. . . .

We see the future as a cooperation of peoples, which implies a dialog of cultures, religions, traditions. We are trying to use this model as a cornerstone for the Earth Charter, in hope that we will create the document addressed to the Planet Earth. . . .

Now we have a perfect chance to use our intellectual, moral and spiritual experience to answer the challenges of the next millennium.[37]

Unfortunately, most people still do not realize that *The Earth Charter* has spiritual as well as political implications. Although it is being presented as a *Bill of Rights* for mankind, if implemented, "the environment" would have far greater rights than people. Humanity would literally become a slave to the earth and to the global regime enforcing these mandates.

It should be understood, *The Earth Charter* which was circulated at Rio+5 was still only a preliminary draft. According to Maurice Strong's Earth Council, the final version is to be presented sometime after June, 1998. Both the Earth Council and Green Cross International are hoping that the United Nations will approve this final version soon after its release, but realize that ratification could take some time. The Rio+5 draft of *The Earth Charter* is presented on the following pages. Although it may appear benevolent at first glance, a careful review of this document will reveal some of its potential dangers. The document's true intent, however, has been concealed by the carefully selected wording of its authors.

Already, great interest has been shown. From June 23 to 27, 1997, the 19th Special Session of the United Nations General Assembly (UNGASS)—billed as "Earth Summit Plus 5"—convened at U.N. headquarters in New York. The main purpose of this meeting was to review the global implementation of U.N. programs presented at the Earth Summit five years earlier. The conference brought together more than 60 heads of state and hundreds of NGOs who agreed that "the implementation of Agenda 21 is vitally important and more urgent than ever."[38] The summit resulted in delegates adopting a "Programme for the Further Implementation of Agenda 21."[39]

On the final day of this Special Session, the Earth Council, together with New York's Interfaith Center, conducted a workshop on *The Earth Charter*. The workshop was a "side event" to remind delegates of *The Charter's* merits while urging them to continue the implementation of its related programs.[40] During the five years between the '92 Earth Summit and this U.N. Special Session, *The Earth Charter* had made significant strides toward being accepted by the "International Community."

– The Earth Charter Benchmark Draft –
Reviewed during the Rio+5 Forum
18 March 1997

Earth is our home and home to all living beings. Earth itself is alive. We are part of an evolving universe. Human beings are members of an interdependent community of life with a magnificent diversity of life forms and cultures. We are humbled before the beauty of Earth and share a reverence for life and the sources of our being. We give thanks for the heritage that we have received from past generations and embrace our responsibilities to present and future generations.

The Earth Community stands at a defining moment. The biosphere is governed by laws that we ignore at our own peril. Human beings have acquired the ability to radically alter the environment and evolutionary processes. Lack of foresight and misuse of knowledge and power threaten the fabric of life and the foundations of local and global security. There is great violence, poverty, and suffering in our world. A fundamental change of course is needed.

The choice is before us: to care for Earth or to participate in the destruction of ourselves and the diversity of life. We must reinvent industrial-technological civilization, finding new ways to balance self and community, having and being, diversity and unity, short-term and long-term, using and nurturing.

In the midst of all our diversity, we are one humanity and one Earth family with a shared destiny. The challenges before us require an inclusive ethical vision. Partnerships must be forged and cooperation fostered at local, bioregional, national and international levels. In solidarity with one another and the community of life, we the peoples of the world commit ourselves to action guided by the following interrelated principles:

1. Respect Earth and all life. Earth, each life form, and all living beings possess intrinsic value and warrant respect independently of their utilitarian value to humanity.

2. Care for Earth, protecting and restoring the diversity, integrity, and beauty of the planet's ecosystems. Where there is risk of irreversible or serious damage to the environment, precautionary action must be taken to prevent harm.

3. Live sustainably, promoting and adopting modes of consumption, production and reproduction that respect and safeguard human rights and the regenerative capacities of Earth.

4. Establish justice, and defend without discrimination the right of all people to life, liberty, and security of person within an environment adequate for human health and spiritual well-being. People have a right to potable water, clean air, uncontaminated soil, and food security.

5. Share equitably the benefits of natural resource use and a healthy environment among the nations, between rich and poor, between males and females, between present and future generations, and internalize all environmental, social and economic costs.

6. Promote social development and financial systems that create and maintain sustainable livelihoods, eradicate poverty, and strengthen local communities.

7. Practice non-violence, recognizing that peace is the wholeness created by harmonious and balance relationships with oneself, other persons, other life forms, and Earth.

8. Strengthen processes that empower people to participate effectively in decision-making and ensure transparency and accountability in governance and administration in all sectors of society.

9. Reaffirm that Indigenous and Tribal Peoples have a vital role in the care and protection of Mother Earth. They have the right to retain their spirituality, knowledge, lands, territories and resources.

10. Affirm that gender equality is a prerequisite for sustainable development.
11. Secure the right to sexual and reproductive health, with special concern for women and girls.
12. Promote the participation of youth as accountable agents of change for local, bioregional and global sustainability.
13. Advance and put to use scientific and other types of knowledge and technologies that promote sustainable living and protect the environment.
14. Ensure that people throughout their lives have opportunities to acquire the knowledge, values, and practical skills needed to build sustainable communities.
15. Treat all creatures with compassion and protect them from cruelty and wanton destruction.
16. Do not do to the environment of others what you do not want done to your environment.
17. Protect and restore places of outstanding ecological, cultural, aesthetic, spiritual, and scientific significance.
18. Cultivate and act with a sense of shared responsibility for the well-being of the Earth Community. Every person, institutions and government has a duty to advance the indivisible goals of justice for all, sustainability, world peace, and respect and care for the larger community of life.

Embracing the values in this Charter, we can grow into a family of cultures that allows the potential of all persons to unfold in harmony with the Earth Community. We must preserve a strong faith in the possibilities of the human spirit and a deep sense of belonging to the universe. Our best actions will embody the integration of knowledge with compassion.

In order to develop and implement the principles in this Charter, the nations of the world should adopt as a first step an international convention that provides an integrated legal framework for existing and future environmental and sustainable development law and policy.

* * *

Earth Council. "The Earth Charter Benchmark Draft." (Web page http://www.ecouncil.ac.cr/rio5/mar18/earthen.html), [Accessed February 11, 1998.]

1998 World Conference on Global Governance

A few years after the initial Earth Summit, the U.N.-funded Commission on Global Governance unveiled its official plan for implementing the one-world agenda. This U.N. plan called for a World Conference on Global Governance to be held sometime in 1998 for the purpose of submitting the necessary treaties and agreements for ratification and implementation by the year 2000. The plan, existing in the form of a 410-page report, published by the Oxford University Press, is entitled *Our Global Neighborhood.*[41]

According to personal conversations with renowned environmental researchers Dr. Michael Coffman (author of *Saviors of the Earth*), and Henry Lamb (publisher of *êco-logic*), global governance— as described in the recommendations of the U.N. Commission— would be a catastrophic act of violence, resulting in the loss of national sovereignty, property rights, and individual freedom, all in the name of saving the environment.

Lamb warns, "The Commission's recommendations would consolidate the power of the United Nations into the hands of a very few individuals." He explains:

> The U.N. Trusteeship Council would be restructured to consist of no more than 23 individuals appointed from accredited NGOs (non-government organizations) such as the International Union for the Conservation of Nature, the World Wide Fund for Nature, and the World Resources Institute. These NGOs are already accredited by the U.N. By international treaty, this reorganized Council would assume "trusteeship" of the global commons.[42]

Many Americans, if they understood these sinister plans, would not support the radical environmental movement. However, under the leadership of the Clinton/Gore Administration, the United States can be expected to facilitate the World Conference on Global Governance and lobby Congress to ratify and implement the treaties necessary to make global government a reality.

An Avoidable Deception

As a result of an effectively waged environmental campaign, humanity has been whipped into a near frenzy over the "deteriorating" condition of the planet. If the situation is really as bad as described by New Age ecologists and the media, then earth's inhabitants had better find an answer soon. But what if the "problems" of global warming, deforestation, and depletion of the ozone are deliberately being overplayed to convince humanity of the need for world government. Could it be that Gorbachev and his allies are creating this "crisis atmosphere" for the express purpose of getting people to accept "a solution" they otherwise might not? Are we stepping into a trap?

If *The Earth Charter* and its supporting programs are implemented, sovereign nations would no longer exist—at least not in the traditional sense. Private property and the ability to choose what to do with your land would be severely limited. The right to decide your child's schooling, and what your child is taught—even at home—would be restricted. This state control would also extend into the realm of personal beliefs. Christianity—saying that Jesus Christ is the only way of reconciliation to God—would not likely be tolerated; in fact, it might be made a crime.

So why is humanity falling for this deception? The answer is simple—the majority of people have rejected the truth of God for a lie. Seeking to "liberate" themselves from a moral God and His holy commandments, most of earth's inhabitants have embraced humanism or pantheism as their world view. These two belief systems are really quite similar. Both reject the reality of a personal God, inevitably resulting in the direct or indirect worship of man or nature.

Nature worship—the elevation of nature (creation) above God (the Creator)—is nothing new. In fact, it was prevalent among the Lucifer-inspired mystery religions of the Old Testament Era. The Bible explains:

> For although they knew God, they neither glorified him as God nor gave thanks to him, but their thinking became futile and their foolish hearts were darkened. Although they claimed to be wise, they became fools and exchanged the glory of the immortal God for images made to look like mortal man and birds and animals and reptiles. Therefore God gave them over in the sinful desires of their hearts to sexual impurity for the degrading of their bodies with one another. They exchanged the truth of God for a lie, and worshipped and served created things rather than the Creator—who is forever praised. Amen. Romans 1:21–25 (NIV)

Throughout history, whenever man chose to worship himself or the pagan deities of nature in place of God, the consequences were severe. Humanity came under the control of false belief systems and those enforcing them. Pantheism, with its earth (or Gaia) worship, has inevitably had the effect of enslaving man. Whether it was the version presented by the Pharaohs of Egypt, the Brahmins of India, or the Caesars of Rome, the result of earth-centered religion was always the same—the enslavement of man under a ruthless, occultic system.

Unfortunately, most leaders of today's environmental movement hold a similar and equally militant world view. According to this view, those who believe in a personal Creator—refusing to make creation their god—are a threat to nature and must be eliminated. Only "enlightened" man (those who have embraced the teachings of occult deities) can evolve to a higher spiritual state, taking the quantum leap into "Godhood" and the New Aquarian Age. In pursuing this goal New Agers falsely believe they are "saving" themselves and the planet.

There are some legitimate concerns over the environment that need to be addressed, but we do not need to unite under a world government to do so. Any existing problems can easily be solved by using common sense, available technology, and a reasonable level of cooperation between nations. If only people would apply God's wisdom, they could avoid Satan's deception and the resulting consequences!

Notes

1. Mikhail Gorbachev, *Gorbachev: Mandate For Peace* (Toronto: PaperJacks, 1987), p. 9.

2. Philip C. Bom, *The Coming Century of Commonism* (Virginia Beach, VA: Policy Books, 1992), p. 113.

3. Mikhail Gorbachev, *Perestroika: New Thinking For Our Country and the World* (New York: Harper & Row, 1987), pp. 35, 66.

4. *Mikhail Sergeyevich Gorbachev—Who Is He?* (Indianapolis, IN: Indianapolis Baptist Temple, October 1996, fact sheet). An identical quote, minus the first sentence, may be found in the following source.

   David B. Funderburk, former U.S. Ambassador to Romania, *Betrayal of America* (Dunn, NC: Larry McDonald Foundation, 1991), p. 61

5. *Mikhail Sergeyevich Gorbachev—Who Is He?*

6. Ibid. For a similar statement by Gorbachev, see Funderburk, *Betrayal of America*, p. 57. For additional quotes by Gorbachev and other contemporary socialist leaders, see the *Soviet Analyst: An Intelligence Commentary*, World Reports Limited, Suite 1209, 280 Madison Avenue, New York, NY 10016-0802 (telephone: 212-599-4560).

7. Richard Nixon, *1999: Victory Without War* (New York: Simon & Schuster, 1988), pp. 29–30.

8. Ibid., p. 32.

9. Samantha Smith, "Gorbachev Forum Highlights World Government," *Hope for the World Update* (Noblesville, IN: Hope for the World, Fall 1995, newsletter), p. 2.

10. Ibid., p. 2.

11. Ibid., p. 2.

12. Ibid., p. 2.

13. Ibid., p. 2.

14. Mikhail Gorbachev, "Environment: Act Globally, Not Nationally," Interview with the *Los Angeles Times*, Thursday, May 8, 1997. Green Cross International, (Web page http://www.gci.ch/GreenCrossFamily/gorby/newspeeches/interviews/laTimes.html), [Accessed March 20, 1998].

15. Green Cross Family, (Web page http://www.gci.ch/ GreenCrossFamily/gorby/gorby.html), [Accessed March 20, 1998].

16. Samantha Smith, Journalist, Testimony of her observations at the State of the World Forum, San Francisco, September 27—October 1, 1995.

17. Smith, "Gorbachev Forum Highlights World Government," *Hope for the World Update*, p. 2.

18. Ibid., p. 2.

19. Mikhail Gorbachev, "The Earth Charter," Speech: Rio+5 Forum, March 18, 1997. Earth Council, P.O. Box 2323-1002, San Jose, Costa Rica. (Web page http://www.ecouncil.ac.cr/rio5/mar18/ gorbachev.html), [Accessed February 10, 1998].

20. Gorbachev, "Environment: Act Globally, Not Nationally," Interview with the *Los Angeles Times*.

21. Al Gore, *Earth in the Balance: Ecology and the Human Spirit* (New York: Plume, 1993), p. 274.

22. International Institute for Sustainable Development, *Youth Source Book on Sustainable Development* (Winnipeg, MB: IISD, 1994), p. 63.

23. Ibid., p. 64.

24. *Report of the United Nations Conference on Environment and Development* (A/CONF.151/26) Annex III, Closing Statements.

25. Ibid.

26. *Report of the United Nations Conference on Environment and Development* (A/CONF.151/26) Annex II, Opening Statements.

27. Elaine Dewar, *Cloak of Green* (Toronto: James Lorimer & Company, 1995), p. 324.

28. Ibid., p. 324.

29. Ibid., p. 326.

30. IISD, *Youth Source Book on Sustainable Development*, p. 64.

31. Hans J. Keller, *Who is Who in Service to the Earth* (Waynesville, NC: VisionLink Education Foundation, 1993), p. i. Also, see Joel Beversluis, *A SourceBook for Earth's Community of Religions* (New York: CoNexus Press and Global Education Associates, 1995), p. 292.

32. IISD, *Youth Source Book on Sustainable Development*, p. 75.

33. Earth Council. For more information on this event visit their web page. (Web page http://www.ecouncil.ac.cr).

34. Earth Council, "Rio+5 Forum - Agenda." Earth Council, P.O. Box 2323-1002, San Jose, Costa Rica. (Web page http://www.ecouncil.ac.cr/rio5/13en.html), [Accessed February 11, 1998].

35. Ibid.

36. Mikhail Gorbachev, "The Earth Charter," Speech: Rio+5 Forum, March 18, 1997. Green Cross International, (Web page http://www.gci.ch/GreenCrossFamily/gorby/newspeeches/speeches/spech18.3.97.html), [Accessed March 20, 1998].

37. Ibid.

38. The Earth Network for Sustainable Development, *The Earth Council at 'Earth Summit +5'*, July 1997. Sent as e-mail from Earth Council's Earthnet (Earth Network mailing list), the Earth Council's monthly e-mail newsletter. (earthnet@terra.ecouncil.ac.cr to Carl Teichrib) Letter on file at Hope For The World.

39. Ibid.

40. Ibid.

41. Henry Lamb, "Conspiracy Theories Laid To Rest As U.N. Announces Plan For 'Global Neighborhood,' " *Hope For The World Update* (Noblesville, IN: Hope For The World, Fall 1996, newsletter), p. 1.

42. Ibid., p. 2.

7

Shaping Global Citizens

"By smooth talk and flattery they deceive the minds of naive people." Romans 16:18 (NIV)

The environmental crisis, although paramount to the purposes of the globalist movement, is not the only reason given to justify the creation of a new world order. The need for a more stable and equitable international financial system, the push to eliminate global hunger and disease, and the quest for lasting world peace are all key arguments in advancing this occult agenda. If the public could be unified around these critical issues, the level of cooperation necessary to achieve a "planetary shift in consciousness" might finally be realized.

Alice Bailey was one of the many mystics who spoke of this coming global transformation and how it would be attained. In her book *The Externalisation of the Hierarchy* she revealed that the Aquarian Age would be ushered in primarily through the efforts of three institutions, which combined would influence every major field of endeavor. These "agents of change" would be Freemasonry, the Education Establishment, and the Apostate Church. Bailey, with help from her spirit guide, wrote:

The three main channels through which the preparation for the new age is going on might be regarded as the Church, the Masonic Fraternity and the educational field. All of them are as yet in relatively static condition, and all are as yet failing to meet the need and to respond to the inner pressure. But in all of these three movements, disciples of the Great Ones are to be found and they are steadily gathering momentum and will before long enter upon their designated task. (emphasis added)[1]

More than two generations have come and gone since Bailey penned these words. The hierarchy, as we have seen, has made significant progress during that time. Today, the "Great Ones" are actively working in all three institutions. Their disciples have embarked upon their "designated task."

I have already examined the activities of the Masonic Lodge in *En Route to Global Occupation*, so the following two chapters will be devoted to exploring developments in the other areas described by Bailey—education and the church. Not coincidentally, the same person is overseeing developments in both areas. As the point man for the United Nations in education and religion, Robert Muller is using environmental issues and other challenges facing mankind to achieve the goals of "the hierarchy."

Robert Muller (1923–)

Born in Belgium in 1923 and raised in Alsace-Lorraine, a province of France bordering Germany, Robert Muller experienced constant political and cultural turmoil during his youth. The Alsace-Lorraine region was ravaged by war on numerous occasions, sometimes existing under the control of Germany, sometimes France. Muller unfortunately lived in this area during its darkest period of history, World War II.

As a young man Robert experienced first hand the effects of war—of being a refugee, of Nazi occupation, and of being captured and placed in a Gestapo prison. As a member of the French Resistance, he had witnessed horrible atrocities and destruction. These nightmarish experiences were fundamental in shaping his world view.

After the war, Muller attended the University of Strasbourg, where he earned a doctorate of law. In 1948 he entered and won an essay contest on "how to govern the world." The prize was an internship at the newly created United Nations.[2] According to Muller, he joined the U.N. "because he wanted to work for peace so that his children and grandchildren would not know the horrors he saw in the war."[3] His intentions appeared to be nothing less than noble.

Muller spent the next forty years of his life working behind the scenes at the United Nations, advocating world government as humanity's only hope for peace. During that time he rose through the U.N. ranks to become one of the organization's most powerful figures, witnessing the creation of thirty-two specialized agencies and playing a personal role in creating eleven of them.[4] Eventually he was promoted to the position of assistant secretary-general. In that capacity, he served as the right-hand man to three U.N. secretary-generals: U Thant, Kurt Waldheim, and Javier Perez de Cuellar.[5] Later, Muller himself would become a candidate for the post of secretary-general.

Although he officially retired in 1986, Muller remains active on numerous fronts. Much of his time is devoted to writing. To date he has authored fourteen books, including *The Birth of a Global Civilization, My Testament to the UN*, and *New Genesis: Shaping a Global Spirituality*. He also serves as the chancellor of the U.N. University for Peace in Costa Rica and is in great demand as a speaker at environmental, educational, "spiritual," and political conferences around the world.[6]

His accomplishments have earned him numerous awards. Recently, he was the recipient of the Albert Schweitzer International Prize for the Humanities and the Eleanor Roosevelt Man of Vision Award.

Most of the year Muller lives on a small farm overlooking the University for Peace. It is located on a "sacred indigenous hill," Mt. Rasur, from which, according to indigenous prophecy, "a civilization of peace will extend to the entire world." Muller and his companion, Barbara Gaughen, refer to themselves as "The Cosmic Couple."[7]

According to Muller's personal biographical summary, he is "a deeply spiritual person" and has been called the "Philosopher" and "Prophet of Hope" of the United Nations.[8] As a top level global statesman, he sees a strong connection between spirituality and politics. In fact, his New Age views—acquired during his years of service at the U.N.—have become the principle driving force behind his political activism.

Muller's stated objectives for the new millennium are sevenfold:

1. To make this planet a paradise.
2. To eradicate from it all the poverty, miseries and errors engendered by power, greed and egotism.
3. To make out of all humans one family.
4. To create a new social, political world order for the centuries to come.
5. To attain a life of fulfillment and happiness for all humans.
6. To achieve a human family in harmony with the Earth and the heavens.
7. To be the ultimate cosmic success of the Universe and God.[9]

His ideals are reflected in the following motto, which appears in some of his written works:

See the world with global eyes.
Love the world with a global heart.
Understand the world with a global mind.
Merge with the world through a global spirit.[10]

A "Grassroots" Globalist

Along with his political involvement at the U.N., Robert Muller has been working to achieve his one-world objectives through lesser known, but important "grassroots" organizations, such as the United People's Assembly (UPA). He has been instrumental in shaping the UPA for the alleged purpose of giving "a voice to all peoples, NGOs and civil society," in the process of creating a world government.[11] As the honorary chairman of the assembly's advisory council, Muller's goal is to establish a People's Assembly within the United Nations by the year 2000.[12]

This exercise is in keeping with U.N. Secretary-General Kofi Annan's call for the creation of a "Millennium People's Assembly" to begin functioning in the year 2000. Annan's proposal was first presented to the General Assembly during his U.N. Reform statement in July 1997.[13] The New Zealand Forum for U.N. Renewal recently reported on the progress of this reform effort, shedding light on its history and direction:

> These proposals get their strength and inspiration from the vision of several UN founding members who, already in 1945, saw the need for a "UN world assembly, elected directly from the people of the world as a whole, to whom the governments who form the United Nations are responsible" as a "completion of the development of the United Nations" (both quotes by Ernest Bevin, former UK Foreign Secretary).[14]

The goal of the U.N.'s founders from the beginning was to develop the organization into a functioning world government in time for the new millenium. But to accomplish this enormous feat, global planners would somehow have to convince the people of the world that they are really the ones in charge and that the U.N. is merely acting on their behalf. Only then might the masses go along with the new world order.

Advancing this notion that humanity is in control, a model United People's Assembly was organized in San Francisco on June 21, 1995, during the fiftieth anniversary of the founding of the United

Nations. Since that time, additional conferences on a People's Assembly have been held. Meetings are currently being planned for Boston, Philadelphia, Los Angeles, London, Paris, Madrid, New Delhi, Bombay, Tokyo, and Wellington to advance this agenda. All of these gatherings are a build up to the Millenium People's Assembly, which, as mentioned, is to convene at the U.N. in the year 2000.[15]

Muller's UPA Advisory Council, which is guiding the process of establishing the People's Assembly, consists of a number of prominent globalists, such as Tim Barner of the World Federalist Association and Barbara Marx Hubbard of the Foundation for Conscious Evolution and The World Future Society.

Advisory Council of the United People's Assembly – 1996

Honorary Chairman, **Dr. Robert Muller**, Chancellor Emeritus
University for Peace,
Ciudad Colon, Costa Rica

Joaquin Antuna, President	**Tim Barner**, Executive Director
Paz Y Cooperacion	World Federalist Association
Madrid, Spain	Washington, D.C., USA
Erskine Childers, deceased	**Barbara Marx Hubbard**, President
Advisor to the United Nations,	The Foundation for Conscious
Author	Evolution
Roosevelt Island, New York, USA	Greenbrae, CA USA
Dr. Ervin Laszlo, President	**Dr. Benjamin Ferencz**
The Club of Budapest	Author, Professor of
Budapest, Hungary	International Law
	New Rochelle, New York, USA
Dr. Harry Lerner, Co-Chair	**Dr. Rashmi Mayur**, President
Campaign for a More Democratic	Global Futures Network
United Nations	Bombay, India
New York, N.Y., USA	
Dr. Hanna Newcombe, Director	**Benton Musslewhite**, President
Peace Research Institute	One World Now
Dundas, Ontario L9H 4E5, Canada	Houston, Texas, USA
Douglas Roche, O.C.	**David Macleod**, Vice President
Parliamentarian and Author,	World Government Org.
Diplomat	Coalition (WGOC)
Edmonton, Alberta, Canada	Kalamazoo, Michigan, USA

* * *

Source: Action Coalition for Global Change, *Welcome to the United People's Assembly*, http://acgc.org/upa/upa.html [accessed March 6, 1998].

Along with Robert Muller and his advisory council, the person who has been most instrumental in coordinating the United People's Assembly is Lucile Green. Her organization, the Action Coalition for Global Change, organized and oversaw the initial UPA meeting in San Francisco.

Muller and Green are close friends who have worked together in the one-world movement for decades. They were among the first globalists to make the environment an issue in the pursuit of world government. To help further their agenda, both became connected with the World Constitution and Parliament Association (WCPA). Green actually joined the WCPA in the early 1960s, becoming one of the organization's trustees.[16]

The WCPA, which was covered extensively in *En Route to Global Occupation*, has been very influential in the area of ecology and has nurtured the development of a pro–world government people's movement since its inception in 1959. Its efforts finally began to pay off in the 1980s, in part because of the growing public concern over the environment. Today, the WCPA, which claims to represent the people of the planet, boasts of a network of more than 430 organizations worldwide.[17]

The New Zealand Forum for U.N. Renewal describes the impact of this type of "people's movement":

> From the early 1980s, NGOs and interested individuals have been joining a worldwide peoples movement to help make the United Nations more democratic, and proposals for the establishment of a UN Second (peoples) Assembly, albeit under different names, have slowly been gathering clarity and momentum. . . . However daunting, this vision can, according to UN senior officials, be realized if we, the people of the United Nations, work with our governments to this end, build broad-based citizen's constituencies and embrace the concept that the UN Charter could come to be seen as the international constitution of all the world's peoples.[18]

By publicly working toward a world government and world constitution, the World Constitution and Parliament Association is playing an indirect but important role in augmenting the efforts of the United Nations. Claiming that the U.N. is not moving quickly enough, the WCPA and its people's network are applying the necessary "grassroots" pressure to speed up the process. This has the affect of creating the false impression that a majority of citizens support the idea of a new world order. It also causes the U.N. to inaccurately appear as a less radical, even conservative organization that is merely responding to the wishes of the people. The WCPA has already supervised the drafting of a model World Constitution—more comprehensive than the U.N. Charter—which it calls A Constitution for the Federation of Earth. Green was the document's fourth signer.[19] Commenting on the significance of this constitution, Green states:

> Based essentially on these East-West principles of inter-dependence, A Constitution for the Federation of Earth has been completed, after ten years' work by people from two dozen countries and all five continents, and signed by 160 participants at an assembly of world citizens in Innsbruck, Austria in June, 1977. This is another important milestone in conscious, deliberate evolution toward a world community. It brings the new world order down from the skies onto the drawing boards, and even proposes a step-by-step plan of action to achieve it. (See Exhibits K-1 and K-2.)[20]

Robert Muller has been very supportive of Lucile Green and the WCPA in general, openly endorsing the organization and its world constitution. In 1992 he stated:

> I support wholeheartedly the brilliant and modern world constitution offered to humanity by the World Constitution and Parliament Association. It is here at the right moment when the world needs a salvation from its present chaos and a metamorphosis into a new, appropriate world order to cope with the massive global problems confronting us. The men and women who gave it birth through hard work and perseverance deserve humanity's gratitude and prompt approval. May God bless this Constitution.[21]

The following letter from the WCPA summarizes some of the organization's plans and activities as of June 1995. Since that time the WCPA's campaign has gained momentum. The organization now has affiliated groups in more than 80 countries.

World Constitution and Parliament Association

**ORGANIZING AGENT for the PROVISIONAL WORLD PARLIAMENT
and for the GLOBAL RATIFICATION AND ELECTIONS NETWORK**
1480 Hoyt St., Suite 31/Lakewood. CO 80215/Ph. 303-233-3548 or 526-0463
Telefax: 303-526-2185 or 233-4800

MEETING IN U.S.A. - AUGUST 1995

To persons who have replied   9th June 1995
to recent information about our campaign

Dear Friends:

During the past several months, several hundred persons have replied by telephone
and letter to our 12 full page magazine advertisements, 30 radio interviews and
other information, and have expressed interest in our program of action to achieve
a democratic federal world government -- able to solve problems peacefully for the
benefit of everybody living on Earth.

As most of you know, who receive this letter, we are preparing for the fourth
session of the Provisional World Parliament, to convene from 26 June to 5 July,
1996. The purpose of the 1996 Parliament is to make rapid progress towards the
establishment of a functioning world federation and world government under the
Constitution for the Federation of Earth.

To help build support for the 1996 Parliament, and to carry forward an on-going
campaign both in the USA and worldwide, we are inviting all interested in the USA
and Canada to a meeting in Colorado in August. The meeting will be 18th, 19th and
the 20th, August, 1995, at the Ramada Denver West in the Colorado Room, 14707
West Colfax Avenue. Registration is required with WCPA for $30.00. (Registration
form on back of page 2)

If you want to help make this campaign succeed, we invite you to the August
meeting in Colorado. If you cannot get to the meeting but want to help, you can do
so by making a contribution, by building support wherever you live, and by getting
an organization of which you are a member to join the Global Ratification and
Elections Network and send a delegate to the 1996 Parliament.

But, please, the August meeting is only for persons who sincerely want to help, and
not for detractors. In a country where armed militia and ultra right groups are
rampant, some of those receiving this letter may be unfriendly to our purposes. We
recognize this hazard. That is why the enclosed reply form is drawn with a
committment to support and assist the achievement of our defined objective. We
must depend on your word of honor in this respect.

'Let Us Raise A Standard To Which The Wise And The Honest Can Repair!'

Exhibit K-1

The importance of our global campaign may be judged in the following light: We aim to accomplish--

- *What was not accomplished by World War One;*
- *What was not accomplished by World War Two;*
- *What was not accomplished by the League of Nations;*
- *What has not and cannot be accomplished by the United Nations;*
- *What has not been accomplished by 50 years of trying to amend or strengthen the U.N.;*
- *What has not been accomplished by thousands of protest demonstrations against the military system.*

We aim to accomplish enduring world peace, total disarmament of war making capabilities, a comprehensive program to save the environment and prevent impending catastrophes from climate changes, a new world economic order designed to give everybody equitable opportunities in life, and to establish those global institutions under federal world government by which the above mentioned problems and all problems which transcend national boundaries can be solved peacefully for the good of all by applied intelligence.

Our aim is to begin World Government soon with more than 70% of Earth included at the start, as defined by the 12 full page advertisements earlier this year.

What we are creating is an immediate and practical alternative to the present chaotic, destructive, unfair, life-threatening and unsustainable course of human affairs on Earth, in which everybody is now trapped.

We hope you want to help this campaign succeed. We shall look for your positive reply.

For ADEQUATE action in time for the Happy survival of humanity on Earth,

Philip Isely

Philip Isely

'Let Us Raise A Standard To Which The Wise And The Honest Can Repair!'

Exhibit K-2

Over the past two decades the WCPA has organized four meetings of a "Provisional World Parliament." These sessions were held in Brighton, England (1982); New Delhi, India (1985); Miami Beach, USA (1987); and Barcelona, Spain (1996). The fifth provisional meeting is tentatively scheduled to be held from March 9–20, 1999, at the Peoples Palace in Baghdad, Iraq.[22] Soon thereafter, global planners expect this concept of a "people's parliament," or "people's assembly" to become a reality within the structure of the U.N., or if not the U.N., then a new, more powerful global governing body yet to emerge.

A tremendous amount of energy and ingenuity has gone into marketing the delusion that the people will be in control of the new order. Hundreds of NGOs have been deployed through the WCPA's network to "represent" humanity. These NGOs have become increasingly visible in their roles, especially since the '92 Earth Summit, where the WCPA participated in the Global Forum. However, what few people seem to realize is that most of the leaders of these NGOs are already staunch advocates of world government who share the U.N.'s views. In some cases, the founders of NGOs have actually worked for the U.N. or are lifetime friends of those who have. (See Appendix G, which lists the "Honorary Sponsors of the Provisional World Parliament" and some of their U.N. connections.)

The public is also generally unaware of the fact that many of these individuals are spiritually motivated. The pantheistic religious views of Muller, Green, and other leaders explain some of the reasoning behind the movement's one-world philosophy. In her book *Journey to a Governed World—Thru 50 Years in the Peace Movement*, Green writes:

> A wholistic, one-world view is emerging from space travel and other miracles of modern technology and from communication. A new consciousness is also emerging from a growing awareness in the West of the wisdom of the Eastern world-view. Buddhism, Hinduism, Taoism and Shinto, while they differ in many respects, portray the world as a multi-dimensional, organically interrelated eco-system of which man is one of many inter-dependent parts. Perhaps we can learn through them to see the world whole, as it really is, and together—West and East—begin to build the foundations of a new world order.[23]

Green recently expressed her delight over the strides made toward this new world order. She made these comments at a world-peace conference held November 7–9, 1997, in Chicago, Illinois. After discussing Muller's UPA Advisory Council and their efforts toward making the one-world vision a reality, she acknowledged the rapid progress of the Assemblies.

There are already signs of life in all of these Assemblies around the world . . . life signs of this embryo about to be born. We even know the date when it will be born, which will be the year 2000. And between now and then, my friends, we are in labor. And there will be pain in labor. Plenty of it, I'm sure. But our labor pains will bring forth a new life in the year 2000.[24]

The dangers of this agenda are obvious. There will be no true representation of the people under the new order. Any appearance of political checks and balances will be a façade intended only to alleviate people's concerns. The top movers and shakers in the one-world movement—like Robert Muller and Lucile Green—share an Eastern, occult world view and will never give true Christians a voice.

Educating for a New World Order

In order to achieve their new planetary civilization, globalists understood early on that they would have to influence the world's educational systems. Only by reeducating our youth to embrace a new set of cosmic values—referred to by Gorbachev, Muller, and other New Agers as the "Global Ethic"—could their political efforts succeed.

Understanding the important role of schools in the development of children, the U.N. embarked on a vigorous campaign to replace traditional Western curricula, which had promoted a strong sense of national identity and a Christian ethic. They proposed a new international curriculum promoting the concepts of world government and pantheistic religion. This new curriculum, it was hoped, would turn children into "global citizens" who would not only embrace the new order but would actively work to help bring it about. Staying true to his spiritual convictions, Robert Muller would take the lead in this effort to redesign education.

The World Core Curriculum

Muller's education agenda was launched in 1975 when an essay he wrote, entitled "The Need For Global Education," appeared in the magazine *New Era*, published by the World Fellowship of Education in London. His essay quickly made the rounds, being distributed by the United Nations Educational, Scientific, and Cultural Organization (UNESCO); the World Affairs Council in Philadelphia (during the U.S. bicentennial); and by numerous educational magazines around the world. According to Muller, this publicity led to an international outcry by educators expressing their need for a global education plan. Allegedly, because of this response, Muller proceeded to draft a document known as *The World Core Curriculum.*

This international curriculum was formally introduced in 1984 by Muller in his book *New Genesis—Shaping a Global Spirituality.* A few years later, unbeknownst to the people of America and the world, *The World Core Curriculum* (WCC) was officially presented to the United Nations.

The World Core Curriculum sets forth the principles that are to govern all of the planet's education programs. The changes recommended in the WCC reflect the heart and soul of today's education-reform movement and have earned Robert Muller the title "Father of Global Education." The U.N., which fully endorses this plan, recognizes it as their position paper on the future course of education worldwide (private and home schooling included). But amazingly, many teachers and administrators remain unaware of the fact that this important document even exists, let alone that it helped inspire the highly publicized GOALS 2000 campaign.

The fact is, today's major education reforms were set in motion by the U.N. in the 1980s and, after gaining the support of key members of the Bush and Clinton administrations, have carefully and systematically been introduced at the state and local levels, where they are now receiving widespread support. The education-reform program currently known as GOALS 2000 was originally introduced under the name America 2000 by Lamar Alexander, Department of Education secretary during the Bush administration. The Clinton administration, after modifying the program slightly, renamed it GOALS 2000. (For more information on the current administration's role in education, see Appendix H.)

It is important to understand that *The World Core Curriculum* is not some obscure document. The U.N. hopes to have the goals of the curriculum fully in place within the next few years, in time for our entrance into global government. To demonstrate its support for this program, the U.N. honored the curriculum's author, Robert Muller, with a special peace prize for education in 1989.

One example of how GOALS 2000 concepts are being implemented at the local level comes from Oregon, where the city of Eugene's 4J School District introduced its EDUCATION 2000 CURRICULUM in 1989 (Exhibits L-1 to L-4). This particular elementary school curriculum is designed for use in Kindergarten through Fifth Grade. Notice the "Curriculum Strands" which have been "adapted from the World Core Curriculum by Robert Muller" (Exhibit L-4, overleaf). In this case the local school authorities knowingly drew their curriculum goals from Muller's WCC.

EDUCATION

DISTRICT 4-J INTEGRATED
CURRICULUM K-5

Exhibit L-1

District 4J Mission

Investing in Students...
Creating the Future...

Eugene's Elementary Program's Mission
To instill in each child -
-a sense of self-worth
-a respect for the earth and all peoples
-and a commitment to the pursuit of life-long
learning

Rationale and Introduction

...With knowledge increasing at exponential rates and demands
for jobs and careers in the next generation shifting from
industrial production to information processing and service,
equipping students with the knowledge and skills they will
need to succeed in the next century demands that schools
modify their current curricula and instructional strategies...
Education 2000, 1988.

Exhibit L-2

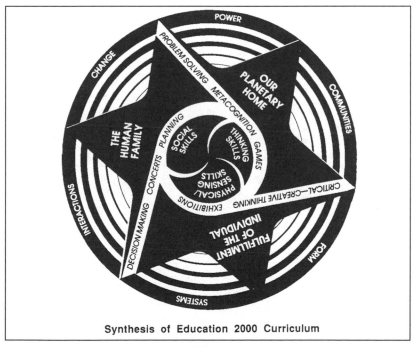

Synthesis of Education 2000 Curriculum

Exhibit L-3

Curriculum Strands

The three curriculum strands are adapted from the World Core Curriculum by Robert Muller, former United Nations Undersecretary General. The strands have been defined as follows:

The Human Family

Within this strand, humanity over time is explored including its universal nature and inherent diversity. This part of the curriculum reflects the richness of cultural heritage and the dignity of all peoples. Students will see themselves as members of an increasingly interdependent, global community, responsible for its future.

The Human Family strand includes some aspects of the traditional content areas of social studies, health education and the arts.

Our Planetary Home and Its Place in the Universe

Responsibility for understanding, preserving and managing our planet is explored within this strand. It provides a framework for the content associated with physical, earth and life sciences, and aspects of social studies, health and art. This content is examined within the context of historical, ethical and aesthetic perspectives.

Understanding and Fulfillment of the Individual

This strand emphasizes self-awareness through an understanding of the physical, social, emotional, and creative aspects of each individual. Experiences which integrate these components lead to a sense of self-worth, creative self-expression and responsible decision-making. Traditional content areas associated with this strand are visual and performing arts, physical education, health, literature, and affective education.

11

Exhibit L-4

The Robert Muller School

What is particularly disturbing about these developments is that Dr. Muller has incorporated many of his New Age religious views into his curriculum. What causes even greater concern is that Muller has been heavily influenced by occultist Alice Bailey. He has a school devoted to the study of her teachings in Arlington, Texas. This institution, although commonly referred to as the Robert Muller School, is officially a branch of The School of Ageless Wisdom, founded in 1974 by Gloria Crook, a Bailey admirer and one of Muller's close friends.

The fact that this school draws heavily from the teachings of Alice Bailey is plainly revealed in the preface of the WCC Manual (Exhibit M-1, *overleaf*). The Manual states:

> The World is indebted to Dr. Robert Muller, Former Assistant Secretary General of the United Nations, author and lecturer, for the formulation of the World Core Curriculum in its skeleton form. It is upon that scaffold combined with the Ageless Wisdom teachings that this present work has precipitated. The underlying philosophy upon which The Robert Muller School is based will be found in the teachings set forth in *the books of Alice A. Bailey by the Tibetan teacher, Djwhal Khul (published by Lucis Publishing Company)*. (emphasis mine)[25]

For more than a decade now, The Robert Muller School has served as a type of testing ground for *The World Core Curriculum* and the teachings of Alice Bailey. Not surprisingly, the school, which is fully accredited, has been certified as a United Nations Associated School. (See Exhibit M-2.) As difficult as it may be to believe, the U.N.'s global education system of the future is being openly modeled after the teachings of a Luciferic trans-channeler and her demonic spirit guide.

In the spring of 1997, Muller decided to go public with his agenda, printing the first issue of *World Core Curriculum Magazine*, a publication devoted exclusively to presenting and promoting his New Age curriculum to the world. A list of Muller's affiliated schools appeared in that introductory issue and is presented in Exhibit M-3.

The same magazine issue went on to feature several revealing articles. The first of these, "A Letter to All Educators in the World," is written by Muller himself. Two of the other articles are written by Gloria Crook. Together they summarize the spiritual goals, activities, and impact of The Robert Muller Schools and the U.N. in the area of education. The articles also reveal how interlocked Robert Muller, the United Nations and Lucis Trust really are. Here are a few highlights:

The world is indebted to Dr. Robert Muller, Former Assistant Secretary General of the United Nations, author and lecturer, for the formulation of the World Core Curriculum in its skeleton form. It is upon that scaffold combined with the Ageless Wisdom teachings that this present work has precipitated.

The underlying philosophy upon which The Robert Muller School is based will be found in the teachings set forth in the books of Alice A. Bailey by the Tibetan teacher, Djwhal Khul (published by Lucis Publishing Company, 113 University Place, 11th floor, New York, N.Y. USA 10083) and the teachings of M. Morya as given in the Agni Yoga Series books (published by Agni Yoga Society, Inc., 319 West 107th Street, New York, N.Y. USA 10025).

The purpose of this presentation is to make available for the use of educators and parents an overview of the practical results of the first year's process with actual application of the World Core Curriculum.

The materials and methodology presented herein emphasize the practical application of concepts dealing with global issues rather than the theoretical approach. The text is designed to be of useful value to the beginning teacher as well as the more experienced.

"The consciousness of universal relationship, of subjective integration and of a proven and experienced unity will be the climaxing gift of the period ahead of us."

<u>Education in the New Age</u>, p. 122

NOTE (1986): After six years of implementation the documentation of the World Core Curriculum process has expanded to include teaching manuals from birth through high school (twelfth year). These will be available after publication which is expected during 1987.

The Robert Muller School was fully accredited in 1985. (See accompanying evaluation after the Bibliography). The school is now certified as a United Nations Associated School providing education for international cooperation and peace. For more information contact:

> *Gloria Crook, Founding President*
> *The Robert Muller School*
> *6005 Royaloak Drive*
> *Arlington, Texas 76016 USA*
>
> *Phone: (817) 654-1018*

Preface

Exhibit M-1

SPEND A WEEKEND AT THE
ROBERT MULLER SCHOOL
INVESTIGATING THE
WORLD CORE CURRICULUM

The school was instituted as a model, having only a few children in each grade level. Fully accredited from birth through high school as an alternative school, it is also Certified as a United Nations Associated School, educating for Peace.

A LIMIT OF 12 PARTICIPANTS PER WORKSHOP!!! see the results of twelve years' implementation of The WORLD CORE CURRICULUM.

ENJOY DIRECT INTERCHANGE WITH THE DIRECTOR AND TEACHING STAFF OF THE SCHOOL AS YOU:
- Examine concepts, methodology
- Gather materials, resources
- Experience World Core Curriculum lesson planning for any level or area of interest
- Have dinner with the high-school students and another dinner with the parents and staff

Start a Robert Muller School!

We will help you! The principal requirements are:

1. The School must begin at birth and might extend as high as practical--through secondary school.

2. The World core Curriculum must be the only implemented curriculum. All academic material will be pre-adjusted to fit into one of the following four categories of the Worldcore Curriculum and thereby improve the students' perspective of universal interdependencies:
- Our Planetary Home and Place in the Universe
- Our human Family
- Our Place in time
- The Miracle of Individual Human Life

3. Parents of the students must be in agreement with the curriculum and willing to involve themselves in the education of their children as citizens of the Planet and the Universe.

Many schools have already been spawned and there will be countless Robert Muller Schools in the future--all around the World! It is time for a New Genesis in education.

Dr.
Robert Muller

Chancellor of the
United Nations University for Peace

The Robert Muller School is a nonprofit entity under IRS Code 501(c)(3). There are no tuitions charged nor donation amounts suggested. Major support for the work of the School is provided through unsolicited, voluntary contributions. Contributions are tax deductible.

Exhibit M-2

This brochure, promoting The Robert Muller School, demonstrates the close connection between the school, Robert Muller, the World Core Curriculum, and the United Nations. Not mentioned in the brochure is the fact that each year the mother school in Arlington, Texas coordinates the popular Global Elementary Model United Nations (GEMUN) program.

The Robert Muller Schools

The following list is of Robert Muller Schools International, or groups, and individuals who are preparing to implement or are promoting The World Core Curriculum. The list is not complete but will be updated periodically. (Jan. 1997)

1. The Robert Muller School
International Coordinating Center
6005 Royaloak Drive
Arlington, Texas 76016 USA
Phone (817) 654-1018
FAX (817) 654-1028

2. Escuela Del Siglo Nuevo
Proyecto Conciencia Planetaria
Fundacion Pio Ronconroni
Uruguay 1037
Piso 5 Dto. 12/3
1037 ARGENTINA
FAX 54. 1.8145264

3. The Yelena Roerich Center
of Aesthetic Education
5. Prospect Mira
Kaliningrad 23000 RUSSIA

4. Prof. Joan Dufour
3406 SW Manning St.
Seattle, WA 98126 USA
Phone (206) 937-5724

5. Instituto de las Americas
Ave. Jardin 606 Fracc. Las fuentos
Piedras Negras. Coah, MEXICO

6. The Fairview Robert Muller School
340 Country Club
McKinney, Texas 75069 USA
Phone (972) 542-5330

7. Angie and Harold Levy
RMS of Blooming Grove
Rt. 1, 9277 NW 1342
Blooming Grove, TX 76626
USA
Phone (214) 987-1546

8. Robert Muller LIFE School
(Panajachel)
PO Box 520972
Miami, FL 33152-0972 USA

9. The Plaza of Light School
Unity Church on the Plaza
707 W. 47th St.
Kansas City, MO 64112 USA
Phone (816) 561-4466

10. Wee Wisdom School
Christ Church Unity
3770 Altadena Avenue
San Diego, CA 92105 USA
Phone (619) 280-2501

11. Manec van der Lugt
Davidhuis
Slotlaan 31
3062 PL Rotterdam
NETHERLANDS
Phone (0) 10-4123442

12. UNITY. Rita Johnson
SJO-401
PO Box 025216
Miami, FL 33102-5216 USA
Phone (506) 226-6051

13. Dr. Richard and Ruth Schneider
Lifeline to the World
Mucherla Global School
Mucherla, A.P. 507128 INDIA
or. Box 20728
Portland, OR 97220 USA
Phone (503) 283-8958

14. Anne MacEwen
8 Cannon Hill Gardens
Colehill Wimborne
Dorset, U.K. BH21 2TA

15. Ferdinand Chadokurenda
Int. Corps Heralding Oneness
UNESCO Centre,
c/o Vuumeve Occult School
P.O. Box 177
Gokwe, ZIMBABWE, Africa

16. Vicki Leslie
1502 NW 17th St.
Gainsville FL. 32605 USA
Phone (904) 462-5908

17. Dr. Catherine Clarke
905 Clear Springs Ct.
Chesapeake, VA 23320 USA
Phone (804) 548-9030

18. The OM RMS
c/o Nikolai Slatin
IPKRO Rm. #38
Tarskaya St. #2
Omsk. RUSSIA 644099
Phone 7-3812-140733

19. Mitch Gold (IAEWP)
2 Bloor St West, 100-209
Toronto, Ontario M4W3F2
CANADA
Phone (416) 924-4449
e-mail mgold@oise.on.ca.

20. Juan Ivan Szemere
Rua Agostinho Cantu
CEP 05501-010
San Paulo. BRAZIL
Ph/FAX 5511 8136945

21. Dara Knerr
144 Martin Drive
Novato, CA. 94949 USA

22. Colegio Huitzil
Maria Victoria Gerbolini
Granicisco Villa N. 102
Col Buenovista
Cuernavaca Moretos MEXICO

23. Lola Kristof
2101 Sacramento St., Apt. 301
San Francisco, CA 94109 USA

24. Caroline Gatehouse
21 Oakridge Rise
Hackham West , AUSTRALIA
5163

25. Stephen P. Thane
Lighted Gateway
L9 Yarrabin St., Melrose
N.S. W. 2085 AUSTRALIA

26. Joanna Mitchell
3300 Old Bullard Rd.
Tyler. Texas. USA 75701
Phone (903) 592-7203

27. Penelope Newcomb
P.O.Box 87
East Charleston, VT 05833
USA

28. Naoko Mira Robinson
10-27 Wakunami, 4-chome
Kanazawa. Ishikawa-Ken
JAPAN 920

29. The Light Community
Montessori School
P. McMillan
c/o PO. Inglewood SA 5133.
AUSTRALIA
Phone 0011 618 389 2383

30. Janet Pliner, Shorewood
Hills Elementary School
1105 Shorewood Blvd.
Madison, WI 53705 USA
pliner@madison.k12.wi.us

31. Whole Child Learning
Garden. Unity Center
San Jose. COSTA RICA

32. Maria - Eri Phocas
Valaoritou 6.
16674 Ano-Glyfada,
Athens, GREECE
Phone: 0030-1-9615596
email: eridim@hol.gr

Exhibit M-3

Excerpts from "A Letter to All Educators in the World" by Robert Muller:

> In the middle of my life I discovered that the only true, objective education I had received was from the United Nations where the earth, humanity, our place in time and the worth of the human being were the overriding concerns. . . . So at the request of educators I wrote the World Core Curriculum, the product of the United Nations, the meta-organism of human and planetary evolution. . . .

> There exist many schools in the world bearing my name or using the World Core Curriculum. Thousands of individuals or groups of educators have acquired the curriculum for study and use. Schools are in process of forming all around the World. . . . It is a curriculum of our universal knowledge which should be taught in all schools of Earth.

> In the meantime, I have concluded that the curriculum could serve as a basic framework for many other applications, the most important example is that of the media. . . . It is the media who are "informing" us and should educate us about the major, very rapid changes which are taking place in the world. But the media do not recognize that they should be educators. They are simply communicators. Well, *they should be the educators of our adult lives until death.* This is why I have also couched the World Core Curriculum into a framework for World Media Coverage which I would like to see taught in all schools of journalism and hung on the walls of all media directors in the world, as a basis of their media coverage and programming. (emphasis mine)[26]

(Author's note: This should not be too difficult considering the fact that many media personalities and owners already have pro-U.N., New Age leanings!)

* * * * *

Excerpts from "The World Core Curriculum In The Original Robert Muller School" by Gloria Crook:

> Sixteen years ago, the first Robert Muller School was formed in Arlington, Texas, to implement Robert Muller's World Core Curriculum and make the results available to educators around the world.

> The mission has been partially accomplished. The School has been fully accredited as an alternative school (birth through

secondary school) and *Certified as a United Nations Associated School*. Teacher Training Conferences have been held since 1989 to assist educators who wish to implement the Curriculum in other schools.

. . . The School has published several books and videos on the use of the Curriculum, including "The World Core Curriculum Manual," and "The WCC Guidebook." These are sold by the School and the UN bookshop. The publications are *also sold by Lucis Trust in London, England*.

. . . Interest in the Curriculum has become Worldwide . . . and educators seeking a curriculum which lends the highest life values, along with academic excellence are supporting the use of the World Core Curriculum.

The World Core Curriculum has been translated into Spanish, Russian, Italian, Dutch, and German. Groups and individuals are using the Curriculum in the United States, Argentina, Russia, Mexico, Guatemala, Costa Rica, Brazil, Africa, Holland, the United Kingdom, India, Canada, Australia, New Zealand, the Philippines, and Ecuador.

The World Core Curriculum *comes from the United Nations* and provides a structure within which a child might find the truth of interdependence and the idea of synthesis to be more than a theory or a wish, but an integral part of our Cosmic existence. Coming generations will find this Curriculum to have played a vital part in the beginning of *a total revolution in the education of the world's young*, forming a structure for a consciousness of non-violence and peace. (emphasis mine)[27]

* * * * *

Excerpts from "How to Start a Robert Muller School" by Gloria Crook:

The principal requirement to become a Robert Muller School is to implement the World Core Curriculum. This is accomplished by fitting every academic subject into one or more of the following categories, relating the subject directly to the life of the individual student, and simultaneously teaching a perspective which is inclusive of the Whole of Existence:

I. Our Planetary Home and Place in the Universe
II. The Family of Humanity
III. Our Place in Time
IV. The Miracle of Individual Human Life

. . . The Curriculum was born out of Robert Muller's 40 year experience with the United Nations, and it will be discovered that an understanding of the United Nations, its structure and purposes, will be a most rewarding factor. *The UN is also a cache of innumerable resources in the implementation of the World Core Curriculum.*

. . . The scope of the curriculum will always be the same; to allow the student to see himself truly, as an integral part of the Cosmos. . . .

At the moment, it seems *the only limitation will be the imagination of the Cosmic-minded and spiritually oriented teaching staff.*

. . . A School can begin with any age-group of children; however it is hoped that *children will be taught the Curriculum from birth and throughout life;* the interdependence of all existence will be foundational to their thinking for a lifetime.

. . . Ideally, the school *will begin at birth, with the parents having used the Balanced Beginnings Program prenatally;* and will continue through the secondary level. In this structure, the student will move directly into college with no break in the continuity of presented perspective. By that time, there will *be an understanding which overrides all false concepts* which are still held among much of the general populace of the world— concepts which have bred separative and prejudiced behavior for most of human history.

. . . The Staff and supporters will be recognized as *those who are bringing about a needed and radical change in the consciousness of the world's children*—they are preparing these children for a synthesis and cooperation of which we can only dream today.

. . . *Strong conviction relating to world interdependence and the need for the global perspective is a foregone prerequisite. A teacher must be naturally consistent in the presentation of this world view.*

. . . The students should be aware as early as possible that *the United Nations is the only planetary Entity* which brings the leaders of the world governments together to work out solutions to world problems. . . .

Too few of the world's teachers have a knowledge of The United Nations, its structure, and how its Specialized Agencies affect every human being. When they have this information, they are much better equipped to teach children how they may contribute ideas for the betterment of the world in which we live. The World Core Curriculum, when implemented correctly, *will cause a student to have a picture of her/himself as one Cosmic Unit,* part of the human species, existing for a limited period of time on the planet Earth, and *contributing to the entire planetary scheme.* (emphasis mine)[28]

* * * * *

If you are disturbed by these remarks and their ramifications, you are not alone. Numerous educators have been hesitant to embrace the WCC because of its obvious New Age overtones. Recognizing this fact, Gloria Crook, in the same article, goes on to address the religious concern. She conjects:

What is the spiritual significance?

Groups often question whether the World Core Curriculum is related to religion.

. . . Each student needs to grasp the wide diversity while holding to the idea of the Unity of the Human Family. They will realize that *every religion is representative of the ways humanity has kept an inner approach to the Infinite, Supreme Being, Intelligence, Spirit, or that ONE, Who is called, by many of us, "God."*

. . . Ultimately, all cultures and parts of the globe will be involved in this pathbreaking work. *Any educators who produce the results depicted here are part of the new world of education.* (emphasis mine)[29]

Crook's veiled explanation, along with raising some serious doctrinal issues, evades the most important questions: Is religion being taught? And if so, what religion is it?

In September 1993, during a newspaper interview with the *Fort Worth Star-Telegram,* Crook admitted that her school introduces its students to practices such as yoga.[30] Yoga, as we have already discovered, is an occult practice rooted in the pantheistic religions of the East. But like most occultists, Crook tries to hide the true origin of these practices under the veil of Christianity, claiming that members of the school believe in God and Jesus Christ.[31] If this is the case, they hold a different view of God and Christ than that taught in Scripture. There is a great difference between believing that Jesus Christ is an ascended master and believing that he is the only Son of God (John 3:16) and the only way of salvation (Acts 4:12).

Crook continues her confusing explanation, stating that the school also embraces the spiritual principles behind all the world's religions.[32] This concept is referred to as "interfaithism" and is widely promoted by The Robert Muller School. In one of its pamphlets the school states, "When some part of Universal Truth has been truly grasped, the Source is recognized to be beyond any scriptural authority."[33]

This underlying doctrine of interfaithism is a complete violation of God's Word. The Bible reveals that it is impossible to accept the beliefs of other religions and simultaneously accept all the teachings of Jesus Christ. Why? Because other religions deny the fact that Jesus is the only way of salvation. In so doing, they minimize the atoning death and resurrection of Christ, falsely teaching that there are other paths to immortality, when in truth there are none. Acts 4:12 (NIV) proclaims, "Salvation is found in no one else, for there is no other name under heaven given to men by which we must be saved." Jesus stated in no uncertain terms, "I am the way and the truth and the life. No one comes to the Father except through me" (John 14:6, NIV). Clearly, The Robert Muller School is not based on Christianity. It is pantheistic.

Even though occult concepts are embedded throughout the school's literature, many educators who have examined this material, I believe, remain unaware of the fact that The Robert Muller School is modeled after the Luciferic principles of Alice Bailey and Lucis Trust. Yet, in some cases, the school's language virtually matches Bailey's comments on the subject of education. Educators should make the connection if they consider the following statements made by Bailey more than fifty years ago:

> I write for the generation which will come . . . at the end of this century; they will inaugurate the frame work, structure and fabric of the New Age . . . which will develop the civilisation of the Aquarian Age."[34]

> The educators who face the present world opportunity should see to it that a sound foundation is laid for the coming civilisation. . . . They must lay an emphatic importance upon those great moments in human history wherein man's divinity flamed forth and indicated new ways of thinking, new modes of human planning and thus changed for all time the trend of human affairs."[35]

> We shall have to train our teachers differently and much time will be lost as we grope for the new and better ways, develop the new textbooks and find the men and women who can be

impressed with the new vision and who will work for the new civilisation."[36]

I have suggested that the textbooks be rewritten in terms of right human relations and not from the present nationalistic and separative angles. . . . To all of these I would like to add that one of our immediate educational objectives must be the elimination of the competitive spirit and the substitution of the cooperative consciousness."[37]

The objective of the new social order of the new politics and the new religion, is to bring about the unfoldment of human consciousness."[38]

It will be apparent to you, therefore, that the whole goal of the future and of the present effort, is to bring humanity to the point where it—occultly speaking—enters into light.[39]

Global Citizenship 2000

Unfortunately, a growing number of top educators are embracing these New Age views. As a result, Dr. Muller is being invited to present his *World Core Curriculum* at major education forums. One such opportunity came in the spring of 1997 in British Columbia, Canada. Carl Teichrib, a Canadian researcher, attended the conference and shared his findings in one of our special reports. The following is his personal account:

> "Welcome . . . Global Citizens!" With these words, Dr. Desmond Berghofer, Chairman of the International Foundation of Learning, officially opened the Global Citizenship 2000 Youth Congress. Between April 4–6, 1997, at the one-thousandth day before the year 2000, the colossal Vancouver Public Library in British Columbia, Canada, became the "visioneering" epicentre of the world. We had gathered to make global history.

> Friday evening, April 4, educators, community leaders, and approximately 150 children congregated in the Library Concourse to celebrate Global Citizenship. This was no ordinary gathering! Philip Owen, Mayor of Vancouver—unable to attend—passed along his support to the Congress. The children, students from British Columbia's lower mainland schools, marched in carrying banners with themes of Global Citizenship. . . .

> In the words of organizer Dr. Geraldine Schwartz, President

of the International Foundation of Learning, the man to inspire and move the Congress was a "planet elder." Dr. Robert Muller took the spotlight to the roar of applause.

Global Citizenship 2000 was a marriage of Robert Muller's *World Core Curriculum*, the "Visioneering" process of Berghofer and Schwartz, and mainstream education. The purpose:

". . . to launch a project to encourage our youth to see themselves as global citizens . . . promoting global education in the curriculum of our schools, and to celebrate the common energy. . . . The central idea of the Congress is that young people be brought together as teams of creative energy, working with their teachers and community leaders to show how and what we all must learn to become global citizens in the 21st century."[40]

These opening ceremonies created, through Robert Muller, the inspiration and "energy" necessary for Saturday's tasks. The next day, we were told, all participants and Global Citizen passport holders would embark on a journey of global "visioneering."

Visioneering the Future

Teichrib goes on to explain the concept of "visioneering" as presented by the conference organizers.

Berghofer's vision discards national borders, unites religions, and brings peace on Earth through a renewed relationship with the planet. Visioneering is an evolutionary concept elevating humanity beyond the traditional to embrace global citizenship. To do this, one must be a "visioneer". That is, one must use the mind's creative energy to elevate attitudes, values and behaviors into proper global frameworks.

In his book, *The Visioneers*, Dr. Berghofer shares more about the thinking behind this process:

"The big truth . . . is that people can choose to become connected through their minds to the energy of universal creative intelligence. If enough do so, they can set in motion a wave of creative initiative to usher in an era of unprecedented harmony and collaboration worldwide."[41]

Visioneering is not a new idea. Chardin, Jung, Price, and Hubbard have all described similar concepts. And, in the occult classic *The Rays and the Initiations*, Alice Bailey explained how the "Art of Visualisation" would enable expressions of human consciousness to materialize. She mentioned three specific areas in which this new type of thinking, or "visualization" would have an impact:

1. Through "the development of the *sense* of vision," a new world occult spirituality will "be definitely seen."
2. "Groups, large wholes and major syntheses will also be visualised, and this will lead to definite expansion of consciousness. Thus the *sense of synthesis* will be unfolded."
3. "All creative art will be fostered by this training (visualisation), and the new art of the future... will be rapidly developed as the training proceeds." (italics Bailey's)[42]

According to Bailey, these developments would all be a direct result of the unfolding of visualization.

Teichrib indicated that "visioneering energy" was the lifeblood of the Congress. Berghofer and Schwartz, he said, referred to this energy often, both on and off the stage. According to Teichrib the main task of participants was to use both Muller's personal inspiration and his *World Core Curriculum* in developing group "visions" toward Global Citizenship. But before their "visioneering" could commence, Muller added his foundational philosophies for proper Citizenship. Teichrib elaborates:

> Introduced as a "planet elder," Muller related how the Earth was overpopulated, how our present lifestyles and values needed to change, and how it was up to the generation present at the Congress to force the world to embrace "Mother Earth."

> On population, Muller boasted that the United Nations had, as a result of warnings to the world, "prevented the birth of 2 billion, 200 million people." He also encouraged the Congress to, "Try to convince your people to reduce the number of children. This is one of the biggest problems we have on this planet."

> Next, Muller laid out a lengthy scenario of unimaginable environmental destruction. He did this in a unique way. In talking to the children, he held a hypothetical dialogue between himself and Mother Earth. This had a staggering effect on the participants.

> "What are you doing to me? How do you think I can continue

to have good oxygen for you? How do you think I'm going to have enough water for you? You are killing me! And in certain projections which have been made by scientists now, some of them say that this Earth will become lifeless and uninhabitable within the next fifty years. So do not forget: That if we continue to live and to waste, and to do all the wrong things which we do today, by your age, maybe this planet will be finished. Never forget this, so that the future of this planet is totally in your hands . . . this is what you have to be taught by your teachers. This is an absolute fundamental knowledge which you must be taught. And remember that when you do something wrong, multiplied by 5.8 billion, this is an incredible quantity of wrong."

Muller continued,

"Now this is why you are here sitting in this room, the generation on which the future life on this planet will depend. Either you change your values, or you don't. If you continue consuming as you do and throwing things away, you will be the responsible generation of having to put an end to all life on this planet. And if you change, if you consider the Earth as being number one, your Mother, then it will change."

Muller went on to tell these Canadian school children,

". . . behave correctly towards the Earth. . . . You are not children of Canada, you are really living units of the cosmos because the Earth is a cosmic phenomena . . . we are all cosmic units. This is why religions tell you, you are divine. We are divine energy . . . it is in your hands whether evolution on this planet continues or not."[43]

Following Dr. Muller's "inspiring" message, every school group was challenged to develop their own "Millennium Project." These plans were part of the visioneering process and would represent their school's contribution to achieving the new global society. Towards the end of the afternoon, each team reported their visioneering results to the Congress. Many of these projects, as expected, took on a spiritual dimension. Teichrib notes:

One school committed itself to starting a school "Inter-faith Council". The team from the Earl Marriott Secondary School presented a drama displaying the philosophy of Global Citizenship. In this drama, a young female student sat on top of a desk, held pine boughs and proclaimed herself "Mother Earth". Encircling her, other female students took turns laying hands on "Mother Earth" and individually confessed their environmental sins. In turn, Mother Earth would forgive each student as the girls committed themselves to change their destructive behavior.[44]

Citizens of Earth

Throughout the conference, Muller used the threat of environmental catastrophe to compel students to become Global, or Earth, Citizens. He emphatically drove home this point.

> You must remember the Earth. I would even say that the word "global education" and the word "global citizens" . . . I'm almost tempted to change the words and to replace them by "Earth education" and by "Earth citizen" . . . we are children of the Sun and we are children of the Earth. . . . You can be the caretakers and the saviors of the world . . . every-day remember your Mother Earth. . . . Do not forget it that from now on you have to be Earth citizens, you have to be the children of Mother Earth.[45]

To ensure that participants would take this call to global citizen-ship seriously, special global passports were issued at the Congress. Several pages from the passport are displayed in Exhibits N-1 to N-3. These passports symbolized the participants' allegiance to Planet Earth. Appearing in the passports and the conference programs was a special poem written by Robert Muller, entitled "Decide to be a Global Citizen." (Exhibit N-4) This poem captured the theme of the conference.

According to Teichrib, one of the participants astutely asked why they were receiving global passports if they were all going to live in a world without borders. Muller explained that this particular pass-port was purely symbolic. However, he went on to share that his inspiration for the passport came from Gary Davis. Davis is the founder of the World Service Authority (WSA). It is from this organi-zation that a real world passport can now be obtained. (A growing number of countries are honoring this document.) Before receiving the WSA passport, one must agree to the Credo for a World Citizen along with accepting an affirmation of global citizenship and allegiance to world government. Part of the affirmation states:

> "As a World Citizen, I affirm my planetary civic commitment to WORLD GOVERNMENT, founded on three universal principles of One Absolute Value, One World, and One

Humanity which constitutes the basis of World Law. As a World Citizen I acknowledge the WORLD GOVERNMENT as having the right and duty to represent me in all that concerns the General Good of humankind and the Good of All." (all capitals in original)[46]

If the world continues on its present course, it may not be long before a majority of Earth's inhabitants are willing to take this oath!

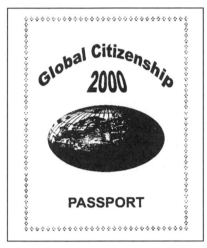

Exhibit N-1

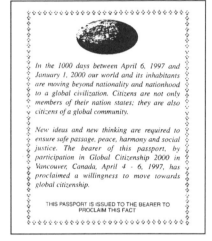

In the 1000 days between April 6, 1997 and January 1, 2000 our world and its inhabitants are moving beyond nationality and nationhood to a global civilization. Citizens are not only members of their nation states; they are also citizens of a global community.

New ideas and new thinking are required to ensure safe passage, peace, harmony and social justice. The bearer of this passport, by participation in Global Citizenship 2000 in Vancouver, Canada, April 4 - 6, 1997, has proclaimed a willingness to move towards global citizenship.

THIS PASSPORT IS ISSUED TO THE BEARER TO PROCLAIM THIS FACT

Exhibit N-2

Issued by
INTERNATIONAL FOUNDATION OF LEARNING | 1 |

Surname _____
Given Name _____
Nationality _____
Date of Birth _____
Sex   Place of Birth _____
Telephone ____ Fax _____
E-mail _____

Issued: APRIL 4, 1997
Expires: APRIL 3, 2000

Please note: If any of the address information above is changed, it is the responsibility of the bearer to notify the International Foundation of Learning. Please contact the International Foundation of Learning as follows:

Address   503-1505 West 2nd Avenue
           Vancouver, BC, Canada V6H 3Y4
Phone   (604) 734-2544 / 738-7766
Fax   (604) 734-9723
E-mail   desgerri@direct.ca

Exhibit N-3

Decide to be a Global Citizen
A good inhabitant of the planet Earth
A member of the great human family
Pray, think, act, feel and love globally
And you will aggrandize yourself
    to the outer limits of being

Know this planet
Love this planet
Care for this planet
For you come from Mother Earth
You are made of her elements
You are the Earth become conscious
    of herself
You are her eyes, her ears, her voice,
    her mind and her heart

Save your mother Earth
    from her matricidal children
    who destroy her
    who divide her
    who spike her with Nuclear arms
    who hold their territories to be
        greater than the globe
    and their groups
        greater than humanity

Unite, global citizens, to save and heal
    planet Earth
And to make our Mother bloom again
As the most beautiful planet
    in the universe.

— Robert Muller —

On April 6, 1997 the world will be 1000 days away from the year 2000. What better time to launch a project to encourage our youth to see themselves as global citizens.

The central idea of the Global Citizenship 2000 Congress is that young people be brought together as teams of creative energy, working with their teachers and community leaders to think, to show how and what we all must learn to become global citizens in the 21st century. This will include not only knowledge to bring economic success in the world's marketplace, but also an appreciation for what must be done to ensure sustainability and peace in an increasingly interdependent world.

Exhibit N-4

Embracing New Age Education

Global Citizenship 2000 was the first conference of its type, and, according to Muller, it won't be the last. Serving as a UNESCO model for proper global citizenship, the Vancouver Congress has opened the doors for many similar events across North America. Indeed, this was the hope of its organizers!

As a result of these and other initiatives, a New Age perspective of global unity is taking hold in the classroom. This trend will likely accelerate as teachers are increasingly exposed to occult philosophy at the university level and at continuing education seminars. Catherine Barrett, former president of the National Education Association, described the anticipated role of teachers in the new millennium.

> Dramatic changes in the way we will raise our children in the year 2000 are indicated, particularly in terms of schooling. . . . We will need to recognize that the so-called "basic skills," which currently represent nearly the total effort in elementary schools, will be taught in one-quarter of the present school-day . . . when this happens . . . and it's near . . . the teacher can rise to his true calling. More than a dispenser of information, the teacher will be a conveyor of values, a philosopher. . . . We will be agents of change.[47]

It is sobering to see how current developments in education are lining up with the plans of Alice Bailey and accomplishing what she said must take place before humanity enters the new world order. The evidence clearly demonstrates that Lucis Trust, Robert Muller, and the United Nations share the same occult vision for the future of mankind. Through the *World Core Curriculum* and its related programs they are determined to mold our children's minds toward accepting their New Age/anti-Christian world view. May God protect the hearts and minds of our young people and give parents wisdom to know how to stand strong against this spiritual assault.

A Parental Challenge

After reading about these developments in education you are probably feeling somewhat overwhelmed. You may be asking yourself, "Is there any hope for our children?" My response is, "Without the Lord – no!" However, Scripture reminds us that with God all things are possible (Matthew 19:26).

God assures Christian believers that He will never leave us or forsake us, even unto the end of the age (Hebrews 13:5 and Matthew 28:20). This means that even when things appear to be completely hopeless, we are never left to face our problems alone. God is always with us. Furthermore, many responsible Christian parents around the world share our concerns.

Although we may be in a minority now, we can take comfort in knowing that someday, (possibly soon) Jesus Christ will return and put an end to man's wicked schemes. Those who have remained faithful to Him will be rewarded. But what do we do until that day arrives?

As the father of four children—ages three to twelve—I would offer the following advice: Be willing to sacrifice some of your modern conveniences to assure a strong Christian educational foundation for your child. If you are not in a position to home school, then consider placing your child in a solid, Bible-based school. For the time being, private schools and home schooling are less affected by the U.N.'s global education policies.

My wife and I have been fortunate for our children to attend a Christian school with high academic standards; a school that is also very supportive of our efforts. However, this type of schooling has not come without a price. We have had to do without certain material possessions to provide this vital education.

Are you willing to give up possessions for the benefit of your child's future? Do you realize that their eternity could be at stake? Remember, we cannot take any material belongings with us when eternity knocks. All of us enter this world and leave it the same way – with nothing. The only things in our lives that really matter are those relationships and commitments which affect eternity. Our children's education definitely falls into this category.

The Bible admonishes us, "Train up a child in the way he should go: and when he is old, he will not depart from it" (Proverbs 22:6). Although the type of education our children receive will not guarantee their entrance into heaven, it certainly will go a long way toward influencing their spiritual choices, if coupled with principled Christian parenting and daily prayer. It all comes down to an act of our will!

If you must send your child to a public school due to circumstances beyond your control, please take the time to discuss with them on a regular basis what they are learning. Review their curriculum. When they are taught theories which run contrary to what the Bible teaches, explain to them why you believe the way that you do, and be prepared to back up your response with facts and Scripture. If you cannot do so, don't expect your child to accept your explanation. The challenge here to all parents is: "Know what you believe and why you believe it!" This involves disciplined Bible study and some well-directed research.

Regardless of what kind of schooling your child receives it is extremely important that you develop a strong relationship with them, involving mutual respect. In order to succeed in this area you must "walk your talk," being consistent in your daily walk with the Lord. More then anything else our children need non-hypocritical role models who serve the Lord wholeheartedly on a day-to-day basis. Although kids will naturally test their boundaries at times, they will generally follow the lead of a good example. Is your example worthy of being followed? If not, you will have a difficult time convincing your child to be any different.

God assures us that He is in control (John 16:33), and holds our future in His hands. He will protect our children if we give them the knowledge—from His Word—that they need to withstand Satan's attacks (Proverbs 2:1–11). However, we must be willing to become lifelong students of God's Word ourselves if we are to properly instruct, edify, and correct our children according to His Will.

Recommended Action:

The *World Core Curriculum* and the "grassroots" activities discussed in this chapter represent only a few of the developments linked to Robert Muller. The U.N.'s initiatives have spawned the creation of dozens of specialized education programs not discussed here. It is critical that parents have a working knowledge of these education reforms along with current classroom curriculum in order to steer their children through this maze of spiritual deception.

To assist parents in taking an effective stand, we have prepared a special report on education which summarizes the most important programs in an easy to understand fashion. This report offers specific steps of action that citizens are urged to take. The report is twenty-eight pages in length and is available free of charge to newsletter subscribers.

To subscribe to our newsletter, simply fill out the form near the end of this book and send it, along with your payment, to:

Hope For The World
P.O. Box 899
Noblesville, Indiana 46061-0899
U.S.A.

Or, call (317)-290-HOPE for subscription information. When calling or writing, please mention that you heard about our newsletter in this book and would like to receive our complimentary issue on education along with our newsletter.

Notes

1. Alice Bailey, *The Externalisation of the Hierarchy* (New York: Lucis Trust, 1957), p. 511.

2. Robert Muller, *2000 Ideas For A Better World: My Countdown on Dreams on Mt. Rasur to the Year 2000 for Your Thoughts and Action*, Fascicle One (Ciudad Colón, Costa Rica: University for Peace), p. ii.

3. International Foundation of Learning, "Dr. Robert Muller," (Web page for the Global Citizenship 2000 Youth Congress http://griffin.multimedia.edu/~gc2000/), [Accessed July 21, 1998], International Foundation of Learning, Vancouver, BC.

4. Ibid.

5. Douglas Todd, "Children told real home is planet Earth," *The Vancouver Sun* (Vancouver, BC: April 4, 1997), p. B3.

6. Muller, *2000 Ideas For A Better World: My Countdown on Dreams on Mt. Rasur to the Year 2000 for Your Thoughts and Action*, p. ii.

7. Ibid., pp. ii–iv.

8. Ibid., p. ii.

9. Ibid., p. ii.

10. Ibid., p. ii.

11. Action Coalition for Global Change, "Welcome to the United People's Assembly," (Web page http://acgc.org/upa/upa.html), [Accessed March 6, 1998], Action Coalition for Global Change, 55 New Montgomery Street, Suite 219, San Francisco, CA 94105.

12. Ibid.

13. New Zealand Forum for United Nations Renewal, *Survey Report: Proceedings of the Third Forum Meeting* (Held at Connolly Hall, Wellington, New Zealand on December 12, 1997), United Nations Association of New Zealand, 192 Tinakori Road, Wellington, New Zealand.

14. Ibid.

15. Carl Teichrib, "A People's World Government. Who's Fooling Who?", *Hope For The World Update* (Noblesville, IN: Hope For The World, Spring 1998, newsletter), p. 7.

16. Philip Isely, WCPA Secretary-General (Lakewood, CO: World

Constitution and Parliament Association, May 5, 1993, letter), Trustees of the WCPA listed on p. 2.

17. World Constitution and Parliament Association, "The Present Direction of the WCPA," (Web page http://www.wcpagren.org/present.html), [Accessed September 16, 1998], World Constitution and Parliament Association, 8800 West 14th Ave., Lakewood, Colorado 80215.

18. New Zealand Forum for United Nations Renewal, *Survey Report: Proceedings of the Third Forum Meeting.*

19. World Constitution and Parliament Association, *A Constitution for the Federation of Earth* (Lakewood, CO: WCPA, 1977), p. 35.

20. Lucile W. Green, *Journey To A Governed World* (Berkeley, CA: The Uniquest Foundation, 1992), p. 35.

21. Robert Muller, as quoted by the WCPA. Muller's endorsement is dated October 13, 1992, and appeared in a WCPA promotional flier entitled *Responsible World Government Is At Least 49 Years Overdue.*

22. WCPA, "Global Ratification and Elections Network," (Web page http://www.wcpagren.org/5thParl.html), [Accessed September 16, 1998].

23. Green, *Journey To A Governed World*, p. 34.

24. Teichrib, "A People's World Government. Who's Fooling Who?", *Hope For The World Update*, p. 8. [Speech by Lucile Green, Saturday, November 7, 1997 on the subject of "NGOs, United Planetary Assembly and Coordinating Citizens Peoples Assemblies." Delivered at the United Peoples Advocates and Global Virtual Assembly World Peace Conference, held at DreamHouse, 1475 W. Berwyn, Chicago, IL 60640-2107. Transcribed from a personal audio taping of the event by Carl Teichrib.]

25. Robert Muller School, *The Robert Muller School World Core Curriculum Manual* (Arlington, TX: Robert Muller School, 1986), Preface.

26. Robert Muller, "A Letter to All Educators in the World," *World Core Curriculum Magazine* (Arlington, TX: The Robert Muller School International Coordinating Center, Spring, 1997), p. 3.

27. Gloria Crook, "The World Core Curriculum In The Original Robert Muller School," *World Core Curriculum Magazine* (Arlington, TX: The Robert Muller School International Coordinating Center, Spring, 1997), p. 5.

28. Gloria Crook, "How to Start a Robert Muller School," *World Core Curriculum Magazine* (Arlington, TX: The Robert Muller School International Coordinating Center, Spring, 1997), pp. 15–17.

29. Ibid.

30. Mary Doclar, "A World of Learning – School Curriculum Adds Peace, Harmony to Math, Science," *Ft. Worth Star-Telegram*, September 30, 1993, p. A18.

31. Ibid., p. A18.

32. Ibid., p. A18.

33. Robert Muller, *The School of Ageless Wisdom* (Arlington, TX: The Robert Muller School, pamphlet), p. 3.

34. Alice A. Bailey, *The Rays and The Initiations* (New York: Lucis Trust, 1960), p. 109. Written by Bailey between 1943 and 1947.

35. Alice A. Bailey, *Education in the New Age* (New York: Lucis Trust, 1954), pp. 46–47.

36. Ibid., p. 87.

37. Ibid., p. 74.

38. Alice A. Bailey, *Esoteric Psychology II* (New York: Lucis Trust, 1942), p. 632.

39. Bailey, *Education in the New Age*, p. 52.

40. International Foundation of Learning, *Education for Global Citizenship: Global Citizenship 2000 Youth Congress Call for Leadership* (Vancouver, BC: International Foundation of Learning, 1997, introductory fact sheet included in the Global Citizenship 2000 Youth Congress promotional packet), p. 1.

41. Desmond E. Berghofer, *The Visioneers* (Vancouver, BC: Creative Learning International Press, 1992), p. 72.

42. Bailey, *The Rays and The Initiations*, p.123.

43. Robert Muller, speech addressed to the Global Citizenship 2000 Youth Congress, Vancouver, BC, April 5, 1997. [Transcribed from an audio tape recorded by Carl Teichrib.]

44. Carl Teichrib, "Global Citizenship 2000: Educating for the New Age," *Hope For The World Update* (Noblesville, IN: Hope For The World, Fall 1997, newsletter), p. 11.

45. Muller, speech addressed to the Global Citizenship 2000 Youth Congress, April 5, 1997.

46. Gary Davis, letter and application form for a World Citizen Registration Card, 1996, (World Service Authority, 1012-14th Street NW, Suite 1106, Washington, DC 20005).

47. Catherine Barrett, former President of the National Education Association, *Saturday Review of Education*, February 10, 1973.

8

The New Religious Order

"The Spirit clearly says that in later times some will abandon the faith and follow deceiving spirits and things taught by demons. Such teachings come through hypocritical liars, whose consciences have been seared as with a hot iron." (1 Timothy 4:1-2, NIV)

While the staging of massive "consciousness raising" events and the teaching of one-world ideals in our schools have contributed toward building global unity, the level of unity necessary to establish a new world order would ultimately require cooperation between the world's major religions. Religious leaders would somehow have to become tolerant of each other's beliefs, or, at the very least, refrain from denouncing one another's doctrines. Interfaithism—the concept that all religions are valid and are merely different pathways to God—would have to become the dominant view.

Ideally, from the standpoint of New Age planners, unity among religious leaders would eventually reach the point where all existing religions could be molded into one synthetic whole. However, for this to become a reality, spiritual leaders would have to surrender some of their most cherished values and tightly held doctrines. Creating this atmosphere of tolerance and compromise has been Robert Muller's main pursuit.

As the U.N.'s "Prophet of Hope," Muller believes that world unity cannot be achieved without a one-world government and a one-world religion. All of his efforts, be they in politics, education, or religion, are, therefore, geared toward the realization of such an ecumenical world system. His spiritual goals, like most of his political activities, are in line with the occult mandates of Alice Bailey and Teilhard de Chardin.

Muller's Spiritual Quest

Although Muller grew up in a Catholic home, he admits that he was not inspired to become a "really spiritual person" until years later, when he joined the U.N.[1] Nevertheless, he feels that his Catholic upbringing prepared him to accept the New Age world view he now holds. In the statement below, Muller describes some of his earliest religious experiences. These recollections came to him after a speaking engagement, during a flight over Iowa.

> As I was looking out of the aircraft into the deep blue sky and over the vast fields of the American Midwest, cherished memories came back to me: I saw myself as a child, lying in my bed in my hometown on the border of France with Germany, listening to the sound of the rain falling on the roof; I remembered the divine moments of early Mass in our old majestic church, the angelic songs of the nuns, the Latin chants and prayers, and the moaning sound of an old organ played by an invalid; I relived my deep communion with God and the universe when I watched the dawning of the day in the hills of Auvergne; I saw in my mind rows of Hindus praying and kneeling before the sun god Surya as he rose above the sacred waters of the Ganges... Be it through meditation, prayer, silence, or song, the miracles of life and resurrection are widely open to each of us every day of God's creation.[2]

Continuing this discourse, he demonstrates his openness toward Eastern meditation, mistaking it as an alternative way of communicating with God.

> Prayer, meditation, and the silent contemplation of nature, reborn each day under the sun's glory, bring us in direct communion with God and the universe. Prayer and meditation are two of the surest and quickest ways to happiness. Through them we reduce our petty arrogance and personal barriers against the streams of life. Letting these streams flow unimpeded through the miraculous point of perception that we are, we feel the greatness of all things, thoughts, sentiments, and dreams. We see everything in harmony and proportion. . . . It is strange that people from the East—

maharishis, yogis, seers, Buddhists, and others—have to come and teach us afresh what we already knew.[3]

According to Muller, a young American college student first helped him to understand meditation. The student gave him a catalogue from Maharishi International University. Muller shares, "I kept the volume and read it in the airplane. I was fascinated by it. I learned how meditation functioned and what it did for the fulfillment of the human person. I discovered that I had been meditating for years without knowing it."[4]

As a lifelong Catholic, he had been practicing meditation for years in the name of Christianity, without realizing the occult origin of this type of meditation. He had been combining Eastern mysticism with the teachings of Catholicism. Apparently, Muller had become convinced that Catholicism and the pantheistic religions of the East have the same spiritual roots, a conclusion also reached by Teilhard Chardin.

Discovering Religion at the UN

Of all the people Muller met at the United Nations, it was Secretary-General U Thant, a Buddhist, who left the deepest impression on his life. In his book, *New Genesis: Shaping a Global Spirituality*, Muller expresses his admiration for this man.

> At the age of forty-six I became director of Secretary-General U Thant's office. Here, for the first time in my life, I met a person who inspired me, a man who was deeply religious, who had a profound spirituality and code of human ethics which he applied to every moment and situation of his day.
>
> . . . I discovered that for U Thant there was no difference between spirituality, religion and life. Life was for him a constant spirituality. I studied Buddhism to understand him better. We became great friends. He was able to teach me what my Catholic priests had always told me, but at that time I hadn't listened. Here, in the middle of my life, was the master, the one who inspired me, someone I could imitate like a father. This has changed my life. Perhaps what we need most at this time are masters who give us the good example. And, like U Thant, they ought to include people in highest office and with wide responsibilities.[5]

Evidently, up until this point, Muller had not found anyone whose life he considered worth emulating. Although he claims that Catholic priests taught him essentially the same philosophy, it was U

Thant's apparent lack of hypocrisy in applying these mystical principles that caused Muller to take note.

Here is a lesson for Christians: Muller was willing to embrace the basic tenets of Buddhism—no matter how incorrect the theology might be—because of the consistent example of the follower. Had Muller, during the course of his life, been influenced in a similar fashion by a single Christian who walked his talk, he might today be a born-again follower of Jesus Christ instead of being an advocate of the New Age.

He continues,

From the moment I became interested in the spiritual dimension of life, everything started to change. . . . I began to read the mystics and understood much more about this new dimension of life consciousness. Some religious people began to be interested in my ideas. I was invited to participate in an East-West monastic encounter. . . .

Later on I was made a member of the East-West Monastic Board. . . . I am learning a great deal from them and they are also learning from me. I found that most monastic orders are organized on the basis of U Thant's cherished four categories of human needs and qualities: physical, mental, moral and spiritual. I learned that he was a monk himself. Buddhists are required to go to a monastery for one month each year. Since he could not go back to a Burmese monastery, he acted as a kind of monk in the United Nations. . . . I would like the whole world to benefit from my experience and to derive the same enlightenment, happiness, serenity and hope in the future as I derived from my contact with U Thant.[6]

Muller reflects,

I would never have thought that I would discover spirituality in the United Nations!... Perhaps spirituality is such a fundamental human need that it always reappears in one form or another in life and throughout history and that we are about to witness now its renaissance in a global, planetary context.[7]

Enlightened by Chardin

Through his associations at the United Nations, Muller, like so many of his colleagues, would eventually come to embrace the teachings of Teilhard de Chardin. In fact, Secretary-General U Thant introduced Muller to Chardin's philosophy. Since Robert Muller continues to serve as the United Nation's leading figure in the area of religious development, we can learn a great deal about the spiritual direction of the U.N.—and the world—by examining his personal theology more closely.

Muller's religious beliefs are best summarized in his book, *New Genesis*. In that book he demonstrates that his spirituality is rooted in Chardinian philosophy by devoting an entire chapter to explaining this Jesuit priest's world view. In addition to Chardin's teachings, Muller has drawn certain principles from the personal life and example of Thant and other popular mystics. Alice Bailey's peculiar terminology is also found throughout his book. Like Chardin, Bailey influenced a great number of U.N. officials over the last half century.

Muller's theology incorporates pantheistic ideas of the human species entering a new period of spiritual evolution, a period of rising planetary consciousness and global living which is expected to result in the perfect unity of the human family. Central to this theology are his views of a divine United Nations and a cosmic Christ. All of these concepts are brought together in *New Genesis*. Muller writes,

> If Christ came back to earth, his first visit would be to the United Nations to see if his dream of human oneness and brotherhood had come true. He would be happy to see representatives of all nations, North and South, East and West, rich and poor, believers and non-believers, young and old, Philistines and Samaritans, trying to find answers to the perennial questions of human destiny and fulfillment.[8]

> There is a famous painting and poster which shows Christ knocking at the tall United Nations building, wanting to enter it. I often visualize in my mind another even more accurate painting: that of a United Nations which would be the body of Christ.[9]

Muller goes on to comment,

> Was it not inevitable that the UN would sooner or later also acquire a spiritual dimension . . . ?

> I have come to believe firmly today that our future peace, justice, fulfillment, happiness and harmony on this planet will not depend on world government but on divine or cosmic government, meaning that we must seek and apply the "natural," "evolutionary," "divine," "universal" or "cosmic" laws which must rule our journey in the cosmos. Most of these laws can be found in the great religions and

prophecies, and they are being rediscovered slowly but surely in the world organizations.

Any Teilhardian will recognize in this the spiritual transcendence which he announced so emphatically as the next step in our evolution.[10]

Muller also quotes from an address he delivered on August 12, 1979, at the Arcane School Conference. The Arcane School was one of the institutions founded by Alice Bailey. In that speech, Muller declared,

> Are we not the partners, the participants, and the instruments of something that goes far beyond us, that was started a long time ago and which will lead to a greater, more beautiful, higher planetary civilization? . . .
>
> I am more and more drawn to some of the very simple but extremely important teachings of the Christ and of all the great prophets and visionaries. I am increasingly convinced that what they foresaw is beginning to become a reality on this planet and that humanity is transcending or metamorphosing itself into what those great dreamers, visionaries and prophets envisioned. This is what I believe I am living in the glass house on the East River of New York City.[11]

In every chapter of *New Genesis*, Muller calls for a U.N.-based world government and a new world religion as the only answer to mankind's problems. Through it all, Muller maintains his status as a Catholic Christian. He finally comes full circle by linking the U.N.'s mission to Catholicism:

> Pope John Paul II said that we were the stonecutters and artisans of a cathedral which we might never see in its finished beauty. I would not have dreamed that when I joined the United Nations a third of a century ago. The scope of the UN has widened in every direction, owing to the imperatives of a new global, interdependent world. But people do not really know how vast and vital its activities are. The tapestry of its work encompasses the total condition of humankind on this planet. All this is part of one of the most prodigious pages of evolution. It will require the detachment and objectivity of future historians to appraise fully what happened in the last third of our century and to understand what the real significance of the United Nations was.[12]

In another book, *My Testament to the UN*, Muller favorably quotes Sri Chinmoy, a Hindu priest, regarding the U.N.'s ultimate destiny:

> No human force will ever be able to destroy the United Nations, for the United Nations is not a mere building or a mere idea; it is not a manmade creation. The United Nations is the vision-light of the Absolute Supreme, which is slowly, steadily, and unerringly illuminating the ignorance, the night of our human life. The divine success and supreme progress of the United Nations is bound to become a reality. At his choice hour, the Absolute Supreme will ring his own victory-bell here on Earth through the loving and serving heart of the United Nations.[13]

The truth of the matter is, the United Nations is not a conception of God. Rather, its spiritual activities are an abomination to Him. The U.N. and its occult-inspired cooperatives will experience the same judgement from the Lord reserved for all ungodly individuals and institutions. It is Jesus Christ who will "ring the victory bell" upon his return (2 Thess. 2:7–12), and it will not be rung through the United Nations!

The Chain of Influence

Along with Teilhard Chardin, Alice Bailey, and U Thant, Robert Muller has been influenced by the mystic Dag Hammarskjöld, the former U.N. secretary-general, and by Father de Breuvery, a Catholic priest who was heavily involved in the affairs of the U.N. While it appears that all of these individuals drew at least some of their ideas from the philosophies of Chardin, none of them was impacted by Chardin more directly than Breuvery.

Muller explains how Chardin influenced the U.N. through Breuvery.

> The thought often crosses my mind that Father Teilhard de Chardin may have influenced him. They shared an apartment in Manhattan, they confessed to each other, said Mass together, and saw each other every day. Father de Breuvery often discussed with Teilhard his work at the UN.

> . . . Teilhard de Chardin influenced his companion, who inspired his colleagues, who started a rich process of global and long-term thinking in the UN, which affected many nations and people throughout the world. I have myself been deeply influenced by Teilhard.[14]

In short, Father Teilhard de Chardin influenced many of the most prominent U.N. leaders of his day, including some of the U.N.'s founding fathers. They, in turn, have impacted hundreds of other U.N. officials and delegates who are today helping to implement Chardin's mystical vision for the future of the world. Muller is only the latest in a chain of Teilhardians who has risen to a position of power at the U.N.; he has already shaped the thinking of countless global leaders.

Teilhard Chardin's influence on Robert Muller has not been a secret. The late Norman Cousins, former president of the World Federalist Association, was well aware of this connection. In the Foreword to Muller's autobiography Cousins wrote,

> Whatever the uncertainties of the future may be, . . . the oncoming generations will . . . need to have special knowledge, certainly; but they will need something far more important: an intense awareness of the conditions under which the values essential to the future of mankind can be created and maintained. They will need living examples of the conspiracy of love that Teilhard de Chardin has said will be essential to man's salvation. Robert Muller is involved in such a conspiracy.[15]

Considering Robert Muller's significant influence at the U.N., it would be wise to take a closer look at what this "conspiracy" entails and exactly what it is that Muller has set out to do. (For important statements by Robert Muller reflecting his views on Christ, inter-faithism, and the U.N., see Appendix I.)

Twentieth-century Ecumenism

New Era Magazine provides the clearest picture of Muller's true intentions. In the November/December 1981 issue of that publication Muller is quoted as saying, "It is necessary that we have a World Government centered on the United Nations." In a follow-up remark he revealed the spiritual basis for this future administration, stating that we can credit the coming World Government to the "influence of the writings of Teilhard de Chardin." While Chardin's impact on the U.N. and world affairs is now well documented, few individuals outside of Chardin's immediate sphere of influence were aware of the fact that he also helped inspire modern-day ecumenism. Nor do people realize that today's ecumenical movement is an integral part of the broader one-world movement.

The seeds for twentieth-century ecumenism were sown in the late 1800s. During that time there was a growing interest in achieving unity for the alleged purpose of building an earthly utopia. Masonic-inspired organizations, ranging from the Hermetic Order of the Golden Dawn to the Theosophical Society, were busy laying the groundwork for the next century, which they hoped might finally usher in their long-awaited new world order.

Against this backdrop, religious leaders from around the world gathered in Chicago for an unprecedented ecumenical event—the 1893 Parliament of the World's Religions (also known as the Parliament of World Religions). The people who attended this international conference came from a variety of faiths. Hindus, Buddhists, Muslims, Roman Catholics, Protestants, and a host of others prayed and dialogued together for seventeen days.[16] Even the Theosophical Society was represented by Annie Besant.[17] This was the largest interfaith leadership conference in the history of the world up to that time.

In the following decades, two catastrophic world wars were fought, each adding to the one-world movement's momentum. World War I resulted in the creation of the League of Nations, and World War II led to the United Nations. Both were created in the name of world peace. These institutions would give the secret societies a focal point around which they could rally religious leaders. The public, worn down from years of war, was ready to accept a new approach to maintaining peace. Teilhard Chardin, Alice Bailey, and other forerunners to Robert Muller would play key roles in presenting the United Nations as the only hope for peace between nations and unity among the world's religions.

Riding this crest of postwar sentiment, global planners seized the moment, attempting to unite the Protestant denominations through one organization. Although the spirit of ecumenism had been alive for decades, the founding of the pro-U.N. World Council of Churches in 1948 marked the beginning of the modern ecumenical era.

Strongly influenced by the Masonic Lodge and with funding from major "old money" sources such as the Rockefeller Foundation, the World Council of Churches (WCC) aggressively embarked on its mission. From the time of its first meeting in Amsterdam, its purpose was clear: to help create the religious atmosphere for achieving a new world order. In a report issued in 1994 at one of its meetings in Jerusalem, the WCC confirmed this intention, stating: "After the Second World War, the establishment of the World Council of Churches in 1948 signalled the resolve of the ecumenical community both to work for the fuller unity of the church and to participate in the struggle for a new just world order."[18]

In a more recent policy statement released in September 1997, the WCC again acknowledged its critical role in the unity movement:

It is impossible to speak of the World Council of Churches apart from the ecumenical movement out of which it grew and of which it is a highly visible part. While the ecumenical movement is wider than its organizational expressions, and while the WCC is essentially the fellowship of its member churches, it serves at the same time as a prominent instrument and expression of the ecumenical movement.[19]

Today, from its headquarters in Geneva, Switzerland, the WCC continues to provide important leadership for the ecumenical movement.

While the efforts of the World Council of Churches have been paramount in bringing the liberal Protestant denominations together, no event would give greater momentum to the ecumenical movement than Vatican II. *The Catholic Encyclopedia* proudly boasts, "The greatest religious event of the twentieth century, whose teachings and clarifications have yet to reach their full impact, was the twenty-first Ecumenical Council, called Vatican II or the Second Vatican Council."[20]

Vatican II, which opened on October 11, 1962 at St. Peter's Basilica in Rome, added fuel to the growing ecumenical movement and helped pave the way for the acceptance of interfaithism. Pope John XXIII resided over the Council's proceedings. According to M. Basil Pennington, a prominent Catholic priest, the Council urged "all Christians . . . to act positively to preserve and even promote all that is good in other religions: Hinduism, Buddhism, and other world religions."[21] To carry out this interfaith directive, the Vatican Council established the Secretariat for Non-Christians, which would eventually be renamed the Secretariat for World Religions.[22]

Years later, Pope John Paul II would take the Council's initiatives a step further by holding an actual interfaith summit in Assisi, Italy (discussed earlier). This 1986 gathering, consisting of leaders from the world's major religions and initiated by the Pope himself, would represent a visible transition from traditional "ecumenism" to the new "interfaithism."

Although these terms are often used interchangeably today, historically the public has viewed ecumenism as an effort aimed at unifying Christian churches. Interfaithism, on the other hand, has been perceived as a broader attempt to unify all of the world's religions. In spite of the public's perception, beneath the surface, ecumenism and interfaithism have been intertwined. The fact is, ecumenism has been used by New Age religious planners as a spring-board to interfaithism. Once most of Christendom has been brought together under a false spiritual unity, it was thought that Christianity might be prepared to go the next step by merging with the other religions.

1993 Parliament of World Religions (August 28 to September 5)

In order to accelerate the move toward religious unity, a special committee was formed in 1988. It's charge was to organize the largest gathering of religious leaders in history, the 1993 Parliament of World Religions, which would serve not only to commemorate the one hundredth anniversary of the original meeting (Chicago, 1893), but also to plan for the world's "spiritual future." Approximately 5,500 religious leaders from a multitude of denominations and religions attended this convention. Another 857 individuals were registered as press.[23]

Besides the major religions and well-known spiritual "traditions," some of those present described themselves as "Catholic Quaker," "Celtic," "blends of many," "inter-religious," or "Hindu Theos-ophy."[24] Also in attendance were voodoo and druid priests, Free-masons, wiccans (witches), snake charmers, Zoroastrian sun wor-shipers, representatives of Lucis Trust, and an assortment of other occultists and Luciferians. This spiritual diversity was evident throughout the Parliament and was reflected in its board of trustees (Exhibit O) and in those who co-sponsored the event (see Appendix J).

The 1993 Parliament programs, like their counterpart meetings of the last century, were held in Chicago. Some of the themes were Interfaith Understanding, The Inner Life, Visions of Paradise and Possibility, and Voices of Spirit and Tradition. During the nine-day gathering, over five hundred seminars, lectures, and workshops were held. Robert Muller delivered the Parliament's first keynote address, forcefully calling for the creation of a "permanent institution" dedicated to pursuing religious unity.[25] The opening and closing plenary sessions complimented his speech and captured the essence of the conference. *The SourceBook for Earth's Community of Religions* elaborates:

> The Opening Plenary was a celebratory pageant of music from East and West, an interfaith processional, welcomes, blessings, and invocations. The Closing Plenary included a keynote address by H.H. the Dalai Lama, invocations from the Parliament Presidents, concluding remarks, performance by a multi-cultural dance company, and a rousing final

Exhibit O

concert by Walter Whitman and the 200-voice Soul Children of Chicago Choir.

Preceding the Closing Plenary was a concert in Grant Park. Arlo Guthrie, Stephen Halpern, a specially formed band of Rastafarian musicians, Tibetan monks performing their timeless chants, and superstar Kenny Loggins all graciously contributed their talents to create a spirit that could not have been bought at any price.[26]

The Templeton Prize

One of the highlights of the Parliament was the awarding of the Templeton Prize for Progress in Religion. Valued at $1.2 million, it is the "world's most prestigious and lucrative . . . ecumenical award."[27] This international prize is bestowed annually upon the individual perceived to be the most "outstanding" religious figure of the year.[28] The decision on who receives the award is made by a group of interfaith leaders with a distinct one-world vision. Historically, this committee has awarded the prize to individuals who display a strong ecumenical outlook. The million-dollar prize, on this occasion, went to Prison Fellowship director Chuck Colson. Other well-known Christian leaders who have received the award include Billy Graham (1982) and Bill Bright (1996).[29]

The first Templeton Prize, awarded in 1973, went to Mother Teresa of Calcutta.[30] Recipients since that time have included Sir Sarvepalli Radhakrishnan, former president of India and Oxford professor of Eastern religions and ethics (1975); Leon Joseph Cardinal Suenens, Archbishop of Malines-Brussels and a pioneer in the Charismatic Renewal Movement (1976); Nikkyo Niwano, a Japanese Buddhist leader (1979); Rev. Professor Stanley L. Jaki, a Benedictine monk and professor of astrophysics at Seton Hall University (1987); Dr. Inamullah Khan, founder and secretary-general of the Modern World Muslim Congress and a vice president of the World Constitution and Parliament Association (1988); Baba Amte, a wealthy Hindu lawyer/humanitarian (1990); The Rt. Hon. Lord Jakobovits, former chief rabbi of Great Britain and the Commonwealth (1991); and Pandurang Shastri Athavale, founder and leader of the Bhagavad Gita-based self-study known as Swadhayaya, which incorporates self-worship (1997).[31]

Sir John Templeton, after whom the award is named, serves on the Parliament's board of trustees and has been closely linked to the Rockefeller family fortune. Along with being the donor of the Templeton Prize, Sir John established The Templeton Foundation in 1987. The foundation serves as an umbrella for a wide assortment of interfaith religious activities, currently funding more than 150 projects, studies, award programs, and publications worldwide.[32] Some of the individuals currently serving on Templeton's board of advisors are Laurance Rockefeller, philanthropist and funder of UFO research; Rev. Glenn Mosley, President and CEO of the Association of Unity Churches; and Mrs. Elizabeth Peale Allen (daughter of the late Norman Vincent Peale), Vice Chairman of the Peale Center for Christian Living and Chairman of the Positive Thinking Foundation.[33]

The Global Ethic

Perhaps the most significant event of the 1993 Parliament was the convening of an inner circle of interfaith religious "authorities." This powerful group, consisting of Robert Muller and his closest allies, dubbed itself the Assembly of Religious and Spiritual Leaders. Developing a consensus "for how people should behave," the Assembly endorsed an interfaith document titled *Towards a Global Ethic, An Initial Declaration*.[34] This document, drafted by Catholic theologian Hans Küng, a friend of Muller's, condemns the "abuses of Earth's ecosystems," poverty, and social injustice. It affirms interdependence, calling for "a common set of core values . . . found in the teachings of the religions." "*The Ethic*," if accepted, would represent "an irrevocable, unconditional norm for all areas of life, for families and communities, for races, nations, and religions." (See Exhibit P-1.)

In his book, *Global Responsibility: In Search of a New World Ethic* (1991), Mr. Küng makes clear that participation in this new "ethic" (religion) will not be optional. He states,

> Any form of . . . church conservatism is to be rejected. . . . To put it bluntly: no regressive or repressive religion—whether Christian, Islamic, Jewish or of whatever provenance—has a long-term future. . . . If ethics is to function for the wellbeing of all, it must be indivisible. The undivided world increasingly needs an undivided ethic. Post modern men and women need common values, goals, ideals, visions. But the great question in dispute is: does not all this presuppose a religious faith? . . . What we need is an ecumenical world order![35]

The Global Ethic, which was signed by Muller and the other interfaith dignitaries present, is emerging as a companion to *The Earth Charter* and is expected to be to religion what *The Charter* is to international politics. Together, these documents are destined to impact and shape the future religious and political course of mankind.

The World Core Curriculum is intended to accommodate both decrees by promoting their ideas through public education.

God, of course, has already given us a set of "global ethics" as part of His created order. These commandments for living are clearly laid out in the Bible (Exodus 20:1–17 and Mark 12:28–31). Unfortunately, as evidenced by the Parliament of World Religions, man would rather create his own set of rules catering to his personal wants and desires than submit to God's authority. The fallen nature of man seems inclined to rally around any system that promises salvation and earthly utopia without repentance and accountability to a personal God.

Exhibit P-1 (overleaf) represents the initial declaration of a Global Ethic. *This declaration is only the first part of a two part document. The second part, called "The Principles of a Global Ethic," provides a complete explanation of the declaration and is found on pages 132 to 136 of* A SourceBook for Earth's Community of Religions. *Some of the subtitles of "The Principles" include:*

"No new global order without a new global ethic!"
"Commitment to a culture of solidarity and a just economic order"
"A transformation of consciousness!"

Exhibit P-2 lists the signers of the Global Ethic. *Notice the diverse religions which are represented.*

Towards a Global Ethic

(An Initial Declaration)

This interfaith declaration is the result of a two-year consultation among approximately two hundred scholars and theologians from many of the world's communities of faith. On September 2-4, 1993, the document was discussed by an assembly of religious and spiritual leaders meeting as part of the 1993 Parliament of the World's Religions in Chicago. Respected leaders from all the world's major faiths signed the *Declaration*, agreeing that it represents an initial effort – a point of beginning for a world sorely in need of ethical consensus. The Council for a Parliament of the World's Religions and those who have endorsed this text offer it to the world as an initial statement of the rules for living on which the world's religions can agree.

The Declaration of a Global Ethic

The world is in agony. The agony is so pervasive and urgent that we are compelled to name its manifestations so that the depth of this pain may be made clear.

Peace eludes us ... the planet is being destroyed ... neighbors live in fear ... women and men are estranged from each other ... children die!

This is abhorrent!

We condemn the abuses of Earth's ecosystems.

We condemn the poverty that stifles life's potential; the hunger that weakens the human body; the economic disparities that threaten so many families with ruin.

We condemn the social disarray of the nations; the disregard for justice which pushes citizens to the margin; the anarchy overtaking our communities; and the insane death of children from violence. In particular we condemn aggression and hatred in the name of religion.

But this agony need not be.

It need not be because the basis for an ethic already exists. This ethic offers the possibility of a better individual and global order, and leads individuals away from despair and societies away from chaos.

We are women and men who have embraced the precepts and practices of the world's religions:

We affirm that a common set of core values is found in the teachings of the religions, and that these form the basis of a global ethic.

We affirm that this truth is already known, but yet to be lived in heart and action.

We affirm that there is an irrevocable, unconditional norm for all areas of life, for families and communities, for races, nations, and religions. There already exist ancient guidelines for human behavior which are found in the teachings of the religions of the world and which are the condition for a sustainable world order.

We Declare:

*W*e are interdependent. Each of us depends on the well-being of the whole, and so we have respect for the community of living beings, for people, animals, and plants, and for the preservation of Earth, the air, water and soil.

We take individual responsibility for all we do. All our decisions, actions, and failures to act have consequences.

We must treat others as we wish others to treat us. We make a commitment to respect life and dignity, individuality and diversity, so that every person is treated humanely, without exception. We must have patience and acceptance. We must be able to forgive, learning from the past but never allowing ourselves to be enslaved by memories of hate. Opening our hearts to one another, we must sink our narrow differences for the cause of the world community, practicing a culture of solidarity and relatedness.

We consider humankind our family. We must strive to be kind and generous. We must not live for ourselves alone, but should also serve others, never forgetting the children, the aged, the poor, the suffering, the disabled, the refugees, and the lonely. No person should ever be considered or treated as a second-class citizen, or be exploited in any way whatsoever. There should be equal partnership between men and women. We must not commit any kind of sexual immorality. We must put behind us all forms of domination or abuse.

We commit ourselves to a culture of non-violence, respect, justice, and peace. We shall not oppress, injure, torture, or kill other human beings, forsaking violence as a means of settling differences.

We must strive for a just social and economic order, in which everyone has an equal chance to reach full potential as a human being. We must speak and act truthfully and with compassion, dealing fairly with all, and avoiding prejudice and hatred. We must not steal. We must move beyond the dominance of greed for power, prestige, money, and consumption to make a just and peaceful world.

Earth cannot be changed for the better unless the consciousness of individuals is changed first. We pledge to increase our awareness by disciplining our minds, by meditation, by prayer, or by positive thinking. Without risk and a readiness to sacrifice there can be no fundamental change in our situation. Therefore we commit ourselves to this global ethic, to understanding one another, and to socially beneficial, peace-fostering, and nature-friendly ways of life.

We invite all people,
whether religious or not,
to do the same.

CHAPTER 23: A GLOBAL ETHIC   131

Exhibit P-1

Members of the Assembly who signed this Initial Declaration at the Parliament

Tan Sri Dato' Seri Ahmad Sarji bin Abdul-Hamid (Muslim, Malaysia)
Prof. Masao Abe (Buddhist, Japan)
Dr. Thelma Adair (Christian, USA)
H.R.H. Oseijeman Adefunmi I (Indigenous, USA)
Dr. Hamid Ahmed (Muslim, India)
Mrs. Mazhar Ahmed (Muslim, India)
Pravrajika Amalaprana (Hindu, India)
Dastoor Dr. Kersey Antia (Zoroastrian, USA)
Mme. Nana Apeadu (Indigenous, Ghana)
Dr. M. Aram (Hindu, India)
Rev. Wesley Ariarajah (Christian, Switzerland)
Dr. A. T. Ariyaratne (Buddhist, Sri Lanka)
Imam Dawud Assad (Muslim, USA)
Jayashree Athavale-Talwarkar (Hindu, India)
H.H. Shri Atmanandji (Jain, India)
H.I.G. Bambi Baaba (Indigenous, Uganda)
Rev. Thomas A. Baima (Christian, USA)
Dr. Gerald O. Barney (Christian, USA)
H.Em. Joseph Cardinal Bernardin (Christian, USA)
Mr. Karl Berolzheimer (Jewish, USA)
Père Pierre-François de Béthune (Christian, Belgium)
Dr. Nelvia M. Brady (Christian, USA)
Rev. Marcus Braybrooke (Christian, UK)
Dr. David Breed (Christian, USA)
Rabbi Herbert Bronstein (Jewish, USA)
Rev. John Buchanan (Christian, USA)
Mrs. Radha Burnier (Theosophist, India)
Rev. Baroness Cara-Marguerite-Drusilla, L.P.H. (Neo-Pagan, USA)
Mr. Blouke Carus (Christian, USA)
Mr. Peter V. Catches (Native American, USA)
Sister Joan M. Chatfield, M.M. (Christian, USA)
H.H. Swami Chidananda Saraswati (Hindu, India)
Swami Chidananda Saraswati Muniji (Hindu, USA)
Ms. Juana Conrad (Bahá'í, USA)
H.H. The Dalai Lama (Buddhist, India)
Swami Dayananda Saraswati (Hindu, USA)
Counsellor Jacqueline Delahunt (Bahá'í, USA)
Dr. Yvonne Delk (Christian, USA)
Sister Pratima Desai (Brahma Kumaris, USA)
Dr. Homi Dhalla (Zoroastrian, India)
Very Rev. R. Sheldon Duecker (Christian, USA)
Prof. Diana L. Eck (Christian, USA)
Dr. Wilma Ellis (Bahá'í, USA)
Hon. Louis Farrakhan (Muslim, USA)
Dr. Leon D. Finney, Jr (Christian, USA)
Rev. Dr. James A. Forbes Jr. (Christian, USA)
Dr. Rashmikant Gardi (Jain, USA)
Mr. Dipchand S. Gardi (Jain, India)
Mrs. Maria Svolos Gebhard (Christian, USA)
Preah Maha Ghosananda (Buddhist, Cambodia)
Dr. Daniel Gómez-Ibáñez (Interfaith, USA)
Dr. Hamid Abdul Hai (Muslim, USA)
Dr. Mohammad Hamidullah (Muslim, Uganda)
B.K. Jagdish Chander Hassija (Brahma Kumaris, India)
Rev. Theodore M. Hesburgh, C.S.C. (Christian, USA)
Prof. Susannah Heschel (Jewish, USA)
Dr. Aziza al-Hibri (Muslim, USA)
Mr. Chungliang Al Huang (Taoist, USA)
Dr. Asad Husain (Muslim, USA)
Dato' Dr. Haji Ismail bin Ibrahim (Muslim, Malaysia)
Prof. Ephraim Isaac (Jewish, USA)
Hon. Narendra P. Jain (Jain, India)
Dastoor Dr. Kaikhusroo Minocher JamaspAsa (Zoroastrian, India)
Very Rev. Frederick C. James (Christian, USA)
Ma Jaya Bhagavati (Interfaith, USA)
Ajahn Phra Maha Surasak Jvnando (Buddhist, USA)
Dr. Chatsumarn Kabilsingh (Buddhist, Thailand)
Abbot Timothy Kelly OSB (Christian, USA)
Mr. Jim Kenney (Christian, USA)
Sadguru Sant Keshavadas (Hindu, India)

Siri Singh Sahib Bhai Sahib Harbhajan Singh Khalsa Yogiji (Sikh, USA)
Dr. Irfan Ahmad Khan (Muslim, USA)
Dr. Qadir Husain Khan (Muslim, India)
Mr. P.V. Krishnayya (Hindu, USA)
Dr. Lakshmi Kumari (Hindu, India)
Prof. Dr. Hans Küng (Christian, Germany)
Mr. Peter Laurence (Jewish, USA)
Ms. Dolores Leakey (Christian, USA)
Rev. Chung Ok Lee (Buddhist, USA)
Mrs. Norma U. Levitt (Jewish, USA)
Rev. Deborah Ann Light (Neo-Pagan, USA)
Mr. Amrish Mahajan (Hindu, USA)
Sister Joan Monica McGuire, O.P. (Christian, USA)
Imam Warith Deen Mohammed (Muslim, USA)
Very Rev. James Parks Morton (Christian, USA)
Mr. Archie Mosay (Native American, USA)
Dr. Robert Muller (Christian, Costa Rica)
Rev. Albert Nambiaparambil, CMI (Christian, India)
Prof. Seyyed Hossein Nasr (Muslim, USA)
Prof. James Nelson (Christian, USA)
Mr. Charles Nolley (Bahá'í, USA)
Rev. Koshin Ogui, Sensei (Buddhist, USA)
Dastoor Jehangir Oshidari (Zoroastrian, Iran)
Dr Abdel Rahman Osman (Muslim, USA)
Luang Poh Panyananda (Buddhist, Thailand)
Ven. Achahn Dr. Chuen Phangcham (Buddhist, USA)
Pravrajika Prabuddhaprana (Hindu, India)
B.K. Dadi Prakashmani (Brahma Kumaris, India)
Mr. Burton Pretty On Top (Native American, USA)
Rev. Dr. David Ramage, Jr. (Christian, USA)
Ven. Dr. Havanpola Ratanasara (Buddhist, USA)
Dr. Krishna Reddy (Hindu, USA)
Prof. V. Madhusudan Reddy (Hindu, INDIA)
Mrs. Robert Reneker (Christian, USA)
Rev. Dr. Syngman Rhee (Christian, USA)
Mr. Rohinton Rivetna (Zoroastrian, USA)
Lady Olivia Robertson (Neo-Pagan, Eire)
Most Rev. Placido Rodriguez (Christian, USA)
Most Rev. Willy Romélus (Christian, Haiti)
Ven. Seung Sahn (Buddhist, USA)
Swami Satchidananda (Hindu, USA)
Ms. Dorothy Savage (Christian, USA)
Rabbi Herman Schaalman (Jewish, USA)
Hon. Syed Shahabuddin (Muslim, India)
Bhai Mohinder Singh (Sikh, USA)
Dr. Karan Singh (Hindu, USA)
Dr. Mehervan Singh (Sikh, Singapore)
Mr. Hardial Singh (Sikh, India)
Mr. Indarjit Singh (Sikh, UK)
Singh Sahib Jathedar Manjit Singh (Sikh, India)
Dr. Balwant Singh Hansra (Sikh, USA)
H.E. Dr. L. M. Singhvi (Jain, USA)
Ms. R. Leilani Smith (Bahá'í, USA)
Ms. Helen Spector (Jewish, USA)
Brother David Steindl-Rast, OSB (Christian, USA)
H.H. Satguru Sivaya Subramuniyaswami (Hindu, USA)
Dr. Howard A. Sulkin (Jewish, USA)
Ven. Samu Sunim (Buddhist, USA)
Hon. Homi Taleyarkhan (Zoroastrian, India)
Mr. John B. Taylor (Christian, Switzerland)
Brother Wayne Teasdale (Christian, USA)
Rev. Margaret Orr Thomas (Christian, USA)
Rev. Robert Traer (Unitarian, UK)
Dr. William F. Vendley (Christian, USA)
Pravrajika Vivekaprana (Hindu, India)
Prof. Henry Wilson (Christian, Switzerland)
Ven. Dr. Mapalagama Wipulasara Maha Thero (Buddhist, Sri Lanka)
Ms. Yael Wurmfeld (Bahá'í, USA)
Rev. Addie Wyatt (Christian, USA)
H.H. Dr. Bala Siva Yogindra Maharaj (Hindu, India)
Baba Metahochi Kofi Zannu (Indigenous, Nigeria)
Dastoor Kobad Zarolia (Zoroastrian, Canada)
Dastoor Mehraban Zarthosty (Zoroastrian, Canada)

Exhibit P-2

215

United Religions

The Assembly of Religious and Spiritual Leaders introduced another initiative with far-reaching implications. The Assembly—following Muller's lead—called for the creation of an international religious authority aimed at unifying all of the world's "faiths" and spiritual "traditions."[36] This proposal, being coordinated through Muller and the U.N., is moving forward under the "United Religions Initiative." (See Exhibit Q.)

Bringing all of the world's religions into cooperation with the United Nations has been Robert Muller's top priority for many years. His passion for this spiritual agenda is apparent in the following statements: "My great personal dream is to get a tremendous alliance between all the major religions and the UN."[37] "I would whole-heartedly support the creation of an institutional arrangement in the UN or in UNESCO for a dialogue and cooperation between religions."[38]

Although Muller's vision is currently still at the conceptual stage, preliminary meetings are already being held. At a 1997 education conference, Muller elaborated on the progression of his concept:

> Let me tell you, that when you have an idea which you consider fundamental and good for humanity, sooner or later you can implement it. So I was invited to the World Parliament of Religions. And I made a speech there which was so well received by all the participants that the idea of creating a United Religions like the United Nations was promoted during the World Parliament of Religions. And then during the 50th Anniversary of the United Nations in San Francisco, we launched again the idea of United Religions and at the end of June there would be a meeting of 200 people from various religions in San Francisco to draft and to give birth, in San Francisco, to a United Religions. . . . I almost cannot believe it that they listened to me! I will be the father of the United Religions![39]

Working closely with Muller on this daring initiative is Rev. William Swing of Grace Episcopal Cathedral in San Francisco. Although Muller is the visionary behind United Religions and the catalyst between the major parties involved, Rev. Swing has become the initiative's figurehead and spokesperson. Swing, who is the residing Episcopal bishop of the Diocese of California, apparently was considered to be the most politically correct Protestant candidate to work with the Vatican, the Gorbachev Foundation, and the United Nations in shepherding this initiative into finalization.

UNITED RELIGIONS INITIATIVE

Fall 1996

Dear Brothers and Sisters,

You are invited to join the United Religions Initiative to help change the world.

This initiative seeks to bring religions and spiritual traditions to a common table, a permanent, daily, global assembly. There, respecting each other's distinctness, they will seek to make peace among religions so they might work together for the good of all life and the healing of the earth.

Already, building on 100 years of interfaith effort, people of many faiths, from many parts of the world have committed themselves to make the UR vision a reality. We share:

1) a deep concern for global crises, such as war, poverty and the destruction of the environment, that threaten life on this planet;

2) a belief that, by gathering in prayerful dialogue on a daily basis and becoming a unified voice for values and a global ethic, the world's faith traditions can be a healing force in regard to these problems;

3) a passion to pray and work for the day when the world's religions gather to work for peace, global ethics, and justice;

4) a commitment to live as a member of the United Religions, building bridges of interfaith understanding and cooperation, locally and globally.

Success requires the participation of leaders of the world's historic religions, and of newer spiritual movements. It requires the hearts and minds of the world's youth. It requires the participation of grassroots people all over the world. It requires your help.

This brochure contains more information about the Initiative, and suggests five commitments to help make this vision a reality.

We hope you will join us. Together we can change the world.

For the People of the United Religions Initiative,

The Rt. Rev. William E. Swing
Bishop
Diocese of California

Ms. Juliet Hollister
Founder,
Temple of Understanding

Dr. Robert Muller
Chancellor,
UN Peace University

Exhibit Q

An Unholy Alliance

The direct involvement of the U.N. in this project has been evident from the beginning. Swing relates how the U.N. first contacted him in 1993 about heading up a worship celebration on its behalf: "Three and a half years ago, a telephone call arrived in San Francisco from the United Nations asking if we, at Grace Cathedral, would host a great interfaith worship service honoring the 50th Anniversary of the signing of the UN Charter in our city." This request is allegedly what prompted Swing to become involved in the United Religions Initiative (URI). He continues, "I got out of bed the next day determined to commit the rest of my life to an initiative that would create a United Religions which would, in appropriately spiritual ways, parallel the United Nations."[40]

As suggested by Swing, the United Religions Organization is intended to be to religion what the United Nations has become to global politics, unifying the world's religions as the U.N. is unifying the world's nations. In a press release dated June 23, 1997, Bishop Swing confirmed these plans: "The URI—if successful—will be a spiritual United Nations. And what better place to give it birth than the Bay Area, which gave birth to the present UN."[41]

Toward this end, proponents of the UR Initiative, operating under the framework of the *Global Ethic*, are preparing a detailed *United Religions Charter* outlining the world's religious future. In a recent interview, Bishop Swing revealed his timetable for the drafting and implementation of this charter: "We want to get the first draft at the end of the 1998 meeting at Stanford. Then in 1999 we want to have the charter finished. And we want to, in the year 2000, have it signed by 60 million people of the world."[42]

United Religions is officially scheduled to begin functioning as an organization on June 26, 2000. Significantly, its headquarters will be in San Francisco, at the Presidio—along with the Gorbachev Foundation.[43] The organization is slated to be fully operational by no later than 2005.[44]

After receiving the call from the U.N., Swing set out to organize the U.N.'s fiftieth anniversary worship service as planned. The U.N. had told him that "they would bring 183 ambassadors of the world to Grace Cathedral," and asked him "to bring representatives of the great religions of the world."[45] According to the *San Francisco Chronicle*, during the service "prayers, chants and incantations were offered to a dozen deities." Children from around the world mingled over thirty "sacred waters [in a] great bowl of unity." This ritual was performed to the accompaniment of music from the earth-worshipping Missa Gaia.[46] This pagan setting would become the platform for Swing to formally present his plan for United Religions. Soon after that meeting, Bishop Swing embarked on an ambitious worldwide campaign to promote the United Religions Initiative. He summarizes his adventure:

> In February of 1996, I started a long trek around the world starting in India with the Mar Thoma in Kerala, the Shankara-charya of Kancheepuram in Madras, Mother Theresa and Dr. Karan Singh in Calcutta, Metropolitan Bishop Vaulos Mar Gregorios, and numerous Baha'i, Sikh, Jain, Moslem, Zoroastrian leaders, and Archbishop Angelo Fernandez in Delhi and the Dalai Lama in Dharamsala. . . . I was able to meet with numerous Muslim religious leaders, ambassadors, writers, politicians, and Supreme Court justices.

> In Egypt, I met with the Orthodox Coptic Pope, Shenouda III, and with Dr. Mohammed Syed Tantawi who, at the time, was the Grand Mufti but has since been elevated to office of Sheik of Alazhar.

> In Jerusalem, I met with Rabbi Mordechai Peron and numerous other rabbis and religious leaders. In Amman, Jordan, with representatives at the only Muslim Interfaith Institute in the world, that of the Crown Prince of Jordan. In Istanbul with the Ecumenical Patriarch Bartholomew. In Geneva with the World Council of Churches. In Tübingen, with The Rev. Dr. Hans Küng. In Rome, with Archbishop Fitzgerald, Cardinal Arinze, and Pope John Paul II. And in England with the Archbishop of Canterbury and Sir Sigmund Sternberg.[47]

Swing's ideas were warmly received, and he was encouraged to continue.

A Vatican Connection

Upon returning from his mission, Swing focused his energies on hosting a Global Interfaith Summit in June 1996. The summit's purpose was to further the UR Initiative and determine how to deal with expected resistance. The conference, held in San Francisco, was co-sponsored by the Gorbachev Foundation and the World Conference on Religion and Peace (WCRP), an organization with strong Catholic representation.[48] While a growing number of people have become familiar with the activities of the Gorbachev Foundation, the U.N., and Robert Muller, very few individuals are even aware of the

WCRP's existence. Yet it is a major player in the global interfaith community.

The World Conference on Religion and Peace started in 1970, with Angelo Fernandes, the Catholic archbishop of New Delhi, India, serving as its first head. As a United Nations non-governmental organization, the WCRP works closely with the U.N. and its various agencies. Among its plans is an international center for conflict resolution, funded by the Rockefeller Foundation.[49]

The first session of the WCRP's sixth General Assembly in 1994 was hosted by the Vatican. Speakers included Hans Küng, Milan's Cardinal Martini, the president of the Rockefeller Foundation, and Roger Cardinal Etchegaray (chief organizer of the Pope's 1986 Assisi interfaith meeting). *Defend Life* reported: "According to *Inside the*

The United Nations/United Religions Alliance

The *Global Ethic* decree is providing the basic "spiritual" framework for the emerging world religion, with the *United Religions Charter* laying out the specific details. *The Earth Charter*, on the other hand, is providing the "political" foundation for the emerging world government – with the *U.N. Charter* and a possible world constitution spelling out the details for implementation. At the center of this alliance between politics and religion are the Gorbachev Foundation and the Vatican.

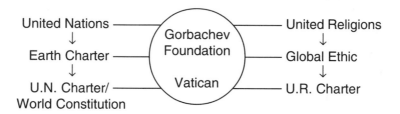

"Do not worry if not all religions will join the United Religions organization. Many nations did not join the UN at its beginning, but later regretted it and made every effort to join. It was the same with the European Community and it will be the case with the world's religions because whoever stays out or aloof will sooner or later regret it."—Robert Muller, speaking at the Parliament of World Religions.

Vatican, the Pope listened to Koranic verses and Jewish, as well as Shinto, Buddhist and Hindu invocations for peace. The conference's final declaration affirmed "the sacredness of the earth and our unity with it."[50]

To the surprise of some Catholics, meetings such as these are now regularly condoned and sponsored by the Vatican. Swing points out, "The Vatican has been actively engaged in this work [interfaith work] for 30 years."[51] This statement confirms the role of Vatican II—thirty years earlier—in launching Catholicism's public interfaith efforts.

Bishop Swing appears to be fully aware of his endeavor's spiritual significance. He asserts, "Interfaith work ultimately becomes dangerous because it threatens every authority: sacred writing, ecclesiastical structures, ethnic purity."[52] This threat pertains particularly to Bible-believing Christians who are unwilling to compromise their sacred beliefs. More than confident of success, Swing states, "The clear fact is that we are on the threshold of global interfaith living. Nothing will stop this or hold it back."[53]

A Vain Undertaking

Together, Robert Muller and Bishop William Swing have become important facilitators for the U.N., the Vatican, and the Gorbachev Foundation in establishing the new religious order. Greatly deluded, they are convinced that they are somehow fulfilling God's plan by merging the world's religions. Muller and his allies are basing their ideas on the false premise that all religions are pathways to immortality.

Building on this faulty foundation, they reckon that since all religions contain some truth, they can draw certain ideas from each of them to create a new synthetic religion. Arguing his case for the new spirituality, Muller proclaims:

> Peace will be impossible without the taming of fundamentalism through a United Religions that professes faithfulness only to the global spirituality and to the health of this planet.[54]

He continues,

> The world's major religions in the end all want the same thing, even though they were born in different places and circumstances on this planet. What the world needs today is a convergence of the different religions in the search for and definition of the cosmic or divine laws which ought to regulate our behavior on this planet. World-wide spiritual ecumenism, expressed in new forms of religious cooperation

and institutions, would probably be closest to the heart of the resurrected Christ.[55]

Muller contends that religions claiming to "have the total truth" missed the real point of Jesus and the other religious "emissaries." He rationalizes:

> The truth that was given by Jesus, by Mohammed, by these emissaries from outer space, they were really basic truths. And they were so great that the cosmos almost incarnated itself. This is why Jesus said, 'I am the incarnation of the divine.' And the Indigenous people, they called it 'Great Spirit.' So there was always this fighting to get the message from the outer universe to give us confidence and to tell us how to behave. This is why practically all the religions have a great contribution to make to the mystery of life. . . . The only trouble is that their followers, the disciples, they created around these spiritual messages a religion.[56]

Muller's belief—that each religion provides part of the truth, and that collectively, the core of the world's religions contain the complete truth—has unfortunately gained widespread acceptance in New Age circles. Proponents conveniently overlook the logical incompatibilities among the religions, especially between Christianity, which teaches that salvation is a gift of God to all who believe in His Son, and pantheism, which teaches that man achieves immortality through his own works and reincarnation.

By building a new religion on the foundation of interfaithism, Muller is in open conflict with the very words of Jesus Christ, including His all important profession that He is the *only* way of salvation (John 14:6). Jesus said in no uncertain terms: "Whoever believes in him [Jesus] is not condemned, but whoever does not believe stands condemned already because he has not believed in the name of God's one and only Son" (John 3:18, NIV). One must either accept Christ's teachings or reject them. There is no middle ground on this matter. Standing before Pilate, awaiting crucifixion, Jesus drove home His message one final time, proclaiming, "Everyone on the side of truth listens to me" (John 18:37b, NIV).

The problem with interfaithism is that it offers a false unity, not a unity based on truth. God's truth is absolute and cannot be modified for the sake of achieving a particular goal. If unity becomes the main pursuit, truth is sacrificed, and participants end up believing a lie for the sake of their cause. True unity comes from God and is a by-product of seeking and believing His truth. It is never an end unto itself.

Clearly, other religions are not pathways to God. To claim that they are is accusing Jesus of being a liar. Moreover, if all religions were inspired by God, everyone's eternity in Heaven would have been secure apart from Christ. One could gain entrance to Heaven by embracing Hinduism, Buddhism, or any other religion. There would have been no need for Jesus to come and pay the penalty for our sins. God would have sent His Son and condemned Him to death for nothing.

But this was not the case. God sent His Son to intervene on our behalf because He loved us, and our sin had to be dealt with. He made a way where there was none. No other religious figure was able to take away our sins—not Buddha, not Zoroaster, not Confucius, nor anyone else. Only Jesus Christ could do so because only He, as God's Son, was perfect. God's justice required a perfect sacrifice to blot out man's sin. John the Baptist accurately said of Jesus, "Behold the Lamb of God, which taketh away the sin of the world" (John 1:29). May we not reject so great a salvation!

Notes

1. Robert Muller, *New Genesis: Shaping a Global Spirituality* (Anacortes, WA: World Happiness and Cooperation, 1982), p. 169.

2. Robert Muller, *Most of All, They Taught Me Happiness* (Garden City, NY: Image Books, 1985), p. 81.

3. Ibid., p. 81.

4. Ibid., p. 80.

5. Muller, *New Genesis*, pp. 169–170.

6. Ibid., pp. 170–171.

7. Ibid., p. 171.

8. Ibid., p. 19.

9. Ibid., pp. 126–127.

10. Ibid., p. 164.

11. Ibid., pp. 117–118.

12. Ibid., p. 48.

13. Gary Kah, "Public Education . . . The Shaping of Global Citizens!," *Hope For The World Update* (Noblesville, IN: Hope For The World, Spring 1997, newsletter), p. 4.

14. Muller, *Most of All, They Taught Me Happiness*, pp. 116–117.

15. Norman Cousins, Foreword to *Most of All, They Taught Me Happiness*, pp. 10–11.

16. Richard Hughes Seager, editor, *The Dawn of Religious Pluralism: Voices from the World's Parliament of Religions, 1893* (La Salle, IL: Published by Open Court in association with The Council for a Parliament of the World's Religions, 1993). Also, Joel Beversluis, editor, *A SourceBook for Earth's Community of Religions* (Grand Rapids, MI/New York: CoNexus Press/Global Education Associates, 1995), p. 111.

17. Peter Washington, *Madame Blavatsky's Baboon* (New York: Schocken Books, 1995), p. 107.

18. Thomas F. Best and Martin Robra, editors, *Ecclesiology and Ethics: Costly Commitment* (Geneva: World Council of Churches, 1995), p. 61. Presentations and Reports from the World Council of Churches' Consultation in Jerusalem, November 1994.

19. World Council of Churches, "Towards A Common Understanding And Vision Of The World Council Of Churches: A Policy Statement," (Web page http://www.wcc-coe.org/wcc/who/cuv-e.html), [Accessed February 9, 1998]. Adopted by the Central Committee of the World Council of Churches, September 1997.

20. Robert C. Broderick, editor, *The Catholic Encyclopedia: Revised and Updated Edition* (Nashville, TN: Thomas Nelson, 1987), p. 596.

21. M. Basil Pennington, *Vatican II: We've Only Just Begun* (New York: Crossroad Publishing Company, 1994), p. 144.

22. Ibid., pp. 146–147.

23. Joel Beversluis, *A SourceBook for Earth's Community of Religions* (Grand Rapids, MI/New York: CoNexus Press/Global Education Associates, 1995), pp. 111–113.

24. Ibid., pp. 113–114.

25. Ibid., pp. 114–116.

26. Ibid., p. 114.

27. Dave Hunt, *A Woman Rides the Beast* (Eugene, OR: Harvest House, 1994), p. 426.

28. John Templeton Foundation, "After the Award: The Legacy of The Templeton Prize," (Web page http://www.templeton.org/prize/pkafter.asp), [Accessed September 16, 1998].

29. John Templeton Foundation, "Templeton Prize Winners, 1973–1997," (Web page http://www.templeton.org/prize/pkwin.asp), [Accessed September 16, 1998].

30. William Proctor, *The Templeton Touch* (Garden City, NY: Doubleday & Company, 1983), p. 121. The authorized account of John Marks Templeton's life and philosophy.

31. John Templeton Foundation, "Templeton Prize Winners, 1973–1997."

32. John Templeton Foundation, "General Information," (Web page http://www.templeton.org/about.asp#4), [Accessed September 16, 1998].

33. John Templeton Foundation, "Board of Trustees," (Web page http://www.templeton.org/thelist.asp), [Accessed September 16, 1998].

34. Beversluis, *A SourceBook for Earth's Community of Religions,* p. 115.

35. Hans Küng, *Global Responsibility: In Search of a New Ethic* (New York: Crossroad Publishing Company, 1990), pp. 23, 35, 69.

36. Beversluis, *A SourceBook for Earth's Community of Religions,* pp. 115–116.

37. Muller, *New Genesis,* p. xiii.

38. Ibid., p. 126.

39. Robert Muller, speech addressed to the Global Citizenship 2000 Youth Congress, Vancouver, BC, April 5, 1997. Transcribed from an audio tape recorded by Carl Teichrib.

40. Bishop William E. Swing, *A Message for all the People* (San Francisco: United Religions Initiative, flier), p. 2.

41. Bishop William E. Swing, *United Religions Initiative,* handout to United Religions Delegates at the Initiative held at Stanford University in San Francisco, June 23, 1997.

42. Bishop William E. Swing, interview with Irvin Baxter, *Endtime Magazine,* July/August 1998 (Web page http://www.endtime.com/bishop.htm), [Accessed November 2, 1998].

43. Don Lattin, "Religious Leaders' Unifying Vision: Bishop leads quest for spiritual version of UN at Presidio," *San Francisco Chronicle,* June 20, 1996.

44. "One-World Church expected in '97," *Defend Life,* reprinted by the *Far Eastern Beacon* (Singapore: ICCC Far Eastern Office, July/August 1997, newspaper), pp. 4–5. *Far Eastern Beacon,* 5 Tavistock Avenue, Singapore 555108.

45. Bishop William E. Swing, interview with Irvin Baxter, *Endtime Magazine.*

46. *San Francisco Chronicle,* as quoted in "One-World Church expected in '97," *Defend Life.*

47. Swing, *A Message for all the People,* p. 3.

48. "One-World Church expected in '97," *Defend Life.*

49. Ibid.

50. Ibid.

51. Swing, *A Message for all the People,* pp. 3–4.

52. Ibid., p. 4.

53. Ibid., p. 4.

54. "One-World Church expected in '97," *Defend Life*.

55. Muller, *New Genesis*, p. 126.

56. Carl Teichrib, "Global Citizenship 2000: Educating for the New Age," *Hope For The World Update* (Noblesville, IN: Hope For The World, Fall 1997, newsletter), p. 10.

9

Crossing the Threshold

"Let no man deceive you by any means: for that day shall not come, except there come a falling away first, and that man of sin be revealed, the son of perdition." 2 Thessalonians 2:3

"And when he shall have accomplished to scatter the power of the holy people, all these things shall be finished." Daniel 12:7b

Determined to build their own utopia, New Age religious leaders have chosen to reject God's plan of redemption in favor of an occult-based world view. However, their world view—including plans for global unification—cannot be realized as long as certain groups oppose their efforts. Since interfaith strategists view Bible-believing Christians as their chief opposition, it should be expected that they would use a variety of tactics to neutralize them—and, if possible, to win them over.

As a result of efforts already underway, a growing number of professing Christians are being seduced, showing a willingness to sacrifice some of their biblical beliefs for the prospect of global peace and unity. This tendency to exchange God's truth for an empty promise has opened the floodgate to all kinds of false doctrines and occult practices to enter our churches. With increasing frequency, false teachings and counterfeit miracles are taking place in the name of Christ. Jesus warned that such deception would occur in the last days: "For false Christs and false prophets will appear and perform great signs and miracles to deceive even the elect—if that were possible. See, I have told you ahead of time" (Matt. 24:24–25, NIV).

Recognizing that the master deceiver and his demons sometimes operate in His name, Jesus admonishes us to use discernment in distinguishing what is genuinely from Him and what is of Satan. He cautioned, "Watch out for false prophets. They come to you in sheep's clothing, but inwardly they are ferocious wolves. By their fruit you will recognize them" (Matt. 7:15-16a, NIV). And John, who was Jesus' closest disciple, instructs us to "test the spirits to see whether they are from God" (1 John 4:1a, NIV). Unfortunately, very few people today are taking these admonitions seriously.

Recently my wife and I viewed a documentary of Hindu swamis in Malaysia placing people into occult trances simply by placing their hands on them. The participants fell backward to the ground, in some cases shaking violently as "the spirit" (a demon) was entering their bodies. Others, while in this hypnotic state, acted and sounded like animals and were able to endure various forms of bodily torture, including puncturing of skin without losing blood. The people involved openly acknowledged that they were engaged in occult practices, the purpose being to please the spirits in order to receive more power.

Similar practices are now being witnessed in churches around the world where a false Jesus and false gospel are being proclaimed. Pastors and evangelists who are leading their flocks into such activities are often well intentioned, not even realizing they are engaging in occult practices. They are convinced that they are serving God because of how these supernatural manifestations were first explained to them by "spiritual" leaders in whom they trusted. Others are deliberately misleading their flocks. Regardless of their motivation, what they are doing is wrong and will some day be severely judged by God. Denouncing the actions of false prophets Jesus declared,

> Not everyone who says to me, "Lord, Lord," will enter the kingdom of heaven, but only he who does the will of my Father who is in heaven. Many will say to me on that day, "Lord, Lord, did we not prophesy in your name, and in your name drive out demons and perform many miracles?" Then I will tell them plainly, "I never knew you. Away from me, you evildoers! (Matt. 7:21-23, NIV)

As the new millennium unfolds and a New Age dawns, Satan's deception will continue to strengthen, each stage becoming more seductive and extreme. With most of the pieces for the new religious order in place, interfaith planners will be targeting Christians as never before. As part of this growing deception, an unprecedented celebration is being staged for the year 2000.

Engaging Evangelicals

Throughout the millennial year, a series of ecumenical events will be held for the alleged purpose of celebrating the two thousandth birthday of Jesus. It all sounds good on the surface. However, upon closer examination, one discovers that some of the main organizers are not Christians and that leaders from other religions will also be participating. The fact is, this year long "party" will be an interfaith spectacle designed to bring the religions together. Since it is taking place in the name of Christ—supposedly to honor Him—Christians are expected to fall in line without question. Few will realize that this celebration is setting the stage for a false Christ, not Jesus Christ.

Nearly two decades ago, Robert Muller called for such a celebration. Anticipating a new millennium and sensing a golden opportunity to further his one-world agenda, he wrote:

> May the kind divine providence help us start a new history and prepare the advent of a new age, a new world, a new philosophy and new human relationships, as we approach the bi-millennium . . .

> The table of contents of a new world encyclopedia is ready. The agenda for the next chapter of humanity is in sight. But this is when the real Teilhardian period begins. . . . On the occasion of Earth Day, I proposed that humanity should hold in the year 2000 a world-wide Bi-millennium Celebration of Life.[1]

Serving as Muller's main link to the evangelical Christian community on this project is his friend Jay Gary. Based in Colorado, Gary is well connected among evangelical groups. Jay Gary has been executive editor with *World Christian* magazine; has worked as a regional coordinator with March For Jesus; has acted as a consultant for New Life 2000, the World Strategy of Campus Crusade; and has participated in a Youth With A Mission writing project.[2] He has authored several books, including *The Star of 2000*, which lays out his vision for the next millennium, including his plan for the upcoming celebration. In his book, Gary favorably quotes Robert Muller, speaks highly of the United Nations, and endorses the World Council of Churches.

Gary is best known for establishing the Bimillennial Global Interaction Network, also referred to as BEGIN. Revealing his ecumenical and interfaith intentions, he describes BEGIN as a "link up with a global network of groups and individuals who are working to insure that the year 2000 is celebrated *as a planetary jubilee by the whole human family."* (italics added)[3] To oversee his endeavor, Gary founded an organization called Celebration 2000.

Gary regularly promotes interfaith leaders, among them Hans Küng and the Pope. In turn, he has been publicly promoted by New Age groups such as Alice Bailey's World Goodwill.[4] As disturbing as his New Age endorsements are, even more troubling is the fact that he has been supported by numerous Christian leaders. Endorsements for Gary and his proposed celebration have been particularly forthcoming from groups within the evangelical unity movement. One example is Promise Keepers, which promoted his book (*The Star of 2000*) in its official magazine *New Man*.[5]

As the largest ecumenical men's movement in history, Promise Keepers is preparing us for the future by bridging the differences between the Protestant denominations and Roman Catholicism. Some leaders of the organization have made the mistake of placing a higher priority on unity than on sound biblical doctrine. Even so, I recognize that there are many fine Christian men who belong to Promise Keepers (PK) and do not support unbiblical teaching. Some of them are close friends of mine. I, myself, had joined PK early on but had some immediate reservations due to the overriding emphasis on unity. I became even more concerned when I noticed that some of the speakers and authors PK promoted had signed the ecumenical declaration *Evangelicals and Catholics Together*.

This document, also known as ECT, was drafted over a period of time by Chuck Colson and a Roman Catholic priest named Richard Neuhaus. As its name implies, ECT calls for spiritual unity between Protestants and Catholics. Although Jesus prayed for love and harmony among Christian believers, longing for them to be as one (John 17:11–23), he never intended this unity to come at the expense of doctrinal purity. The ECT document, together with organizations such as Promise Keepers, is disregarding doctrinal boundaries that God has established.

Instead of bringing down doctrinal walls, God calls us to build them up to preserve His truth. Yet, few remain who are willing to do so. Today's spiritual state is amazingly reminiscent of the condition of Israel during Ezekiel's time. God lamented, "I looked for a man among them who would build up the wall and stand before me in the gap on behalf of the land so I would not have to destroy it, but I found none" (Ezek. 22:30, NIV).

The walls being torn down today are paving the way for tomorrow's global celebration and acceptance of a false Christ.

* * * * *

Doctrinal Differences

There is nothing wrong with unity as long as it is centered on God's truth. The problem with the unity being pursued by Catholic and Protestant leaders is that it replaces God's truth with a man-made theological hybrid based on Catholic teaching and tradition. As the outline below demonstrates, Roman Catholic doctrine does not line up with God's Word. The following eight points are from the *Catechism of the Catholic Church*, released in April, 1995. Comments, unless otherwise noted, are by Pastor Phil Arms of Houston, Texas.[6]

1. Baptism: The Catechism states, "Through baptism we are freed from sin and reborn as sons of God" (p. 342). "The Lord Himself affirms that baptism is necessary for salvation" (p. 352).
Water has never saved anyone. [Although the Scriptures command Christians to be baptized, we are saved from sin by accepting Christ's atonement on the Cross.]

2. Tradition: The Catholic Church does not derive her certainty about all revealed thoughts from Holy Scriptures alone. The Catechism declares that both Scripture and Tradition must be accepted and honored with equal sentiments of devotion and reverence (p. 31). These traditions can be retained, modified, or even abandoned under the guidance of the church magistration (p. 32).
Timothy 3:16 says, "All Scripture is given by inspiration of God, and is profitable for doctrine, for reproof, for correction, for instruction in righteousness." We do not use traditions or saints for our doctrine, it must be the Bible.

3. Transubstantiation: This says that Christ is literally, physically present, and the Communion becomes his Body. The Catechism teaches in the most blessed sacrament of the Eucharist, the body and blood, together with the soul and divinity, of our Lord Jesus Christ and, therefore, the whole Christ is truly, really and substantially contained (p. 383).
Hebrews 10:10–12 states, "He paid for our sins one time offered His body once for all." The Catholic "bread & wine" do not mystically turn into Jesus once ingested. This is blasphemous!

4. Confession to a priest: The Catechism teaches, "Confession to a priest is an essential part of the sacrament of penance" (p. 405).
Ephesians 2:18, "Through Jesus we have access by one Spirit unto

the Father." No priest is needed to confess to God and renew our mind. Again, this is apostate. [I Timothy 2:5 states that Jesus Christ is the only mediator between God and men.]

5. Devotion and prayer to Mary: The Catechism teaches that like the beloved disciple we welcome Jesus' mother into our homes, for she has become the mother of all the living. We can pray with and to her. The prayer of the church is sustained by the prayer of Mary and united with in hope (p. 706). The Catechism also holds strongly to the sinlessness of Mary, her perpetual virginity, and her bodily ascension into heaven.

Romans 3:23, "All have sinned and come short of the glory of God." All means ALL, including Mary.

6. Purgatory: The Catechism teaches that Purgatory is the final purification of the elect. The Church formulated her doctrine of Purgatory at the Councils of Florence and Trent. This teaching is also based upon the practice of prayer for the dead (p. 291).

Hebrews 9:27, "Appointed to man once to die and after this the judgement." There is no second chance for Heaven after death.

7. The Mass: The Catechism teaches a continuing renewal of Calvary and Christ's sacrifice. The Eucharist is thus a sacrifice because it re-presents (makes present) the sacrifice of the Cross.

Catholics teach salvation by works. Salvation is a free gift and you do not receive it nor keep it by working for it. Romans 6:23.

8. Idolatry: The Catechism condones the images of Mary and the Saints. There is the lauding of the "Contemplation of Sacred Icons" and encouragement for churches to display "Holy images" of our Lord, Mary, angels, and the saints (p. 329).

There is also encouragement to have statues and images in our homes. This is idol worship. You cannot sanctify idols. First Thessalonians 1:9, ". . . you turn from idols to God." Idol worship is condemned throughout the Word of God.

Some of my good friends are Roman Catholic. We have worked together side-by-side in exposing the New Age movement. These particular friends are born again and do not believe in purgatory, do not pray to Mary or the "patron saints," and do not believe in the infallibility of the Pope. They accept Jesus Christ as the only way of salvation, embracing the Bible as it is without adding the traditions and rituals of the Catholic Church.

Recognizing the doctrinal fallacies of Catholicism, they have chosen to remain in their local parishes for the time being, hoping to bring about positive changes. Although I can appreciate what they are doing, they will unfortunately not succeed in altering the structure and long held doctrinal positions of the Roman Catholic Church. The Vatican has demonstrated an historic resolve in maintaining its structure, rituals, and beliefs.

* * * * *

Roman Catholicism

Ever since Vatican II, where the idea of a global millennial celebration was first conceived, the papacy's goal has been to achieve full unity between Protestants and Catholics by the year 2000.[7] The upcoming millennial event was intended to be a victory party of sorts, celebrating the unification of Protestants under the Church of Rome. Recognizing that this unity might not be completely achieved by the start of the new century, the Vatican, at the very least, would see this celebration as a vital step in that direction.

Within the Vatican this celebration is officially known as "The Great Jubilee of the Year 2000" and is scheduled to begin in late 1999.[8] More than a birthday party for Jesus, this Jubilee signifies a larger concept. During Old Testament times, every fiftieth year was designated as a Year of Jubilee, at which time everyone's outstanding debt was cancelled, providing a fresh financial start. (See Leviticus 25.)

The Vatican, as part of its agenda, seeks to resurrect this idea. Pope John Paul II proposes "the Jubilee as an appropriate time to give thought, among other things, to reducing substantially, if not canceling outright, the international debt which seriously threatens the future of many nations."[9] Though this idea is attractive to many, the Jubilee could be used for the purpose of establishing a new global monetary system. This would be particularly appealing to a world in a state of economic recession. Along with debt cancellation, the authorities could offer low or no interest loans—but at what price? Could the collateral be our freedom?

Global Ambitions

In addition to bringing Protestants under its domain, the Vatican has a larger mission of uniting all of the world's religions. This mandate is reflected in several of the Pope's messages. Sharing part of his Jubilee interfaith vision, Pope John Paul declares,

The eve of the Year 2000 will provide a great opportunity, especially in view of the events of recent decades, for inter-religious dialogue. . . .

In this regard, attention is being given to finding ways of arranging historic meetings in places of exceptional import-ance like Bethlehem, Jerusalem, and Mount Sinai as a means of furthering dialogue with Jews and the followers of Islam, and to arranging similar meetings elsewhere with the leaders of the great world religions.[10]

The Vatican has established Jerusalem and Rome as the centers for its worldwide Jubilee. As part of this celebration John Paul is planning a personal pilgrimage to the Holy Land.[11] His visit is intended to further the peace process and is expected to consolidate Vatican influence in the region. Delegates commissioned by the Pope have already met with leading Israeli and Palestinian officials con-cerning his trip.

This upcoming trip will hold special significance. A growing number of religious leaders believe Pope John Paul II will finally bring peace to the Middle East and the world. One such leader is George Huntston Williams, former professor at Harvard Divinity School. In his classic biography, *The Mind of John Paul II*, Williams makes a provocative statement concerning the Pope's potential role as a global savior. Reflecting on a harrowing experience from the Pope's youth, he remarks,

How he conducted himself in a tense situation in his native Cracow two score years ago may be prophetic of how in some tense situation for our planetary city in the coming score of years he may with comparable steadiness of nerve deliver a saving word for all mankind.[12]

Professor Williams concludes his book on a similar note, posing a profound, in-depth scenario:

One can imagine some parlous moment in the evolution of humanity, ever in constant peril now of utter destruction, when the present Servant of the Servants of the Lord might with personal magnanimity and moral magnitude, forthright and supple in the languages of our planet, interpose himself by God's grace, between mankind and the awesome power of imminent Holocaust, possibly *usque ad mortem*. He has been given a mandate from on high and by spiritual magnet-ism he has gained the authority to speak and to act on behalf of all humankind.[13]

Whether it be through the efforts of the current or a future pope, statements such as these suggest that the Holy See is destined to play a major role not only in "bringing peace" but in introducing the new political and religious order.

Quotes by Pope John Paul II

THE APPROACHING END OF THE SECOND millennium demands of everyone an examination of conscience and the promotion of fitting ecumenical initiatives so that we can celebrate the Great Jubilee, if not completely united, at least much closer to overcoming the divisions of the second millennium.[14] (uppercase in original)

It is necessary for humanity to achieve unity through plurality, to learn to come together in the one Church, even while presenting a plurality of ways of thinking and acting, of cultures and civilizations.[15]

I believe in the Church. We place the Church on the same level as the Mystery of the Holy Trinity and the mysteries of the Incarnation and the Redemption.[16]

UNIVERSAL BY NATURE, [THE CATHOLIC CHURCH] is conscious of being at the service of all and never identifies with any one national community. . . . She is mindful of—indeed she knows that she is the depository of—God's design for humanity: to gather all people into one family.[17] (uppercase in original)

In a divided world, the unity of the Catholic Church, which transcends national boundaries, remains a great force, acknowledged as such even by its enemies and still present today in world politics and international organization. Not everyone is comfortable with this force . . .[18]

The fact that Pope John Paul has become highly revered in religious circles is made evident by author Malachi Martin, a former Jesuit priest. Regarding the Pope's claim to moral and religious leadership of the human race, Martin states: "All realize, seemingly, that he is in a category superior to the Dalai Lama, the Patriarch of Constantinople, the Archbishop of Canterbury, Billy Graham, any renowned itinerant Indian swami, or any other religious leader who travels."[19]

Not only is the Pontiff revered by his religious peers, he is highly esteemed by all segments of society, including many within the Protestant realm. This Pope, more than any other, has particularly endeared himself to evangelical Christians. This unique relationship has been born largely out of their appreciation for his strong stance against abortion. However, most Evangelicals remain unaware of John Paul's acceptance of evolution and his strong devotion to Mary. It is widely expected that he will publicly elevate Mary to the status of co-redeemer in the near future.[20]

While many Evangelicals have embraced the Pope as a spiritual ally, he is only returning the favor in public. Privately, he continues to hold Bible-believing Christians in contempt. In a Sunday mass in Venezuela, Pope John Paul called on parish workers to intensify their efforts against "the threat from evangelical Protestantism."[21] As disturbing as this may be, there are political realities concerning this pope that are equally troubling.

Political Ties

Among those working with the Pope to establish the new global civilization are Robert Muller, the United Nations, and Mikhail Gorbachev. As a top U.N. official, Muller was appointed to oversee Pope John Paul's first visit to the U.N. in 1979. Anticipating this major event, Muller wrote,

> I expect the Pope to lift the hearts of all international servants of the UN and of its specialized agencies and programs . . . bring forth new visions in philosophy, sociology, ideology and spirituality centered on the UN's noble objective of "unity in diversity."[22]

Muller was not disappointed by the Pope's mission. In his address before the U.N. General Assembly, John Paul offered the following words of endearment and encouragement:

> As a universal community embracing the faithful . . . the Church is deeply interested in the existence and activity of the Organization whose very name tells us that it unites and associates nations and States. It unites and associates: it does not divide and oppose. This is the real reason, the essential reason, for my presence among you.[23]

In appreciation for Robert Muller's dedicated efforts in making his visit a success, the Pope personally presented him with a "magnificent golden pectoral crucifix," which would serve as a continuous reminder of their time together.[24]

Muller is aware of the Vatican's special partnership with the U.N. Describing this religious-political alliance he states:

The Church vastly surpasses that of the young United Nations and its agencies. This is why the Holy See has become so close to the United Nations, offering its vision, help and experience in the solution of most difficult world problems. . . . What marvelous opportunities the UN, its agencies and its world conferences offer Catholics to participate in the making of a better world! The Holy See has fully understood it and maintains important missions at the seats of all the UN agencies. His Holiness is always ready to help the United Nations in its endeavors.[25]

One way the Vatican is helping the U.N. is by training its future diplomats. Through Seton Hall University's international program on diplomacy, the Vatican has an unusual arrangement with the United Nations. Seton Hall has allied itself with the United Nations Association (U.S.A.) to educate tomorrow's global leaders to operate within the U.N. system. As one of the largest Catholic Universities in the U.S., Seton Hall is the only institution of its type holding this special status. (See Exhibit R.)

This close partnership further implies that the U.N. is serving as a political instrument of the Vatican. Aware of this spiritual/political alliance, former U.N. Secretary-General Dag Hammarskjöld articulated that "there were two Popes on this planet: a spiritual Pope in Rome and a civilian Pope in New York, namely, the Secretary-General of the UN."[26]

Mikhail Gorbachev holds a similar view regarding the position of the pope and the U.N. secretary-general. He considers Pope John Paul II as "the world's highest moral authority."[27] And though Gorbachev is not the leader of the United Nations, he has been working closely with this global governing body on the implementation of *The Earth Charter*.

Together, Pope John Paul and Mikhail Gorbachev have already received credit for bringing an end to the Cold War, and now, together they are building the new world order. Gorbachev's relationship to the Pope was made evident during their first meeting in Rome on December 1, 1989. At that time Gorbachev knelt at the pope's feet and "asked pardon for all the crimes he had committed in his life."[28] During that historic meeting, Pope John Paul invited the Russian leader to join him in ending global confrontation and building "universal solidarity."[29] They have been in close contact ever since.

MANAGE THE WORLD
BECOME A GLOBAL LEADER

Seton Hall University, one of the largest Catholic universities in the U.S., offers a distinctive opportunity for students interested in pursuing careers in global leadership. Seton Hall's School of Diplomacy and International Relations (SODIR) is the only school in the USA that has a special alliance with the United Nations Association of the United States of America. It offers a unique undergraduate curriculum with special emphasis on the United Nations system.

SODIR's program, leading to a Bachelor of Science in International Relations, provides comprehensive undergraduate education to students from around the world. Symposia with world leaders and distinguished international lecturers, study abroad, and internships in government, international businesses, and organizations prepare you for a variety of global diplomacy and management career opportunities. Beginning in August 1998, SODIR will also offer a Master of Arts in International Relations.

To learn more about SODIR and to better understand the process for applying to U.S. universities, high school students, parents, teachers, guidance counselors, university students and professors are invited to attend an

OPEN MEETING
THURSDAY, 18 DECEMBER, 7:00 - 9:00 P.M.
Urdaneta Room, Intercontinental Hotel
1 Ayala Avenue, 1226 Makati City

For more information on Seton Hall's School of Diplomacy and International Relations and to R.S.V.P. for the Open Meeting, call 893-4431, FAX: 893-3876 or call the U.S. directly (001) 973-275-2515, FAX: 973-275-2519, e-mail: diplomat@shu.edu

SETON HALL
UNIVERSITY

The Catholic University in New Jersey — Founded in 1856 • 400 South Orange Ave., South Orange, NJ U.S.A. 070970 • http://www.shu.edu

Exhibit R

Gorbachev describes his special affection for this Pope:

> I have carried on an intensive correspondence with Pope John Paul II since we met at the Vatican in December 1989....
>
> The sense of mutual affection and understanding which resulted from our meeting is to be found in each of our letters.
>
> I cannot help but say that we share a desire to move forward and complete what we began together. . . .
>
> When I was with him, I realized that the pope had also played a role in what we came to call the new political thinking. . . .
>
> What I have always held in high esteem about the pope's thinking and ideas is their spiritual content, their striving to foster the development of a new world civilization.
>
> Besides being pope, John Paul II is also a Slav, and, of course, that too was conducive to our mutual understanding.
>
> However, I remain convinced that the closeness of spirit that was established between us was of much greater significance than the fact that we both are Slavs. . . .
>
> It can be said that everything which took place in Eastern Europe in recent years would have been impossible without the pope's efforts and the enormous role, including the political role, which he played in the world arena.[30]

After years of working together, Mikhail Gorbachev continues to regard John Paul II as his closest ally in building a new planetary civilization. Malachi Martin recognizes the vision of these two global leaders:

> John Paul and Gorbachev both understand already what practical working structures are needed to create a geopolitical system among nations. They have long since seen clearly that geopolitics must and will transfer national politics to a global plane. . . . They have long since understood that no nation of the world will remain in the next century as it has been or is in this century.[31]

The Jesuit Order
In addition to being allied with major world figures such as Mikhail Gorbachev, Pope John Paul has at his disposal a number of formid-

able institutions. One of the organizations assisting the Pope in his monumental undertaking is the Jesuit order, the most prestigious and powerful secret society of Roman Catholicism. This organization, referred to by some as the CIA of the Vatican, has been working closely with the papacy for centuries.

Unlike other popes before him, John Paul has publicly acknowledged his undisputed leadership of this order. In an address to the society in October 1981, he reminded the Jesuits of their special vow of obedience to the office of the Pope.[32]

Recently, with the help of a U.S. Congressman's office, we were able to obtain a copy of the "Ceremony of Induction and Extreme Oath of the Jesuits" from the U.S. Library of Congress. The following excerpts from this oath reveal the unquestionable loyalty of the Jesuits to the Pope and their commitment to eradicate Protestantism.

> I, . . . Now, in the presence of Almighty God, the Blessed Virgin Mary, the blessed Michael the Archangel, the blessed St. John the Baptist, the holy Apostles St. Peter and St. Paul and all the saints and sacred hosts of heaven, and to you, my ghostly father, the Superior General of the Society of Jesus . . . declare and swear, that his holiness the Pope is Christ's Vicegerent and is the true and only Head of the Catholic or Universal Church throughout the earth; and that by virtue of the keys of binding and loosing, given to his Holiness by my Saviour, Jesus Christ, he hath power to depose heretical kings, princes, states, commonwealths and governments, all being illegal without his sacred confirmation and that they may safely be destroyed. Therefore, to the utmost of my power, I shall and will defend this doctrine and His Holiness' right and custom against all usurpers of the heretical or Protestant authority . . . and all adherents in regard that they be usurped and heretical, opposing the sacred Mother Church of Rome.

> . . . I do further promise and declare, that I will have no opinion or will of my own, or any mental reservation whatever, even as a corpse or cadaver, (*perinde ac cadaver*,) but will unhesitatingly obey each and every command that I may receive from my superiors in the Militia of the Pope and of Jesus Christ.

> . . . I furthermore promise and declare that I will, when opportunity presents, make and wage relentless war, secretly or openly, against all heretics, Protestants and Liberals, as I am directed to do, to extirpate and exterminate them from

the face of the whole earth. . . . I will secretly use the poisoned cup, the strangulating cord, the steel of the poinard [sic] or the leaden bullet, regardless of the honor, rank, dignity, or authority of the person or persons, whatever may be their condition in life, either public or private, as I at any time may be directed so to do by any agent of the Pope or Superior of the Brotherhood of the Holy Faith, of the Society of Jesus.

In confirmation of which, I hereby dedicate my life, my soul and all my coporeal [sic] powers, and with this dagger which I now receive, I will subscribe my name written in my own blood, in testimony thereof; and should I prove false or weaken in my determination, may my brethren and fellow soldiers of the Militia of the Pope cut off my hands and my feet, and my throat from ear to ear, my belly opened and sulphur burned therein, with all the punishment that can be inflicted upon me on earth and my soul be tortured by demons in an eternal hell forever!

All of which I . . . do swear by the blessed Trinity and blessed Sacrament, which I am now to receive, to perform and on my part to keep inviolably; and do call all the heavenly and glorious host of heaven to witness these my real intentions to keep this my oath.[33] (See Appendix K for the complete Jesuit Oath.)

How far will this Pope go—working with his inner circle—to consolidate the Church of Rome's worldwide spiritual and political authority?

The New World Religion

The growing involvement of the Vatican and its allies in politics and religion reminds one of Alice Bailey's prediction that the new world order would be ushered in with the help of a universally-accepted church. Bailey explained that the New Age would "rest upon the foundation of a newly interpreted and enlightened Christianity . . . being universal in nature."[34] The occult prophetess also stated that there were no major distinctions "between the One Universal Church (Catholicism), the sacred inner Lodge of all true Masons, and the innermost circles of the esoteric societies."[35] She indicated that they would all be working together through a global governing body to achieve their goal.

While it is helpful to understand the plans of occult leaders so that we do not succumb to their deception, we must turn to the Final Authority—God's Word—to know exactly what will take place. The

Bible prophesies that the Antichrist and his accomplice, the false prophet, will, through deception and flattery, bring the world's religions and nations together—uniting them under a new spiritual/political order (Rev.13; Daniel 7, 11).

According to Scripture, the Antichrist and his close ally will be in direct contact with the demonic realm, having Satan's complete power at their disposal. They will be able to perform "great and miraculous signs, even causing fire to come down from heaven to earth in full view of men" (Rev. 13:13b, NIV). Together, they will lead mankind in an all-out rebellion against God. Through this endeavor the Antichrist—representing Satan on earth—will succeed in gaining the worship of most of the earth's inhabitants.

> The dragon [Satan] gave the beast his power and his throne and great authority. . . . Men worshiped the dragon because he had given authority to the beast, and they also worshiped the beast and asked, "Who is like the beast? Who can make war against him?". . . And he was given authority over every tribe, people, language and nation. All inhabitants of the earth will worship the beast—all whose names have not been written in the book of life belonging to the Lamb that was slain from the creation of the world. (Revelation 13:2b,4,7b, 8, NIV)

Those who refuse to participate in this abomination will suffer the consequences:

> He was given power to make war against the saints and to conquer them. . . . He who has an ear, let him hear. If anyone is to go into captivity, into captivity he will go. If anyone is to be killed with the sword, with the sword he will be killed. This calls for patient endurance and faithfulness on the part of the saints. (Revelation 13:7a, 9, 10, NIV)

Those who participate in the rebellion, and take the mark of the beast, will experience a far greater punishment:

> . . . If any man worship the beast and his image, and receive his mark in his forehead, or in his hand, The same shall drink of the wine of the wrath of God, which is poured out without mixture into the cup of his indignation; and he shall be tormented with fire and brimstone in the presence of the holy angels, and in the presence of the Lamb: And the smoke of their torment ascendeth up for ever and ever: and they have no rest day nor night, who worship the beast and his image, and whosoever receiveth the mark of his name. (Revelation 14:9b–11)

Why would God's judgement be so severe against those who take the mark or worship the beast? Because by engaging in this activity they will be giving allegiance to Satan and making his reign on earth possible.

The blatant demonic nature of this global rebellion was described by Alice Bailey, who worked her whole life to bring it about:

> The spiritual Hierarchy [demonic realm] of the planet, the ability of mankind to contact its Members and to work in cooperation with Them, and the existence of the greater Hierarchy of spiritual energies of which our tiny planetary sphere is a part—these are the three truths upon which the coming world religion may be based.[36]

> . . . The new religion will be one of Invocation and Evocation, of bringing together great spiritual [occult] energies and then stepping them down for the benefiting and the stimulation of the masses. The work of the new religion will be the distribution of spiritual energy.[37]

The occult religion that Bailey envisioned would be promoted and enforced through a geopolitical system—possibly the United Nations or a new, more powerful global organization yet to emerge. She stated:

> The new world religion must be based upon those truths which have stood the test of the ages . . . they are steadily taking shape in human thinking, and for them the United Nations fights.[38]

This political body, Bailey predicted, would be the vehicle for the "new" religious order to achieve its "ancient" spiritual goals.

The new world religion foreseen by occultists throughout the centuries would be built upon the ancient pantheistic ideas of Eastern mysticism—drawing heavily from Buddhism, but containing a certain top-dressing or public appearance of Christianity. This, as we shall see, is the interfaith strategy of Roman Catholicism, which is universal in nature, acting as a bridge between Christianity and pantheism.

Historical Summary

Pantheistic thought had its roots in Satan's first lies to Adam and Eve—that they could be as God and that they would never die. From the moment the first man and woman partook of the forbidden fruit, Satan's deception grew, and sin increased. By the time of Noah, man had become so thoroughly corrupt and intermingled with the demonic realm that God sent the Flood.

After the Flood, it took only a few generations before man had again embraced the occult. This was evidenced by the building of the Tower of Babel, which is believed to have been the first ziggurat, an occult worship tower with a shrine at the top. Throughout the cradle of civilization, the occult mysteries flourished.

All of the ancient mystery religions during the Bible era were pantheistic. Pantheism originated in the city of Babylon in Mesopotamia and from there spread rapidly in all directions to cover the face of the earth. Hinduism is one of the offshoots of the original Babylonian pantheism (via the Aryans of ancient Persia). And Buddhism is an offshoot of Hinduism. All of the Eastern religions of today are ultimately traceable to ancient Babylon, where the post-Flood rebellion against God began.

These occult forces completely surrounded Israel. To the west were the Egyptian Mysteries (also known as the Mysteries of Osiris). To the south were the Arabian Mysteries; the chief god of this pantheon was called Allah. To the east were the Babylonian and Persian Mysteries (respectively known as the Mysteries of Semiramis and the Mithraic Mysteries, or Zoroastrianism). To the north were the

Assyrian and Phoenician Mysteries (including Baal worship) and later on, the Mysteries of Greece and Rome (referred to as the Mysteries of Eleusis, Dionysus, Bacchus, etc.). All of these pantheistic religions—at their base—were the same.

Although God had scattered the people from Babylon during the building of the Tower of Babel, this did not put an end to occultism; it only slowed its progress. As new civilizations arose in Egypt, Persia, India, etc., the occult practices of old were revived. The people had merely taken their beliefs and practices with them.

Although some changes and modifications had taken place in these "new" mysteries to suit the developing cultures of the various language groups, the basic tenets and practices remained the same. All of the ancient mysteries, for example, had a priesthood that ruled the country or empire in association with the appointed priest-king. In order to enter the priesthood, one had to go through a series of secret occult rituals and initiations. When an initiate reached the highest level (or inner circle) of the priesthood, the secret doctrine was revealed. It always included the worship of Lucifer, more frequently referred to in the mysteries as the God of Hades, or the God of the Underworld, and usually symbolized by the serpent or dragon. This should have sent a clear message to the people of the day that their religions were satanically inspired. By the time of Abraham and Lot, the human state had degenerated to the point where God once again intervened. Those were the days of Sodom and Gomorrah, when perversion and immorality reached new heights.

Although Abraham was himself not perfect, he was a man who sought to do right before God. Because he and his family were the only ones left who were willing to acknowledge God, God honored Abraham's faith by choosing to create a nation from his seed. God would work through Abraham and his descendents, the Israelites, to keep His truth and the way of righteousness alive in the midst of a spiritually darkened world. After a few hundred years, when Abraham's seed had sufficiently multiplied, there were enough Israelites to constitute a physical nation. At that time, God led His people out of Egypt through His servant Moses.

The history of Israel would be one of victory and defeat. When the Israelites were obedient to God they prospered, and none of their pantheistic neighbors could stand against them. However, when the Israelites began to fall for the spiritual lies of the surrounding nations, these same powers oppressed them. God sent a steady stream of holy prophets to teach Israel His ways and to warn them of what would happen if they did not obey. Much like the relationship between a loving father and his child, while longing for his child (Israel) to be obedient, there were times when that child was rebellious and needed to be disciplined before something much worse happened.

The Israelites, through Moses, were instructed to bring regular animal offerings or sacrifices before God. These sacrifices symbolized the payment for their sins, reminding them that the result of sin is death. These offerings were also symbolic of the ultimate sacrifice of Jesus Christ, whose death would pay the penalty for the sins of the entire world at the appointed time.

After the proper groundwork had been laid, God sent His Son. The message of forgiveness and the promise of eternal life to those who believe in Christ would be sent forth from Israel to all nations. Although this gospel (the good news) spread in all directions, it was not accepted by all peoples and met with more resistance in some places than in others. Those missionaries who carried the message into Babylon, Persia, and India were violently rejected; only a small number of people believed and received the truth there. The hold of Satan on these countries was so complete that, to this day, only a small percent of the Orient believes in Christ. For example, Hinduism (the oldest surviving pantheistic religion) is still being practiced by a majority of India's inhabitants.

The story would be different in the Mediterranean where the gospel was accepted by large numbers of people in spite of fierce persecution against those who believed in Christ. Within a few generations there were so many Christians in this region that the high priests of the Mysteries of Greece, Rome, and Egypt began to lose their control. The teachings of Christ went head-to-head against the pantheistic beliefs and occult practices of the priests, exposing them for what they were. Finally, the occult priests were forced to go underground in order to keep their secret knowledge and traditions alive.

These occult teachings have been handed down from generation to generation. They were preserved in the Western world by the secret societies of Europe, which were a continuation of the ancient occult priesthoods. Satan's plan was to keep his priesthood and secret doctrines alive until, being sufficient in number and power, the priesthood could once again seize control over his lost territories.

Gnosticism, the most effective and widely accepted form of pantheism, was more deceptive and clever than the others, developing the occult's only major counter-explanation to the person and message of Christ. The Gnostics were the chief adversaries of the Apostle Paul and the early Church, relentlessly pursuing Christians wherever they went, long before the mystery religions began to crumble.

According to Masonic historian Albert Pike, Gnosticism was an offshoot of Kabalism—an oral occult tradition which was adhered to by a minority of the Jews. At some point, which remains uncertain, these occult teachings were reduced to writing, and the Kabalah was born. On page 626 of *Morals and Dogma*—the most esteemed work of Freemasonry—Pike states, "The Kabalah is the key of the occult sciences; and the Gnostics were born of the Kabalists."

Kabalism was merely a unique version of the ancient mysteries specifically designed to deceive God's chosen people. Unlike other mystery religions, its teachings dealt specifically with Israel, offering occult explanations to the revelations of the prophets—complete with a mystical interpretation of Israel's history. Moses, for example, was presented in their teaching as an occult figure whose purpose was to initiate the Israelites into the "enlightened," more advanced teachings of Egypt, rather than the biblical teaching that he was the righteous prophet of God who led the Israelites out of bondage.

If Kabalism could be viewed as the occult counter-explanation of the Old Testament, Gnosticism—existing as a further development of Kabalism and addressing Satan's "new problem" posed by the risen Christ—would serve as the main occult attack against the New Testament. Thus, Kabalism and Gnosticism together, composed a type of occult parallel to the Old and New Testaments.

Gnosticism initially attracted a strong Jewish element. However, it rapidly gained Gentile followers until it soon became a predominantly Gentile movement. Gnosticism gained favor with the ancient priesthoods, becoming a magnet for many occult adepts. Branches of Gnosticism were the first significant secret societies in the centuries following Christ, with various degrees or levels of initiation, and the inner circle of initiates worshipping Satan.

As the followers of Christ increased throughout the Roman Empire, so did the persecution. Believers were relentlessly pursued by various Gnostic sects and the pagan Roman system. In spite of this, and partly because of it, Christianity multiplied and spread.

By the time of Constantine (around 300 AD), Christianity's potential as a political force was recognized. The Roman Empire utilized the integration of Christianity to consolidate its authority. To achieve this consolidation, the pagan Emperor Constantine—in an unprecedented move—lifted the ban against Christianity and placed believers in various offices throughout the empire. Constantine's plan of unification worked, and a politically "Christianized Rome" was born. Without realizing the full implications, Christianity had been wed with a pagan system. Meanwhile, antagonism continued toward true Christians, although to a lesser extent.

From the time of Constantine's conception of a "universal" Church, its ceremonies, beliefs, and practices reflected the strong pantheistic influence of its pagan roots. For example, the concept of monks and monasteries existed for hundreds of years within Buddhism, long before "Roman Christianity" was born. It is interesting to note that the pope's two-pointed headdress, the Mitre, is virtually identical to that worn by ancient Babylonian priests. The veneration of Mary is similar to the goddess worship of the ancient mystery religions (Semiramis in Babylon, Isis in Egypt, Diana in Greece, Cybele in Rome, etc.). And purgatory, while not identical to reincarnation, is a big step in that direction—promoting the idea of being able to work out one's salvation after death.

Even some of the medieval Church's symbols were borrowed from the ancient mystery religions. The all-seeing eye of Lucifer exists in many churches and shrines in Europe—often located above the altar. The ancient obelisk in Saint Peter's Square (Rome) was transported from Egypt, where it was formerly used in fertility worship and represented male sexuality. These examples show how the medieval Church blended the ancient mysteries with certain Christian concepts to form a type of "Christianized" paganism.

In the 1100s and 1200s, a gradual renewal of the true gospel in Europe prompted persecution from the "official" Church. This led to one of the bloodiest periods in known history. For the next few hundred years, the Vatican's pursuit of "heretics" was relentless. The Roman church was able to maintain and enhance its political strength by torturing and executing Christians who opposed them. Truly Christian groups such as the Waldenses and Albigenses, who would not bow to Rome's authority, were hunted down and put to death. This persecution of the saints has been recorded in *Foxes Book of Martyrs* and other historical writings.

This was also the time of the Crusades and medieval religious orders. The Order of the Knights of the Temple—also known as Knights Templars—came into existence in 1118. The Knights Templars, under the blessing and protection of the papacy, grew in stature and power.

As a military order the Knights Templars played a leading role in a series of Crusades aimed at defeating the Muslims and conquering Jerusalem. These Crusades resulted in unspeakable atrocities against Jews, Arabs, and Christians throughout Europe and the Middle East. During the following two centuries, the Knights Templars—

entrusted with great wealth by European nobility—became the world's most influential bankers.

While they were perceived by many as a genuine, devout Christian order, it was later discovered that they were a secret Luciferic society operating under the guise of Christianity. Surprised and outraged, most Europeans felt betrayed. Although Pope Clement V initially protected the order, public opinion modified his position. To avoid further embarrassment the Pope reluctantly agreed to their punishment. After a bitter and prolonged trial overseen by King Philip IV of France, several of the order's top leaders—including Grand Master Jacques de Molay—were sentenced to death for their crimes. Those Templars who escaped punishment went underground and would later resurface under a different name, to carry on their religious agenda.

As a result of the Templar scandal, the disaster of the Crusades, Rome's continued abuse of power and wealth, and the ever-increasing persecution of true Christians—fear, anger, and distrust grew among Europeans. After centuries of bondage to Rome, an increasing number of people began to openly seek religious freedom. In 1517, a Catholic priest who had witnessed the excessive opulence, corruption, and apostasy of the Church, took a stand. In defiance of Rome, Martin Luther nailed his 95-point thesis to the door of the castle church in Wittenburg, publicly denouncing the errors of Catholicism. The Protestant Reformation had begun.

In spite of the severe persecution of Protestant Reformation leaders, the "heretical" movement grew. The "Church's" influence became threatened. To counter the Reformation, the Papacy launched a new round of Inquisitions against all who rejected her authority. A new order called the Society of Jesus was created to attack the powerful new movement as millions began to search the Scriptures for God's truth.

This "secret" order of Catholicism—also known as the Jesuits—was founded in 1534 by Ignatius Loyola, and would become the "eyes and ears" of the Vatican. Its supreme aim would be the destruction of Protestantism which was based on the doctrine of "Sola Scripture" (only Scripture), and declared that the only authority for Christians must be Jesus Christ himself, according to the Bible. To accomplish this feat the Society would work through education, political blackmail, and brute force. From their inception, the Jesuits would be used as the main weapon against uprisings.

The medieval order of the Knights Templars, on the other hand, would re-emerge in 1717 as the order of Freemasonry.* The Masonic Lodge represented the beginning of an occult revival in Western society. Although rooted in Catholicism, Freemasonry was publicly cast as the arch-rival of Rome. This perception would allow the order to penetrate Protestant circles—the ultimate goal being to bring the "lost sheep" back under Vatican authority.

Various organizations were established to accomplish the order's objectives. The most infamous Masonic offshoot of the 18th Century was the Illuminati, founded in 1776 by Adam Weishaupt. Weishaupt, a Bavarian, had been both a high-level Freemason and a Jesuit. His society, like that of the Knights Templars, consisted of initiates who had been "illumined" by the secret teachings of Lucifer—hence the name "Illuminati." Even though the Illuminati would only exist for a decade before being exposed, its impact during that short time was significant. It had infiltrated some of the highest political and financial circles of Europe and the United States. The "brotherhood's" purpose was to create a Luciferic world order. After the Illuminati was exposed, its initiates continued to operate within the Masonic hierarchy.

During the century that followed, a wide variety of occult societies were established. These groups included the Theosophical Society, the Hermetic Order of the Golden Dawn, the Ordo Templi Orientis and a host of other "illuminized" orders and fraternities—all founded by high-level Freemasons. It was largely through these Masonically-inspired organizations that the New Age movement was born.

Since the beginning of this movement in the late 1800s, the one-world agenda has gained steady momentum. Today, both the Jesuits and Freemasons are working through their network to achieve unity under a new religious and political order. The revived Roman empire foretold in Scripture (Daniel 7–8) is taking shape; and the age-old "mystery Babylon" religious conspiracy, master-minded by Satan, is nearing completion (Rev. 17). Thankfully, Satan's reign will last only for a short time. The battle between God and Satan over man's eternal destiny—which began with Adam and Eve—will finally end when Jesus Christ returns.

---

* Most Masons do not realize what their order is all about at its highest levels. This is largely because they have not taken the time to read their own historical and philosophical works. A more detailed history of the Knights Templars, their public demise, and the founding of Freemasonry, is provided in my book *En Route To Global Occupation*.

Conclusion

We are now witnessing the final stages of Satan's lawless endeavor. Having lost his high position in Heaven, this fallen angel has remained determined to enslave humanity and receive its worship. At stake is his ego—and our souls. Who will be Satan's chosen vessel to rule the world? How, and when, will he come to power? And what will happen to those who question his authority?

It is possible that once the new civilization is in place, the earthly instruments used to build it will be supplanted by one more powerful. If so, could the "lawless one" be a satanic entity posing as an extraterrestrial being? Could this be why he is referred to as the "beast" in Revelation?

There are many possible scenarios of how the Antichrist and his hierarchy will come to power. With terrorism on the increase, Middle East tensions mounting, and international financial markets in chaos, it is not difficult to imagine how one or more of these situations could be manipulated to usher in the new world order.

If the world is thought to be on the brink of disaster, humanity could be convinced to embrace a new set of ideals to replace the old. Given the right circumstances, people might be willing to surrender some or all of their freedoms in exchange for a system promising peace and security. Terrorized and fearful of the future, they might be prepared to accept an international government and a new world religion.

Whether the "global civilization" is actually birthed in the year

2000—as many occultists would like—remains to be seen. But if current world trends continue, major changes can be expected in the months and years ahead. Regardless of what takes place, one thing is certain: Nothing will happen until God allows it.

Ultimately God is in control, and He is still working through knowledgeable, obedient Christians to oppose Satan's efforts. Since true Christians will not, and cannot, embrace the pagan teachings presented by the New Age, there can be no "complete" acceptance of the new world religion and it's system of global government as long as Christians are alive and refuse to compromise.

New Agers understand this very well. While they are heralding the prospect of "global peace," the worldwide persecution of Christians is on the increase and will continue to grow as the new occult order approaches. Jesus said,

> A time is coming when anyone who kills you will think he is offering a service to God. They will do such things because they have not known the Father or me. I have told you this, so that when the time comes you will remember that I warned you. (John 16:2b–4a, NIV)

In the days ahead, God's people should expect to pay a price for their loyalty to Christ. Some, as Jesus said, will be put to death. Even now, more than a quarter of a million Christians are martyred annually. But there is hope. Even though Christians may endure difficulties in this world and experience persecution for a time, those who remain faithful will receive a great reward. Being in the Lord's presence forever will far outweigh any of this life's pain.

For those who choose to conform, the new world order will seem attractive—at first. The promise of global peace and prosperity will be most alluring. However, once individuals have embraced this seductive world system, they will be in Satan's grasp. The door to spiritual freedom will close, and there will be no escape. They will have to suffer the consequences of their decision forever.

Urging us to make the right choice, Jesus said:

> Enter through the narrow gate. For wide is the gate and broad is the road that leads to destruction, and many enter through it. But small is the gate and narrow the road that leads to life, and only a few find it. (Matthew 7:13,14, NIV)

God's perfect will is for all to enter through the narrow gate. But the ultimate choice regarding your spiritual destiny remains in your hands. You must decide whether or not you will follow Jesus Christ as your Lord.

God's Incredible Love

God created man sinless. However, He gave us the freedom to make decisions; this included the right to choose between obeying God or following the empty lies and temptations of Lucifer (Satan).

The moment that Adam fell for Satan's deception, his seed became corrupted. As a result, every future human would be born into sin and would wage a life-long struggle between doing what he knows is right (obeying his spiritual conscience) and doing what is wrong (yielding to the sinful nature of his flesh). Contrary to popular belief, sin is not only learned, it is also inherited. Romans 5:12 (NIV) states that "Sin entered the world through one man, and death through sin, and in this way death came to all men, because all sinned." (Also see Rom. 3:23.)

When Satan succeeded in getting man to disobey God, it gave him the right to condemn our souls; this fallen angel became our accuser. According to Scripture, he stands accusing us before God day and night (Rev. 12:10).

By yielding to Satan's temptation and choosing to live a life independent of God's will, man inflicted upon himself the penalty for sin, which is death (Rom. 6:23). Death, according to Scripture, includes permanent separation from God and eternal damnation in Hell.

Man's sin, therefore, presented what appeared to be an insurmountable problem, since only that which is perfect may enter Heaven and live forever with God. This standard of perfection had to be maintained, or Heaven itself would have become corrupt. (This is why Lucifer and his conspiring angels were dealt with accordingly.)

God could have allowed all of us to go to Hell, a punishment we justly deserve. But because of His great love, He chose instead to intervene by paying the penalty for our sins Himself. God came to earth in the flesh, in the body of Jesus Christ, to suffer and die in our place on the cross. "But God demonstrates his own love for us in this: While we were still sinners, Christ died for us" (Rom. 5:8, NIV).

God paid the ultimate price so that we might be set free from the hold of death and have eternal life. This, completely undeserving though we are, is God's gift to us. He did not have to do this but chose to do it anyway.

Such an act of mercy runs completely contrary to the thinking of the human mind. We are not accustomed to receiving something for nothing. It seems unfathomable that God would do something like this for us simply out of mercy or love. That the very Creator of the universe would humble Himself by coming to earth as a man, to be mocked and scorned, and to die a grueling death at the hands of His own creation in order to save them, is incomprehensible. It defies all human logic. It can only be understood as an act of extraordinary, unjustifiable love!

> Who hath delivered us from the power of darkness, and hath translated us into the kingdom of his dear Son: In whom we have redemption through his blood, even the forgiveness of sins. (Col. 1:13–14)

> Once you were alienated from God and were enemies in your minds because of your evil behavior. But now he has reconciled you by Christ's physical body through death to present you holy in his sight, without blemish and free from accusation. (Col. 1:21–22, NIV)

This is the good news of the gospel! There is nothing we can do to earn eternal life, for it cannot be obtained through works or human effort. It is purely a gift from God to us.

> The gift of God is eternal life through Jesus Christ our Lord. (Rom. 6:23b)

> For by grace are ye saved through faith; and that not of yourselves: it is the gift of God: Not of works, lest any man should boast. (Eph. 2:8-9)

The "gift" of salvation is available only through Jesus Christ, because He is the only one who, as a perfect being—God in the flesh—was able to pay the necessary price for our sins. It took a perfect sacrifice to overcome Satan's claim to our souls.

> For there is one God, and one mediator between God and men, the man Christ Jesus; Who gave himself a ransom for all, to be testified in due time. (I Timothy 2:5–6; also read John 3:36 and Acts 4:12)

If Jesus is man's only hope for salvation, and if we are unable to earn this gift through our own efforts, then what must we do to receive it? We must believe that only Jesus paid the penalty for our sins through His shed blood.

> Yet to all who received him, to those who believed in his name, he gave the right to become children of God. (John 1:12, NIV)

It's Your Decision

If you sincerely wish to accept the gift of eternal life through Jesus Christ, simply pray to God in your own words. Confess to Him that you are a sinner and would like to be forgiven. Tell Him that you accept His Son, Jesus Christ, as your Savior, and that you believe His sacrifice on the cross was sufficient to cleanse you of your sins. Thank God for what He has done, and ask Him to help you live a life of obedience that would honor Him. God will hear your prayer if it comes from a sincere heart!

If you have just accepted Jesus as your Savior, you now have eternal life. Satan no longer has a claim to your soul. You are at peace with God and have entered into a permanent relationship with Him. The quality of this relationship, however, is up to you. Please allow God to have "complete" control of your life!

If you are already a Christian, here are some words of advice and encouragement:

Stand firm.

The Apostle Paul, in his letter to the Corinthians, wrote, "Be on guard; stand firm in the faith; be men of courage; be strong. . . . Let nothing move you. Always give yourselves fully to the work of the Lord" (I Corinthians 16:13; 15:58b, NIV).

Paul's exhortations to the church in Corinth still apply to us today. Although it appears that an anti-Christian world government is imminent, we should not help bring it about by "throwing in the towel." We must raise a standard of righteousness while proclaiming the truth of Jesus Christ for the sake of those who will listen. It is because so few people are speaking out to warn others, that the New Age movement is making such progress in these days. As James emphasized, "Faith without works is dead" (James 2:26). There is much work to be done!

- Inform Christian friends about the deceptive teachings of the New Age, as many of the false doctrines of pantheism and the occult are now subtly making their way into some of our churches.
- Be involved in your schools by examining the curricula and working for change where it is needed.
- Share the truth about the current world situation with members of your family, with friends and neighbors. Keep them posted of important developments while living a positive Christian example.
- Pray for the salvation of unsaved loved ones and tactfully share

the message of Christ with them. Your faithful words may affect their eternal destiny.

- Pray for your elected officials. There are still some godly people in government trying to hold back the tide. They need your prayers and encouragement.

It takes both spiritual preparedness and physical action to live effectively for God. Therefore, be consistent in your walk. Spend time with the Lord daily by praying to Him and reading His Word.

Maintain a sense of urgency.

There are two ways to respond to the information contained in this book. One is to panic and become overwhelmed; the other is to allow this information to instill a healthy sense of urgency. This second reaction is God's desire for us. Reflecting on the urgency of life, someone once said, "You should treat every day as if it's your last one, because one of these days you're going to be right." The fact is, we will not be on this earth forever, so we must do what we can with the time that we have.

Stay focused on doing God's will. Millions of people need to be reached with the hope of Jesus Christ. Their souls are at stake—and time may be much shorter than any of us realize.

And do this, understanding the present time. The hour has come for you to wake up from your slumber, because our salvation is nearer now than when we first believed. The night is nearly over; the day is almost here. So let us put aside the deeds of darkness and put on the armor of light. (Romans 13:11–12, NIV)

Don't lose hope.

The Word of God offers us tremendous encouragement and hope. We know that any suffering in this world will be temporary. It will not continue indefinitely. The Apostle Paul assures us of this fact in 2 Thessalonians 2:8, where he describes the glorious return of Jesus, along with the destiny of the satanic world ruler and his kingdom:

And then shall that Wicked be revealed, whom the Lord shall consume with the spirit of his mouth, and shall destroy with the brightness of his coming.

Even if we do face death as a result of physical persecution, we can take comfort in knowing that we have an incredible eternity with God ahead of us. Although Satan can make our lives difficult and may be responsible for persecuting us in this life, he cannot destroy our souls. If we trust Jesus as Savior, our destiny in Heaven has been sealed. No matter what happens to us, in the end, we win!

> In all these things we are more than conquerors through him that loved us. For I am persuaded, that neither death, nor life, nor angels, nor principalities, nor powers, nor things present, nor things to come, Nor height, nor depth, nor any other creature, shall be able to separate us from the love of God, which is in Christ Jesus our Lord. (Romans 8:37-39)

As Christians, therefore, we have great reason for hope. This is not a time for fear. This is a time for faith and determination! We know that God is in control and will have the final say. So let us boldly move forward, living obedient lives and proclaiming the good news of Jesus Christ in whatever time remains!

He which testifieth these things saith,
"Surely I come quickly." Amen.
Even so, come, Lord Jesus.
(Revelation 22:20)

Notes

1. Robert Muller, *New Genesis: Shaping a Global Spirituality* (Anacortes, WA: World Happiness and Cooperation, 1982), front cover, pp. 168, 20.

2. Rev. David C. Kanz, Ingrid Guzman and Steven P. Smith, *An Urgent Report: Celebration 2000 and Jay Gary* (Milwaukee, WI: VCY/America Radio Network, 1995), p. 2.

3. Jay Gary, *Jay Gary Author and Consultant*, personal bio sheet (Colorado Springs, CO: Celebration 2000).

4. *World Goodwill Newsletter* (New York: World Goodwill, no. 3, 1993), p. 7.

5. *New Man* (Lake Mary, FL: Strang Communications, August 1995), p. 85. The official magazine of Promise Keepers.

6. Phil Arms, *Phil Arms Ministries Newsletter* (Alief, TX: Phil Arms Ministries, September 1997), p. 4. Phil Arms Ministries, P.O. Box 770, Alief, TX 77411-0770.

7. Pope John Paul II, *Tertio Millennio Adveniente*, "As the Third Millennium Draws Near," (Web page for the Catholic Information Network, http://www.cin.org/jp2ency/tertmill.html), [Accessed November 30, 1998].

8. Ibid.

9. Ibid.

10. Ibid.

11. H.B. Patriarch Michel Sabbah Latin Patriarch of Jerusalem, "Preparations for the Jubilee Year 2000," (Web page for Franciscan Cyberspot - Towards the Jubilee Year, http://198.62.75.1/www/ofm/jub/JUBpast.html), [Accessed November 30, 1998].

12. George Huntston Williams, *The Mind of John Paul II* (New York: The Seabury Press, 1981), p. xiii.

13. Ibid., p. 352.

14. Nick Bakalar and Richard Balkin, editors, *The Wisdom of John Paul II: The Pope on Life's Most Vital Questions* (New York: HarperCollins Publishers, 1995), pp. 96–97.

15. John Paul II, *Crossing The Threshold of Hope* (New York: Alfred A. Knopf, 1994), p. 153.

16. Ibid., p. 174.

17. Bakalar and Balkin, *The Wisdom of John Paul II*, p. 96.

18. John Paul II, *Crossing The Threshold of Hope*, pp. 169–170.

19. Malachi Martin, *The Keys of This Blood* (New York: Touchstone, 1990), p. 490.

20. Kenneth L. Woodward, "Mary," *Newsweek*, August 25, 1997, pp. 49-55.

21. CNN News Service, "Pope Ends Latin American Tour," (Web page for Christus Rex Information Service, http:// www.christusrex.org/www1/news/es2-11-96.html), [Accessed November 30, 1998].

22. Muller, *New Genesis*, pp. 113–114.

23. Ibid., p. 111.

24. Ibid., p. 110.

25. Ibid., p. 149.

26. Ibid., p. 101.

27. Mikhail Gorbachev at the Vatican, December 1, 1989, as quoted by Malachi Martin, *The Keys of This Blood*, p. 491.

28. Catholic Information Network, "Sister Lucia Interview on Russia and Third Secret," *CINBVM*, October 6, 1997 (Web page for the Catholic Information Network, *CINBVM* Archives, http:// www.cin.org/cinbvm/v1n70.html), [Accessed December 5, 1998].

29. Pope John Paul II, *The Vatican-Soviet Summit* (Web page for the Catholic Information Network, Catholic History FTP Site, File: *Soviet.zip*, http://www.cin.org/ftphist.html), [Accessed December 5, 1998].

30. Mikhail Gorbachev, "Pope played significant role in changing world," *The Denver Post*, March 9, 1992, p. 2A.

31. Martin, *The Keys of This Blood*, pp. 278–279.

32. James Hitchcock, *The Pope and the Jesuits: John Paul II and the New Order in the Society of Jesus* (New York: The National Committee of Catholic Laymen, 1984), pp. 1, 186.

33. "The Ceremony of Induction and Extreme Oath of the Jesuits" is located in the Library of Congress, Washington, D.C., Library of Congress Catalog Card # 66-43354. A nearly identical version of this

oath may be found in the U.S. House Congressional Record, 1913, p. 3216. The oath was originally made public in 1883.

34. Alice A. Bailey, *The Rays and The Initiations* (New York: Lucis Trust, 9th printing, 1993), p. 533.

35. Alice A. Bailey, *The Externalisation of the Hierarchy* (New York: Lucis Trust, 7th printing, 1982), p. 513.

36. Ibid., p. 416.

37. Ibid., p. 401.

38. Ibid., p. 404.

APPENDIX A

The Tibetan's Views on Jews and Christians

(As channeled through Alice A. Bailey)

Alice Bailey and Lucis Trust have had a long history of promoting ideas that run contrary to the historical teachings of Orthodox Christians and Jews. Bailey's devious character is reflected in her pronounced, but cleverly rationalized, anti-Jewish and anti-Christian statements which permeate her writings. Her remarks at times are maliciously hostile.

She justifies the atrocities of the two world wars, including the Holocaust, in all its horror, as necessary developments in preparing the way for the coming New Age. Bailey also attempts to redefine the person of Jesus Christ and His teachings in order to fit her agenda. For example, she tries to explain away the atoning work of Jesus on the cross by teaching that man is divine and doesn't need redemption. What is further distressing is how she refers to Jews and Bible-believing Christians as belonging to the Forces of Darkness. In short, she turns the truth upside down, calling good, evil, and evil, good.

Bailey's false teachings should be obvious to any student who is firmly grounded in the Bible. However, her statements often contain certain grains of truth which add to the subtlety of her message. This is typical of how Satan operates. He masquerades as an angel of light (2 Corinthians 11:14), masterfully weaving his web of deception around traces of truth (twisting the truth). Jesus did not call him the "father of lies" for nothing (John 8:44).

Satan's tactics are evident throughout Bailey's channeled writings. Many of her darkest statements, for example, contain *positive* references to "the Christ"—thereby potentially confusing the reader. We know, however, that these references are not to the person of Jesus Christ. Rather, Bailey considered the title of Christ something that could be earned. According to her doctrine, humans are simply gods in the making who can attain the "Christ-consciousness." This belief is particularly appealing to pantheists.

But, according to Bailey, "the Christ" also has a second, more esoteric meaning, which she reveals on page 558 of *The Externalisation of the Hierarchy*:

> The Tibetan [Djwhal Khul] has asked me [Alice Bailey] to make clear that when he is speaking of the Christ he is referring to His official name as Head of the Hierarchy. The Christ works for all men, irrespective of their faith; He does not belong to the Christian world any more than to the Buddhist, the Mohammedan or any other faith. There is no need for any man to join the Christian Church in order to be affiliated with Christ. The requirements are to love your fellowmen, lead a disciplined life, recognise the divinity in all faiths and all beings, and rule your daily life with Love. A.A.B.

Bailey's use of "the Christ" in this context is simply a disguised reference to who, according to Scripture, would be termed "the Antichrist" (1 John 2:18). It is a further example of how Bailey and the Tibetan have inverted the truth.

Having strongly warned the reader of Alice Bailey's deceitful tactics, I will allow her words—as allegedly received from the Tibetan Master—to speak for themselves.

Jews Are Posed as the Problem

I am considering the world problem, centering around the Jews as a whole. (*The Externalisation of the Hierarchy* [January 1939], p. 74).

The Jew, with his emphasis upon his position as one of the 'chosen people,' has stood symbolically throughout the centuries as the representative of the wandering, incarnating soul, but the Jewish people have never recognised the symbolic mission with which their race was entrusted, and they have taken to themselves the glory and the honour of the Lord's elect. The Jew made this mistake and, as an Oriental race, the Jews have failed to hold before the Orient the divine nature of mankind as a whole, for all are equally divine and all are the Lord's elect. (*The Destiny of the Nations* [1939], pp. 34–35)

It may interest you to know that the Christ has not yet decided what type of physical vehicle He will employ should He take physical form and work definitely upon the physical plane. He waits to see what nation or group of nations do the most work, and the most convincing work, in preparation for His reappearance. He will *not*, however, take a Jewish body as He did before, for the Jews have forfeited that Privilege. The Messiah for Whom they wait will be one of Christ's senior disciples, but it will *not* be, as originally intended, the Christ. Symbolically, the Jews represent (from the point of view of the Hierarchy) that from which all Masters of the Wisdom and Lords of Compassion emerge: materialism, cruelty and a spiritual conservatism, so that today they live in *Old Testament* times and are under the domination of the separative, selfish, lower concrete mind.

But their opportunity will come again, and they may change all this when the fires of suffering at last succeed in purifying them and burning away their ancient crystallisation, thus liberating them to the extent that they can recognise their Messiah, Who will *not*, however, be the world Messiah. The Jews need humility more than any other nation. By humility they may learn something of value. (*The Rays and the Initiations*, 1st ed. [1960], pp.705–706)

There are certain areas of evil in the world today through which these forces of darkness can reach humanity. What they are and where they are I do not intend to say. I would point out, however, that Palestine should no longer be called the Holy Land; its sacred places are only the passing relics of three dead and gone religions. The spirit has gone out of the old faiths and the true spiritual light is transferring itself into a new form which will manifest on earth eventually as the new world religion. . . . Judaism is old, obsolete and separative and has no true message for the spiritually-minded which cannot be better given by the newer faiths . . . the Christian faith also has served its purpose; its Founder seeks to bring a new Gospel and a new message that will enlighten all men everywhere. Therefore, Jerusalem stands for nothing of importance today, except for that which has passed away and should pass away. The "Holy Land" is no longer holy, but is desecrated by selfish interests, and by a basically separative and conquering nation. (*The Rays and the Initiations* [1943–1947], p. 754)

The World Tension Analyzed

The tension in the world today, particularly in the Hierarchy, is such that it will produce another and perhaps ultimate world crisis, or else such a speeding up of the spiritual life of the planet that the coming in of the long-looked-for New Age conditions will be amazingly hastened. . . .

The area of difficulty—as is well known—is the Near East and Palestine. The Jews, by their illegal and terroristic activities, have laid a foundation of great difficulty for those who are seeking to promote world peace . . . the Jews have partially again opened the door to the Forces of Evil . . . Palestine is no longer a Holy Land and should not be so regarded. . . .

It is the Zionists who have defied the United Nations, lowered its prestige and made its position both negative and negligible to the world. It is the Zionists who have perpetrated the major act of aggression since the formation of the United Nations, and who were clever enough to gain the endorsement of the United Nations, turning the original 'recommendation' of the United Nations into an order. The rule of force, of aggression and of territorial conquest by force of arms is demonstrated today by the Zionists in Palestine, as well as the demonstration of the power of money to purchase governments. These activities run counter to all the plans of the spiritual Hierarchy and mark a point of triumph of the forces of evil. (*The Rays and the Initiations* [April 1947], pp. 428–430 and 681)

The Forces of Darkness are powerful energies, working to preserve that which is ancient and material. . . . They work to prevent the understanding of that which is of the New Age; they endeavor to preserve that which is familiar and old, to counteract the effects of the oncoming culture and civilisation, to bring blindness to the peoples and feed steadily the existing fires of hate, of separateness, of criticism and of cruelty. . . .

Our earth humanity and the group of human beings who are far more ancient in their origin than we are, will form one humanity and then there will be peace on earth. . . .

The solution will come . . . when the races regard the Jewish problem as a humanitarian problem. . . . He [the Jew] must let go of his own separative tendencies and of his deep sense of persecution. [Remember, this was written in 1939, during the Nazi Era.] He will do this latter with great facility, when he grasps, as a race, the significance and inevitability of the Law of Karma, and . . . realises that the law is working out and incidentally releasing him for a greater future. (*The Externalisation of the Hierarchy* [January 1939], pp. 75–78)

"The War" Was Deemed Good
(The Death and Destruction Was Necessary)

The great energy of purification [Shamballa forces] is regenerating humanity, and of this the wide spread fires which have been such an outstanding characteristic of this war (1914-1945) are the outward and visible sign. Much evil is being burnt out through the revelation of the appalling character of that evil, and through this, unity is being produced. . . . The energy of destruction has its side of beauty when the spiritual values are grasped. (*The Rays and the Initiations* [April 1943], p. 86, ref. p. 76)

This world crisis, with all its horror and suffering, is—in the last analysis—the result of successful evolutionary processes. . . . Today we are watching the death of a civilisation or cycle of incarnation of humanity. . . . Wornout religious dogmas and the grip of theology and the orthodox churches have no longer sufficed to hold the allegiance of the potent, inner, spiritual life. . . . There is everywhere a cry for change and for those new forms in the religious, political, educational and economic life of the race which will allow . . . better spiritual expression. Such a change is rapidly coming and is regarded by some as death—terrible and to be avoided if possible. It is indeed death but it is beneficent and needed . . .

That humanity is bringing about this needed change in unnecessary, cruel and painful ways is indeed true. . . . Nevertheless, for the progress of the soul . . . death is inevitable, good and necessary. . . . But we need to remember that the worst death of all . . . would be if a form of civilisation or a body form became static and eternal; if the old order never altered and the old values were never transmuted into higher and better ones, that would indeed be a disaster . . .

This stage of death and of birth . . . can be easily grasped by the esotericist as he studies the world war in its two distinctive periods: 1914 to 1918, and 1939 until 1942. The first stage . . . was most definitely the death stage; the second stage, in which we now find ourselves, is literally the stage of birth—the birth pangs of the new order and of the new civilisation . . .

Such a dying is ever a painful process. Pain has always been the purifying agent, employed by the Lords of Destiny, to bring about liberation. The accumulated pain of the present war and the inherited pain of the earlier stage (begun in 1914) is bringing about a salutary and changing world consciousness. The Lord of Pain has descended from His throne and is treading the ways of earth today, bringing distress, agony and terror to those who cannot interpret His ends. (*The Externalisation of the Hierarchy* [September 1939], pp. 113–116)

Others again may have faint glimmerings of this new approach to God and service, which—again I say—can and must remake, rebuild, and rehabilitate the world. . . . Those who seek to evoke the Shamballa force, are approaching close to the energy of fire. . . . Fire was an outstanding aspect of the war. . . . This was the great menacing and chosen means of destruction in this war. This is a fulfillment of the ancient prophecy, that the attempt to destroy the Aryan race will be by means of fire, just as ancient Atlantis was destroyed by water. But, fiery good will and the conscious focused use of the Shamballa force, can counter fire by fire, and this must be done. (*Esoteric Astrology*, 1st ed. [1951], pp. 586–587)

To many of you . . . the World War was a supreme disaster, an agony to be averted in the future at any cost, a dire and dreadful happening indicative of the wickedness of man and the incredible blind indifference of God. To us, on the inner side, the World War was in the nature of a major surgical operation made in an effort to save the patient's life. A violent streptococcic germ and infection had menaced the life of humanity (speaking in symbols) and an operation was made in order to prolong opportunity and save life, *not* to save the form. This operation was largely successful. The germ, to be sure, is not eradicated and makes its presence felt in infected areas in the body of humanity.

Another surgical operation may be necessary, not in order to destroy and end the present civilisation, but in order to dissipate the infection and get rid of the fever. It may not, however, be needed, for a process of dissipation, distribution and absorption has been going on and may prove effective. Let us work towards that end. But at the same time, let us never forget that it is the *Life*, its purpose and its directed intentional destiny that is of importance; and also that when a form proves inadequate, or too diseased, or too crippled for the expression of that purpose, it is—from the point of view of the Hierarchy—no disaster when that form has to go. Death is not a disaster to be feared; the work of the Destroyer is not really cruel or undesirable. (*Education in the New Age*, 1st ed. [1954], pp. 111–112)

The Planned Destruction of Western Civilization (Judeo-Christian Culture)

The Hierarchy is deeply concerned over world events. . . . The New Age is upon us and we are witnessing the birth pangs of the new culture and the new civilisation. This is now in progress. That which is old and undesirable must go and of these undesirable things, hatred and the spirit of separation must be the first to go. (*The Externalisation of the Hierarchy* [28 September 1938], pp. 61–62)

The Hierarchy is struggling hard with the so-called "forces of evil," and the New Group of World Servers is the instrument. . . . The forces of evil are . . . the entrenched ancient ideals . . . which must now disappear if the New Age is to be ushered in as desired. The old established rhythms, inherent in the old forms of religion, of politics and of the social order, must give place to newer ideals, to the synthetic understanding, and to the new order. The laws and modes of procedure which are characteristic of the New Age must supersede the old, and these will, in time, institute the new social order and the more inclusive regime. (*Esoteric Psychology II*, 1st ed. [1942] pp. 630–631)

They [France, Germany, Italy, Spain and Portugal] have . . . reacted to that force [Shamballa Force] through the medium of certain great and outstanding personalities who were peculiarly sensitive to the will-to-power and the will-to-change and who . . . have altered the character of their national life, and emphasised increasingly the wider human values. The men who inspired the initiating French revolution; the great conqueror, Napoleon; Bismarck, the creator of a nation; Mussolini, the regenerator of his people; Hitler, who lifted a distressed people upon his shoulders; Lenin, the idealist; Stalin and Franco are all expressions of the Shamballa force and of certain little understood energies. These have wrought significant changes in their day and generation . . .

We call these people dictators, demagogues, inspired leaders, or just and wise men, according to our peculiar ideology, tradition, attitudes to our fellowmen and our particular political, economic and religious training. But all these leaders are . . . in the last analysis, highly developed personalities. They are being used to engineer great and needed changes and to alter the face of civilisation . . .

Blame not the personalities involved or the men who produce these events before which we stand today bewildered and appalled. They are only the product of the past and the victims of the present. At the same time, they are the agents of destiny, the creators of the new order and the initiators of the new civilisation; they are the destroyers of what must be destroyed before humanity can go forward along the Lighted Way. (*The Externalisation of the Hierarchy* [1939], pp. 133–135)

I write for the generation which will come . . . at the end of this century; they will inaugurate the framework, structure and fabric of the New Age . . . which will develop the civilisation of the Aquarian Age. This coming age will be as predominantly the age of group interplay, group idealism and group consciousness as the Piscean Age has been one of personality unfoldment . . . for the will of the individual will voluntarily be blended into group will. (*The Rays and the Initiations* [1943–1947], p. 109)

It will be for humanity then to precipitate and stabilise the appearing good, and this they will learn to do through the utilisation of the third Shamballa energy—the energy of organisation. The new world will be built upon the ruins of the old. The new structure will rise. (*The Rays and the Initiations* [1943–1947], p. 88)

Christianity to Be Conquered or Redefined

I refer to that period which will surely come in which an *Enlightened People* will rule; these people will not tolerate authoritarianism in any church . . . they will not accept or permit the rule of any body of men who undertake to tell them what they must believe in order to be saved. . . . (*The Reappearance of the Christ* 1st ed. [1948], pp. 164–165)

World unity will be a fact when the children of the world are taught that religious differences are largely a matter of birth; that if a man is born in Italy, the probability is that he will be a Roman Catholic; if he is born a Jew, he will follow the Jewish teaching; if born in Asia, he may be a Mohammedan, a Buddhist, or belong to one of the Hindu sects; if born in other countries, he may be a Protestant and so on. He will learn that the religious differences are largely the result of man made quarrels over human interpretations of truth. Thus gradually, our quarrels and differences will be offset and the idea of the One Humanity will take their place. (*Education in the New Age* 1st ed. [1954], p. 88)

Recognition of the successful work of the New Group of World Servers will be accorded by the Hierarchy, and the testimony of the recognition will be the appearing of a symbol in the aura of . . . the entire group. This will be a symbol projected by the Hierarchy, specifically by the Christ. . . . It is "the mark of a Saviour" and it will embody the mark or indication (the signature as medieval occultists used to call it) of a new type of salvation or salvage. Up till now the mark of the Saviour has been the Cross, and the quality of the salvation offered has been freedom from substance or the lure of matter and from its hold—a freedom only to be achieved at a great cost. The future holds within its silence other modes of saving humanity. The cup of sorrow and the agony of the Cross are well-nigh finished. Joy and strength will take their place. Instead of sorrow we shall have a joy which will work out in happiness and lead eventually to bliss. (*The Rays and the Initiations*, 1st ed. [1957], pp. 233–234)

There is, as you well know, no angry God, no hell, and no vicarious atonement . . . and the only hell is the earth itself, where we learn to work out our own salvation. . . . This teaching anent hell is a remainder of the sadistic turn which was given to the thinking of the Christian Church in the

Middle Ages and to the erroneous teaching to be found in the Old Testament anent Jehovah, the tribal God of the Jews. Jehovah is *not* God. . . . As these erroneous ideas die out, the concept of hell will fade from man's recollection and its place will be taken by an understanding of the law which makes each man work out his own salvation . . . which leads him to right the wrongs which he may have perpetrated in his lives on Earth, and which enables him eventually to "clean his own slate." (*Esoteric Healing*, 1st ed. [1953], p. 393)

The failure of Christianity can be traced to its Jewish background (emphasised by St. Paul), which made it full of propaganda instead of loving action, which taught the blood sacrifice instead of loving service, and which emphasised the existence of a wrathful God, needing to be placated by death, and which embodied the threats of the Old Testament Jehovah in the Christian teaching of hell fire.

This situation is one which the Christ is seeking to alter; it has been in preparation for His instituting a new and more correct presentation of divine truth that I have sought—with love and understanding—to point out the faults of the world religions, with their obsolete theologies and their lack of love, and to indicate the evils of Judaism. The present world faiths must return to their early simplicity, and orthodox Judaism, with its deep-seated hate, must slowly disappear; all must be changed in preparation for the revelation which Christ will bring. (*The Externalisation of the Hierarchy*, 1st ed. [1957], pp. 542–543)

It can be expected that the orthodox Christian will at first reject the theories about the Christ which occultism presents; at the same time, this same orthodox Christian will find it increasingly difficult to induce the intelligent masses of people to accept the impossible Deity and the feeble Christ which historical Christianity has endorsed. A Christ Who is present and living, Who is known to those who follow Him, Who is a strong and able executive and not a sweet and sentimental sufferer, Who has never left us but Who has worked for two thousand years through the medium of His disciples, the inspired men and women of all faiths. . . . Who has no use for fanaticism or hysterical devotion but Who loves all men persistently, intelligently and optimistically, Who sees divinity in them all and Who comprehends the techniques of the evolutionary development of the human consciousness . . . these ideas the intelligent public can and will accept. (*The Externalisation of the Hierarchy*, 1st ed. [1957], pp. 589–590)

APPENDIX B

Clinton, Rockefeller and UFOs

Americans were surprised a few years ago to discover that President Clinton supports the theory of life on Mars. His position on this subject was made known in August 1996, during a press conference. At the same conference Clinton revealed that the United States was launching an unmanned space craft, scheduled to land on Mars on July 4th, 1997—"Independence Day!"

While many people saw the "life on Mars" announcement on television, few Americans were aware of the fact that it came after the president's meeting with Laurance Rockefeller in Jackson Hole, Wyoming—the site of the Rockefeller family ranch. Laurance, now in his eighties (and the only living brother of David) had been urging Bill Clinton to acknowledge the reality of UFOs for some time. These details surfaced in an article printed in "UFO Magazine," published by Quest Publications in the United Kingdom.

The article, entitled "Rockefeller-Financed UFO Report Sent to World Leaders," revealed that Mr. Rockefeller financed the creation of a special 169 page document on UFOs which he distributed to a very select audience; namely, heads of state and other key world figures. According to the article, "only 1,000 copies of the special briefing were printed, and it will not be offered for sale." The magazine described Laurance Rockefeller as an "environmental activist and venture capitalist" who "is also interested in the whole area of spiritually." It pointed out that he majored in philosophy at Princeton.[1]

The influence Rockefeller wields over Bill Clinton must be substantial, since the President risked public ridicule by making his announcement. Then again, if over 70 percent of Americans believe in life on other planets, as polls suggest, perhaps the timing of his announcement wasn't so risky after all. His statements—undoubtedly calculated—came shortly after the release of the blockbuster feature film *Independence Day*, which focuses on the world's response to an "extraterrestrial visitation."

Interestingly, on August 22, 1996, CNN Headline News revealed how humanity would "officially respond" to alien beings, should they decide to visit earth. According to this CNN segment, which came only days after Clinton's announcement, world leaders would follow a three step procedure: **First**, there would be an international consultation among world leaders—no nation would be permitted to respond unilaterally. **Second**, a united global response would be given. **Third**, this response to extraterrestrials would occur *only* through the United Nations.

I sat stunned in front of my television as I learned of these details. I was even more astonished when the same CNN segment revealed that world leaders had reached this consensual agreement for a unified response more than two decades ago.

Since President Clinton made his statements, a variety of new prime time programs dealing with aliens and the paranormal have been launched on network television, the most popular of these being *Strange Universe* and *X-Files*. Is humanity being "set-up"? Are we being conditioned to accept a powerful delusion? The Bible warns of a huge deception that would be thrust upon humanity in the last days. Paul prophesied, "They perish because they refused to love the truth and so be saved. For this reason God sends them a powerful delusion so that all will be condemned who have not believed the truth but have delighted in wickedness" (2 Thess. 2:11–12, NIV).

Could it be that a staged visitation by "threatening" extraterrestrials will be used to unite mankind (under a world government) against a common enemy? Or, could it be that humanity will be commanded to unite under a global system by these alleged beings, who—claiming to be more "highly evolved" than we are—must know what is best for us and are merely intervening to prevent mankind from destroying himself? Either scenario could work given the gullibility of a godless humanity. Or, what if these beings are real? If so, they would be nothing more than manifested demons (beasts).

God could permit such beings to materialize for a period of time because of man's wickedness and rampant involvement in the occult.

Sound far-fetched? According to Genesis chapter six, it happened during the time of Noah. God sent the Flood in response to man's out-of-control practices, demonstrated and climaxed by man's direct interaction with manifested demonic beings. In Matthew 24:37 (NIV) Jesus warned, "As it was in the days of Noah, so it will be at the coming of the Son of Man." Could Jesus' words, among other things, have referred to a global manifestation of demons, taking place immediately prior to His return to earth to destroy this occult world order? (2 Thessalonians 2:1–12) Only time will reveal how the remainder of human history will unfold. But no matter what happens on this earth we can take comfort in knowing that our eternity is secure through Jesus Christ—if we believe on Him!

Note

1. "UFO Briefing Document Shows Best Available Evidence: Rockefeller-Financed UFO Report Sent To World Leaders," *UFO Magazine* (Otley near Leeds, UK: Quest Publications, July/August 1996, Special Edition), pp. 35–38. With a readership of almost one million, *UFO Magazine* is one of the largest publications on UFO phenomena in the world.

APPENDIX C

Nostradamus: The Man, The Mystic

– Facts In Brief –

Personal data:
- Born: December 13, 1503
- Location: St. Remy, France
- Died: July 2, 1566
- Full name: Michel de Notredame

Appearance/Disposition:
- slightly under medium height
- robust, yet nimble and vigorous
- a large and open forehead
- a straight, even nose
- pleasant grey eyes which "blazed when he was angry"
- a long, thick beard
- cheeks were always red
- talked little
- had an inquiring mind
- possessed a remarkable memory and spent much time in thought
- only slept four or five hours a night
- his joking was joyous, yet biting[1]

Early theological background:

– His family had converted to Catholicism from Judaism before his birth. His two grandfathers, both of whom were physicians in royal households, were also Kabalistic scholars and keepers of "forbidden" ancient magic rituals. The young Nostradamus was heavily influenced by these two men.[2]

– Along with passing down Kabalism, they taught the young Nostradamus "astrology and herbal folk medicine." Bernie Ward, author of *Nostradamus: the man who saw tomorrow*, reveals,

> Both men were clairvoyant themselves, a gift that Nostradamus obviously inherited and that the grandfathers secretly encouraged. Nostradamus learned as a child that he was descended from a long line of clairvoyants and that prophecy was his destiny.[3]

Schooling:

– Nostradamus studied at Avignon, which contained a vast library of books on astrology and the occult. According to Ward, "Much of what he later predicted came from his natural clairvoyance reinforced by his deep knowledge of astrology."[4]

– He also studied and received a medical degree at Montpellier.[5]

As physician:

– Nostradamus, following family tradition, became a physician around the time of the Black Plague. Using herbal remedies and common sense treatments such as clean water and bedding, Nostradamus was influential in saving many lives.[6]

– He was appointed "physician in ordinary" at the French court by Charles IX. This occurred after his psychic reputation had gained attention throughout Europe.[7]

Pre-eminent historical issues of Nostradamus' day:

– There was an on-going Islamic threat. During his time Islamic Turks were a powerful adversary, pushing themselves into the European front. The Turks, meanwhile, were dealing with attacks from Persia on the eastern front.

– Conflicts were also taking place between the various political factions in Europe; the most dramatic being the duel between "the French and the colossal Habsburg empire, which seemed about to add even England to the rest, or to break up completely."

– The Roman Catholic Church was under "doctrinal attack" by the Calvinists and other Anabaptist movements, as well as the Luther-

ans. It fought these "heretics" through imposed Inquisitions. Their bloody outcomes added to the deep tensions of the day.
– European migrations into the Western Hemisphere and, to some extent, into the East had begun.[8]

A famous "second sight" story:

– While on the road, Nostradamus met a group of lowly friars. Nostradamus dropped to his knees and kissed the robe of one of the friars. When asked why he was doing this, he replied, "I must bend a knee before his Holiness." It was forty years later—and nineteen years after the seer's death—that this lowly friar became Pope Sixtus V.[9]
– The 19th century Nostradamus commentator, Torne-Chavigny, made the following interesting observation:

> He [Nostradamus] approved of the ceremonies of the Roman Church and held to the Catholic faith and religion, outside of which, he was convinced, there was no salvation . . .[10]

Quatrains:

– Nostradamus wrote his prophecies in rhyming four-line verses called quatrains. He called these collected quatrains *The Centuries*. He wrote a total of ten Centuries, each of them being composed of one hundred quatrains.[11]

As a seer:

– In 1550 he started using his psychic powers in a more public way. He published the first of many annual almanacs which included prophecies for the coming year.[12]
– Nostradamus described his fortune-telling methods as follows:

> Sitting alone at night in secret study, (a brass bowl) rests solitary on the brass tripod. A slight flame comes out of the emptiness, making success that which would have been in vain.

> The wand in the hand is placed in the middle of the legs of the tripod. He sprinkles with water both the hem of the garment and its (his) foot. Fear, a voice runs trembling through the sleeves (of his robe). Divine splendor; the God sits nearby.[13]

– More than likely Nostradamus learned of this technique—staring into a brass bowl and receiving predictions—from the ancient occult writings of Jamblichus, who authored a classical work on old magic. Nostradamus' opening two quatrains are almost an exact replica of the pages of Jamblichus.[14]

– His first two quatrains, from *Century 1*, are as follows:

1. Being seated by night in secret study,
   Alone resting on the brass stool:
   A slight flame coming from the solitude,
   That which is not believed in vain is made to succeed.

2. With rod in hand set in the midst of Branchus,
   With the water he wets both limb and foot:
   Fearful, voice trembling through his sleeves:
   Divine splendor. The divine seats himself near by.[15]

Magic:

– Nostradamus was widely suspected of witchcraft.[16] Researcher, Edgar Leoni, states, "He vigorously denounces magic, undoubtedly with his cheek barely able to contain his tongue . . . he was obviously hip-deep in magic."[17]

– Nostradamus constantly used astrology to confirm his predictions; as he noted to his son, Caesar Nostradamus, in the preface to *The Centuries*.[18]

– It is obvious that Nostradamus was heavily involved in occultism— including ritual magic and astrology. He indirectly admitted this fact in the following message to his son:

> Although this occult Philosophy was not condemned, I did not desire that you should ever be faced with their unbridled promptings. I had at my disposal many volumes which had been hidden for a great many centuries. But dreading what use might be made of them, after reading them I consigned them to the flames. As the fire came to devour them, the flame licking the air shot forth an unusual brightness, clearer than natural fire. It was like the light of lightning thunder, suddenly illuminating the house, as if in sudden conflagration.[19]

Places mentioned in his prophetic quatrains:

– "Most of the quatrains which mention place names mention French names."

– "Nostradamus is first, and above all, the Oracle of France."

– After France, Italy is mentioned more than any other country.

– He mentions "the Empire" often.

> A 16th-century writer, prophet or otherwise, who mentions "the Empire" could only mean the Holy Roman Empire. . . .

Of Russia, the Middle and Far East and the Americas there is next to nothing.[20]

Accuracy and theme of predictions:

– In *Nostradamus and His Prophecies*, Leoni points out:

> Although there are indeed some quatrains that are very vague, very general or even meaningless, an overwhelming proportion of them do predict a certain combination of historical events. But alas, not many of the events seem to have occurred since 1555, or are likely to occur any more now.
>
> . . . It seems that in the huge mass of predictions that can be found in the prose outline, there is not a single successful prophecy. The dating of the calamities serves to discredit him completely in this work. On the other hand, in the verse quatrains, where he rarely binds himself with any temporal bonds, there occur some successful predictions which, if lucky guesses, are very lucky indeed. This is not to deny that the quatrains also contain some quite clear predictions that were never realized and are never likely to be.[21]

– The following is an example of a Nostradamus prose prediction that did not come to pass. It is found in his preface to *The Centuries*, as written to his son, Caesar Nostradamus.

> From this moment, before 177 years, 3 months and 11 days have passed, by pestilence, long famine, wars and, most of all, by floods, the world will be so diminished, with so few remaining, that no one will be found willing to work the fields, which will remain wild for as long a period as they had been tilled.[22]

Who sought his "predictions"?

– As a psychic he gained the attention of French Queen Catherine de Medicis, who viewed Nostradamus favorably. His "powers" were known throughout Europe, drawing the attention of other notables, such as Charles IX.[23] Bernie Ward relates, "Despite the threat of the Inquisition, Nostradamus' fame grew. People, especially the nobility, demanded his uncannily accurate horoscopes and advice."[24]

Who seeks his predictions now?

– Ward acknowledges, "Today, there is an almost universal curiosity over what Nostradamus actually foresaw about the world we live in."[25]

– The fact is, many occult historians, through outright "prophetic" fabrications and stretched interpretations, have made Nostradamus appear much more accurate than he really was. In spite of recent exposés discrediting the accuracy of many of "the prophet's" predictions, the public seemingly can't get enough of Nostradamus. His writings are sold at major bookstores around the world. Publications on the man and his predictions can be found on supermarket shelves. Television personalities quote him. Documentaries, movies, books, magazines, and the internet all have contributed, to some extent, to the tremendous upsurge in his popularity. Nostradamus, unfortunately, is becoming a household name.

Notes

1. Edgar Leoni, *Nostradamus and His Prophecies* (New York: Wings Books, 1982), p. 38.

2. Bernie Ward, *Nostradamus: the man who saw tomorrow* (New York: Globe Digest/Globe Communications, 1997), p. 14.

3. Ward, *Nostradamus*, p.15.

4. Ibid., p. 15.

5. Alfred Lawrence Hall-Quest, *Collier's Encyclopedia*, vol.17 (New York: Macmillian Education Company, 1985), p. 680.

6. Ward, *Nostradamus*, p.15.

7. Hall-Quest, *Collier's Encyclopedia*, p. 680.

8. Leoni, *Nostradamus and His Prophecies*, p. 552.

9. Ward, *Nostradamus*, p. 16.

10. Leoni, *Nostradamus and His Prophecies*, p. 38.

11. Ward, *Nostradamus*, p.17.

12. Ibid. p.16.

13. Ibid., pp. 16-17.

14. Leoni, *Nostradamus and His Prophecies*, p. 107.

15. Ibid., p. 133.

16. Ward, *Nostradamus*, p. 17.

17. Leoni, *Nostradamus and His Prophecies*, p. 107.

18. Ibid., p. 125.

19. Ibid., pp. 125–127.

20. Ibid., p. 109.

21. Ibid., p. 110.

22. Ibid., p. 129.

23. Hall-Quest, *Collier's Encyclopedia*, vol. 17, p.680.

24. Ward, *Nostradamus*, p. 17.

25. Ibid., p. 20.

APPENDIX D

Shirley MacLaine: A Cayce Connection

On January 18-19, 1987, the ABC television network aired *Out On A Limb*, a mini-series which chronicled Shirley MacLaine's personal spiritual adventure. During this five-hour odyssey, the viewing audience was introduced to concepts of reincarnation, trans-channeling, legends of Atlantis, extraterrestrials, yoga, and astral projection (out-of-body experiences). Through this one endeavor, millions of people in search of spiritual reality were given a counterfeit answer. The only prerequisite for accepting MacLaine's metaphysical theology was to reject the reality of Satan, sin, and a personal God to whom we are accountable. To a me-oriented, "if it feels good, do it" generation, this proposition was like frosting on the cake.

Shirley didn't stop with her television special. She planned to help thousands more to "get in touch with their Higher Self" through a series of highly publicized seminars scheduled for every major city in the country, beginning with Virginia Beach. Why Virginia Beach? Because it is the home of the Association for Research and Enlightenment (A.R.E.), the institution dedicated to preserving Edgar Cayce's "readings."

Cayce's organization was instrumental in Shirley's quest to find "her true self." She, like thousands of other seekers, was led into the world of the occult through the books promoted by A.R.E. In the organization's January 1987 newsletter she reflected, "As I read about Edgar Cayce and his 'psychic readings,' I found myself fascinated with the idea that they might be true and certainly a good set of life values for consideration."

Titles included in A.R.E's 1987 Annual Bookstore Edition were: *Numerology and the Divine Triangle, Pyramid Power, Cosmic Crystals: Crystal Consciousness and the New Age, A Vision of the Aquarian Age, Gods in the Making,* and *The Goddesses in Every Woman.* They also featured books by Carl Jung, John Randolph Price, and Shirley MacLaine. So it was only natural that Shirley wanted to honor Cayce and his organization by launching her New Age proselytizing tour at the home of this famous occult seer.

APPENDIX E

The Quartus Foundation

Exhibit 1-A provides an overview of the Price's foundation, while exhibits 1-B and 1-C display the front pages of two of their newsletters—*The Quartus Report*, edited by John, and *The Quartus InBetweener*, which is overseen by Jan. These exhibits shed further light on the Price's beliefs and reveal how they blend Christian terminology with occult philosophy.

 The Quartus Foundation, Inc.

P.O. Box 1768 · Boerne, Texas 78006-6768 · (830) 249-3985 · Fax (830) 249-3318

ABOUT QUARTUS

The Quartus Foundation was established in 1981 by John and Jan Price, and incorporated tax exempt in 1983.

The word "Quartus" denotes the four-square aspect of each individual: spiritual, mental, emotional, and physical. The foundation is a research and communications organization with the stated purpose of probing the mysteries of Age-less Wisdom and integrating those interminable truths with spiritual metaphysics. By combining the dynamics of mind with the unlimited potential of universal laws, the ancient principle of *energy follows thought* is confirmed. With this understanding as a key, a door opens to a new philosophy of life that is both practical and rewarding.

Quartus publishes the bimonthly *Quartus Report*, written by the Prices and supplemented by articles from contributors.

As a subscriber-member you will receive much helpful information to enable you to realize your own unlimited potential and make dramatic changes in your life.

Quartus also publishes Jan Price's *InBetweener*--a newsy letter with words of wisdom and updates of special happenings. It is sent to members on those months between the *Quartus Report*.

Other subscriber benefits include the powerful *Quartus Prayer Network* where members' challenges are lifted into the Light of Reality where they can be dissolved quickly and in peace, advance notice of the annual *Quartus Mystery School* and other workshops conducted by John and Jan, and the opportunity to come together on December 31st of each year for *The World Healing Day Event*-- the global mind-link that the Prices originated in 1986.

Exhibit 1-A

286

Quartus Report©

September-October 1997, Vol. XVI

The *Quartus Report* is a publication of The Quartus Foundation Inc.
P. O. Box 1768 Boerne, Texas 78006-6768 U.S.A. (210) 249-3985

FAX No. 830-249-3318

CONTENTS

The Path of Light

by John Price

It's time to dispel the darkness, to come out from under the shadow of false beliefs that have imprisoned humanity for aeons. With this thought in mind, I have attempted to write what I consider Truth from my perspective, my understanding. In periods of meditation I have reached deeply into that Core Reality that we share as the one Universal Spirit. Whenever there was a missing piece in the cosmic puzzle, I have opened an imaginary book called forth from mind and read from the pages. For historical references I went to the ancient, sacred books of the Egyptians, Assyrians, Hebrews, Hindus, Chinese, and Greeks. Hopefully the message provides sufficient continuity to show us not only the reason for the darkness, but also the path of light for our escape. Let us begin.

The Genesis Conception

In the beginning, of which there was not, the Eternal IS in Self-absorbed contemplation beheld Itself as All, not an image, but as infinite absolute Reality.

This Self-Knowing of Creative Being as *I*, the Genesis

Exhibit 1-B

The **Q**uartus InBetweener©

Summertime 1997

"Above all, clothe yourselves with love, which binds everything together in perfect harmony."--Colossians 3:14

Have a Love Affair With Yourself

Have you told you lately that you love you? Have you thought about how wonderful you are? Do you know that within your very being is the creative power of the universe? You are constantly creating your experience by your belief in who and what you are. That which you believe about yourself is what you express and it radiates out to all you encounter. You experience just exactly what you believe you deserve. So what are you experiencing? Is that what you really believe you deserve?

I'd like to introduce you to yourself. You are the image of God. Infinite love, power, wisdom and life--all that we know God to be--created you in Its image and likeness. All that God is, you are. All that you are is God. This pulsating, powerful, universal creative energy chose to express Itself into form for the complete joy and fulfillment of Itself. It loves Itself and It calls Its creation good!

Universal creative energy is unlimited and cannot be confined to one shape, but for our purposes let's imagine a great round ball of vibrating energy, and let's say it's God. This ball of energy projects itself in various places, pressing outward. These outpressings, or expressions, are all a part of the whole mass, but each one is different, unique, individual. That's what you are: God individualized--not separate, still the allness, but pressed out as a distinct being of consciousness. You are the self-expression of infinite Being, and infinite Being is where Its self-expression is.

We're all projections of the invisible presence into visibility. Each projection has its own individuality to express, but each is still part of the whole. So we are one with God, and if we are one with God, we can't love God without loving ourselves. And if we are one with God, we have to be one with our neighbor, so our neighbor is ourself. You can't love anyone until you love yourself.

Court yourself as you would one for whom you feel great love. Tell yourself nice things, like "I'm a fantastic, loveable person. I'm perfect in every way and I deserve the best of everything. Nothing is too good for me to have, or be, or experience.

I AM is the name of God. When I speak the words I AM, I do not take the name of God in vain. I look within to my Higher Self and I see such beauty and sweetness--and I realize what a wondrous being I am. God is the creative energy of all that is. God is the life of my soul, my body, my complete ex-

Exhibit 1-C

APPENDIX F

Quotes on the Global Environmental Movement

Intentional Manipulation

In searching for a new enemy to unite us, we came up with the idea that pollution, the threat of global warming, water shortages, famine and the like would fit the bill. . . . All these dangers are caused by human intervention and it is only through changed attitudes and behaviour that they can be overcome. The real enemy, then, is humanity itself.[1]

—Alexander King/Bertrand Schneider (founder/secretary-general of the Club of Rome), *The First Global Revolution.*

During any "issue-attention-cycle" in environmental campaigning, there is a phase in which the issue needs to be strategically exaggerated in order to establish it firmly on an agenda for action.[2]

—Robin Mearns (co-director of the Environment Group and Fellow of the U.K. based Institute of Development Studies), "Environmental Entitlements: Towards Empowerment for Sustainable Development."

Fifty years is ample time in which to change a world and its people almost beyond recognition. All that is required for the

task are a sound knowledge of social engineering, a clear
sight of the intended goal—and power.[3]
 —Arthur C. Clarke (world-renowned scientist, author,
futurist), *Childhood's End.*

Education has been advanced as significant in bringing about
changes in attitudes, behaviour, beliefs and values. . . . In
order to redirect behaviour and values towards institutional
change for sustainable development there is a need to investi-
gate strategic options in relations to educational philosophies, scope for propagation and adoption, and groups most
likely to be susceptible to change.[4]
 —Naresh Singh/Vangile Titi (program director at the
International Institute for Sustainable Development/
research officer at the International Institute for Sustainable Development), editors, *Empowerment For Sustainable
Development: Toward Operational Strategies.*

Children have to take an active role in shaping their own
destiny. . . . One way is to influence their parents. Schools are
having an enormous impact on children, making them more
aware of environmental issues than many of their parents.
Those parents are important people—lawyers, labourers,
doctors, homemakers, politicians—that is, the people who
make up all of society. These environmentally concerned
children then must affect the most important adults in
society. . .[5]
 —David Suzuki (famous Canadian ecologist), *Time To
Change.*

A world society cannot be haphazard. Since there are no
precedents, it cannot be traditional at this stage of development. It can only be deliberative and experimental, planned
and built up with particular objectives and with the aid of all
available knowledge concerning the principles of social
organization. Social engineering is a new science.[6]
 —Scott Nearing (outspoken socialist and advocate of
world government, author), *United World.*

A Religious Motivation

What we do about ecology depends on our ideas of the man-
nature relationship. More science and more technology are
not going to get us out of the present ecological crisis until we
find a new religion, or rethink our old one.

. . . as we now recognize, somewhat over a century ago science and technology . . . joined to give mankind powers which . . . are out of control. If so, Christianity bears a huge burden of guilt. . . . Our science and technology have grown out of Christian attitudes toward man's relation to nature . . .

No new set of basic values has been accepted in our society to displace those of Christianity. Hence we shall continue to have a worsening ecological crisis until we reject the Christian axiom that nature has no reason for existence save to serve man.

By destroying pagan animism, Christianity made it possible to exploit nature in a mood of indifference to the feelings of natural objects. . . . The spirits in natural objects, which formerly had protected nature from man, evaporated.[7]
    —Lynn White, Jr. (Professor of History at the University of California) "The Historical Roots of Our Ecologic Crisis."

What was it that enabled Eskimo shamen, their minds a product of the taiga, tundra, and sea ice, to travel on spirit journeys under the ocean and to talk with the fishes and the potent beings who lived on the bottom? How did the shamen develop the hypnotic power they employed in their seances? What can we learn from the shamen who survive about thought transference and ESP? The answers are in the arctic wilderness still left to us . . .

New perspectives come out of the wilderness. Jesus, Zoroaster, Moses, and Mohammed went to the wilderness and came back with messages. It was from the wilderness, and the people who knew wilderness, that the first concern about pollution and environmental decay came.[8]
    —Kenneth Brower (prolific environmental writer, closely linked to the Earth Island Institute), "Wilderness."

It seems evident that there are throughout the world certain social and religious forces which have worked through history toward an ecologically and culturally enlightened state of affairs. Let these be encouraged: Gnostics, hip Marxists, Teilhard de Chardin Catholics, Druids, Taoists, Biologists, Witches, Yogins, Bhikkus, Quakers, Sufis, Tibetans, Zens, Shamans, Bushmen, American Indians, Polynesians, Anarchists, Alchemists . . . the list is long. All primitive

cultures, all communal and ashram movements . . . it would be best to consider this a continuing "revolution of consciousness" . . . life won't seem worth living unless one's on the transforming energy's side.[9]
—Keith Murray (Ecologist at the Berkeley Ecology Center), "Suggestions Toward an Ecological Platform."

Global Government The Goal

The search for a new paradigm should be a search for synthesis, for what is common to and unites people, countries, and nations, rather than what divides them.

The search for such a synthesis can succeed if the following conditions are met.

First of all, we must return to the well-known human values that are embodied in the ideals of the world religions and also in the socialist ideas that inherited much from those values.

Further, we need to search for a new paradigm of development that is based on those values and that is capable of leading us all toward a genuinely humanistic or, more precisely, humanistic-ecological culture of living.

Finally, we need to develop methods of social action and policy that will direct society to a path consistent with the interests of both humanity and the rest of nature.[10]
—Mikhail Gorbachev (former leader of the Soviet Union; President of the Gorbachev Foundation—Moscow Headquarters; Chairman of the Gorbachev Foundation/USA; and President of Green Cross International), *The Search for a New Beginning.*

The environment, perhaps more than any other issue, has helped crystallize the notion that humanity has a common future. The concept of sustainable development is now widely used and accepted as a framework within which all countries, rich and poor, should operate. The aspect that particularly concerns us is the global governance implications.[11]
—The Commission on Global Governance (a U.N. allied NGO), *Our Global Neighborhood.*

It is simply not feasible for sovereignty to be exercised unilaterally by individual nation-states, however powerful. It is a principle which will yield only slowly and reluctantly to the imperatives of global environmental cooperation.[12]

—Maurice Strong, (U.N. Secretary-General of the 1972 Stockholm Conference on the Human Environment [the first "Earth Summit"] and the 1992 Rio Earth Summit; member of the Commission on Global Governance; and overseer of U.N. Reform initiatives).

We have recognized the need for cooperative global action. All nations are affected by the actions of others. All nations must now work together to find global solutions to global problems.[13]

—Jean Chrétien (Prime Minister of Canada), *Opening of the World Conservation Congress,* October 14, 1996.

We need a new way of governing the whole planet. The problems we face today are bigger than any single country.[14]

—Children's Task Force on Agenda 21, *Rescue Mission Planet Earth.*

Achieving world peace requires establishment of governmental institutions for creating, enforcing, and interpreting world law, arrived at through an equitable and democratic decision-making process. In short, it requires the institutions of global government . . .[15]

—World Federalist Association, *1996 WFA Statement of Values and Beliefs.*

We are going to end up with world government. It's inevitable. . . . There's going to be conflict, coercion and consensus. That's all part of what will be required as we give birth to the first global civilization.[16]

—James Garrison (President, Gorbachev Foundation/ USA).

Ancient institutions and systems of belief which have brought us to the present moment are being shattered by the force of change, compelled to either renew themselves or perish. This is so because what is arising within and around us is nothing less than the birth of the first global civilization. It is our generation, in our time, to which has fallen the great task of its birthing and first definition.[17]

—James Garrison.

As long as the original covenant that Noah made with the "Heavenly Landlord" remains in force, His rainbow is still in the sky and we earthly tenants are not evicted from this planet, there is at least the possibility of "A Constitution for the World." In view of the rate at which events are now moving, I would even put a small amount of money on it being initiated by the year 2000.[18]

> —Lucile W. Green (signer of the WCPA *Constitution for the Federation of Earth*, futurist, global activist, author).

A Militant Approach

We, in the green movement, aspire to a cultural model in which killing a forest will be considered more contemptible and more criminal than the sale of 6-year-old children to Asian brothels.[19]

> —Carl Amery (German Greens).

I got the impression that instead of going out to shoot birds, I should go out and shoot the kids who shoot birds.[20]

> —Paul Watson (founder of Greenpeace).

Childbearing [should be] a punishable crime against society, unless the parents hold a government license. . . . All potential parents [should be] required to use contraceptive chemicals, the government issuing antidotes to citizens chosen for childbearing.[21]

> —David Brower (first executive director of the Sierra Club; founder of Friends of the Earth; and founder of the Earth Island Institute).

The first task is population control at home. How do we go about it? Many of my colleagues feel that some sort of compulsory birth regulation would be necessary to achieve such control. One plan often mentioned involves the addition of temporary sterilants to water supplies or staple food. Doses of the antidote would be carefully rationed by the government to produce the desired population size.[22]

> —Paul Ehrlich (population control advocate, author), *The Population Bomb*.

Isn't the only hope for the planet that the industrialized civilizations collapse? Isn't it our responsibility to bring that about?[23]

> —Maurice Strong (U.N. environmental leader).

The world has cancer, and that cancer is man.[24]

> —Merton Lambert, (former spokesman for the Rockefeller Foundation).

If I were reincarnated I would wish to be returned to earth as a killer virus to lower human population levels.[25]
—Prince Philip (Duke of Edinburgh, leader of The World Wildlife Fund).

A total population of 250-300 million people, a 95% decline from present levels, would be ideal.[26]
—Ted Turner (media mogul and United Nations advocate).

The human race could go extinct, and I for one, would not shed any tears.[27]
—Dave Foreman (founder of Earth First!).

Notes

1. Alexander King and Bertrand Schneider, *The First Global Revolution: A Report by the Council of the Club of Rome* (New York: Pantheon Books, 1991), pp. 104–105.

2. Robin Mearns, "Environmental Entitlements: Towards Empowerment for Sustainable Development," Naresh Singh and Vangile Titi, editors, *Empowerment For Sustainable Development: Toward Operational Strategies* (Halifax, NS/Winnipeg, MB: Fernwood Publishing/International Institute for Sustainable Development, 1995), p. 51.

3. Arthur C. Clarke, *Childhood's End* (New York: Ballantine Books, 1953), p. 69.

4. Naresh Singh and Vangile Titi, *Empowerment For Sustainable Development*, p. 27.

5. David Suziuki, *Time To Change* (Toronto: Stoddart Publishing, 1994), p. 225.

6. Scott Nearing, *United World* (New York: Island Press, 1944), p. 221.

7. Lynn White, Jr., "The Historical Roots of Our Ecologic Crisis," Garrett de Bell, editor, *The Environmental Handbook: Prepared For The First National Environmental Teach-In* (New York: Ballantine/Friends of the Earth Book, 1970), pp. 21–25.

8. Kenneth Brower, "Wilderness," Bell, *The Environmental Handbook*, p. 148.

9. Keith Murray, "Suggestions Toward an Ecological Platform," Bell, *The Environmental Handbook*, p. 331.

10. Mikhail Gorbachev, *The Search for a New Beginning: Developing a New Civilization* (San Francisco: HarperSanFrancisco and the Gorbachev Foundation/USA, 1995), pp. 60–62.

11. The Commission on Global Governance, *Our Global Neighborhood* (Oxford: Oxford University Press, 1995), p. 208.

12. Maurice Strong, as quoted by Henry Lamb, "Conspiracy Theories Laid To Rest As U.N. Announces Plan For 'Global Neighborhood'," *Hope For The World Update* (Noblesville, IN: Hope For The World, Fall 1996, newsletter), p. 2.

13. Canadian Prime Minister Jean Chrétien, *Opening of the World Conservation Congress*, speech, October 14, 1996.

14. Children's Task Force on Agenda 21, *Rescue Mission Planet Earth: A Youth Edition of Agenda 21* (London: Peace Child Charitable Trust and Kingfisher Books, 1994), p. 81.

15. World Federalist Association, *1996 WFA Statement of Values and Beliefs, as quoted in The Quarterly Newsletter of the World Federalist Association*, April 1996, p. 6.

16. James Garrison, quoted by Dr. Dennis L. Cuddy, "Ruling Elite Working Toward World Government," *The Daily Record*, Dunn, NC, October 17, 1995, p. 4.

17. James Garrison, *State of the World Forum*: 1997 Program Overview, p. 1.

18. Lucile W. Green, *Journey To A Governed World: Thru 50 Years in the Peace Movement* (Berkeley, CA: The Uniquest Foundation, 1991), p. 139.

19. Carl Amery, as quoted by Dixie Lee Ray, *Trashing the Planet* (Washington, D.C: Regnery Gateway, 1990), p. 169

20. Paul Watson, as quoted by Dixie Lee Ray, *Trashing the Planet*, p. 166.

21. David Brower, as quoted by Dixie Lee Ray, *Trashing the Planet*, p. 169.

22. Paul Ehrlich, *The Population Bomb* (New York: Ballentine, 1968), p. 135.

23. Maurice Strong, as quoted by Daniel Wood, "The Wizard of Baca Grande," *West* (Toronto: West is a division of the Globe and Mail, May, 1990, magazine) p. 47.

24. Merton Lambert, *Harpeth Journal*, December 18, 1962.

25. Prince Philip, as quoted by Kathleen Marquardt, "Are You Ready for Our New Age Future?" *Insiders Report* (American Policy Center, December 1995).

26. Ted Turner, as quoted by Donald McAlvany, *The McAlvany Intelligence Advisor*, June 1996. MIA, P.O. Box 84904, Phoenix, AZ 85071.

27. Dave Foreman, *The People's Agenda*, March/April 1992.

APPENDIX G

Sponsors of the Provisional World Parliament

The following list of Provisional World Parliament sponsors reveals the close connection between the "people's" world government movement and the United Nations. You will notice that a high percentage of these sponsors—many of them founders of Non-Government Organizations—have held key positions within the U.N. Another list, consisting of Non-Government Organizations which are supportive of the World Constitution and Parliament Association's efforts, may be accessed on the worldwide web at http://www.wcpagren.org/present.html.

Honorary Sponsors
Of The Provisional World Parliament

(While endorsing the aims and objectives of the Provisional World Parliament, Honorary Sponsors do not necessarily agree with all of the specific details of the bills and resolutions which the Parliament may adopt.)

Egil Aarvik,
> Norway; Chrmn. Norwegian Nobel Cttee.; M.P. since 1961; Pres. Lagting (upper house par.); Min. Social Affairs 1965-70.

Dr. Norman Z. Alcock,
> Canada; Nuclear Physicist; x-Pres. Canad. Peace Research Inst.

Sheikh Mohammad Abdullah,
> India; Chief Minister of Jammu and Kashmir; was Pres. All-India States Peoples Conf.; Delegate to U.N.

Alexey A. Abrikosov,
> U.S.S.R.; Physicist; Lenin Prize 1966; Corrs. Mem. USSR Academy Scs.; Prof. Landau Inst.. Theoretical Physics.

Nicholas Y.B. Adade,
> Ghana; Lawyer; was Minister Justice, Dir. Ghana News Agency; Dir. Ghana Commercial Bank.

Dr. Adebayo Adedeji,
Nigeria; U.N. Under-Sec. Gen. and Exec. Sec. Economic Comm. for Africa; Pres. African Assn. Public Adminis.

Chief J.O. Agboye,
Nigeria; Pres. Nigerian Inst. Administrative Mgmt., Nigerian Society Commerce, and Inst. Internal Auditors.

Aziz Ahmed
Pakistan; Min. Foreign Affairs 1971-77; Ambas. USA 1959-63; Chrmn Press Trust Pakistan; many other diplomatic posts.

Mohsin Ahmed Alaini,
Yemen Arab Republic; twice Prime Minister; three times Foreign Min. Ambas. UK, France, USA, USSR, UN, W. Ger.

Justice Zvi Bar-niv,
Israel; Judge and Pres. Nat'l Labor Court; x-Solicitor General.

Dr. Richard Bedggood,
New Zealand; Prof. Education; V. Pres. Int'l. Community Educ. Assn.

Prof. Suri Bhagavantam,
India; Prof. Physics; Univ. V. Chancellor; Pres. Cttee. on Science and Technology in Developing Countries.

Prof. S. O. Biobaku,
Nigeria; Dir. Inst. African Studies, Univ. Ibadan; V. Chancellor Univs. Ife and Lagos; Pres. Historical Society Nigeria.

Dr. A. H. Boerma,
Netherlands; Dir.-Gen. Food and Agriculture Org. of U.N. 1968-76; Dir. of F.A.O. programs since 1948.

Prof. Goran Von Bonsdorff,
Finland; Prof. Political Sc. Univ. Helsinki; Author, "World Politics in Age of Technology."

Fr. Phil Bosmans,
Belgium; Priest; Radio Call-in Couns.; Author, "Give Happiness A Chance."

Dennis Brutus,
South Africa; Poet; Dir. World Campaign for Release S. African Pol. Prisoners; V. Pres. Union of Writers of African People.

Hon. Gordon M. Bryant,
Australia; M.P. 1955-1980; Cabinet Min. 1972-75; U.N. Delegate.

Chief Mangosuthu Gatsha Buthelezi,
Kwazulu, S. Africa; Chief Minister; Leader S. Africa Black Alliance; Leader 5,000,000 Zulus.

Prof. Adriano Buzzati-Traverso,
Italy; Dir. Inst. Genetics, Univ. Pavia 1946-62; Sr. Sc. Advisor UN Environment Prgm; WHO Advisor.

Prof. Henri Cartan,
France; Prof. Math, Univ. Paris 1940-75; Pres. European Assn. Teachers (Fr.) 1957-75; Pres. Mvmt. Federaliste European.

Vedat Celik,
Cyprus; was Deputy Prime Min. and Min. Foreign Affairs, Turkish Fed. State Cyprus; TFSC Rep. to UN; Mem. Legislature.

Khub Chand,
India; Ambas. and High Commr. to Many Countries of Europe, Africa and Mid-East; Consultant for International Development.

Hon. Yeshwant Vishnu Chandrachud,
India; Chief Justice of Supreme Court.; President of India Law Inst., and International Law Assn.

Dr. Josef Charvat,
Czechslovakia; Prof. Medicine; on Scien. Council Ministry of Health.

Augustine Namakube Chimuka,
Zambia Asst. Secretary Gen., Organization of African Unity; many posts with Ministry Foreign Affairs.

Ramsey Clark,
U.S.A.; Lawyer; U.S. Attorney Gen. 1967-69; Prof. Law. Brooklyn Law School.

Everett R. Clinchy,
U.S.A.; Pres. Nat'l Conf. Christians and Jews 1928-58; x-Pres. Council on World Tensions; x-Pres. Inst. Man and Science.

Prof. Conrnelis De Jager,
Netherlands; Astronomer; Gen. Sec. Int'l. Astronomical Union 1967-73; was Pres. Int'l Council Scient. Unions.

Hitendra Desai,
India; M.P.; Min. Works and Housing 1976-77; Min. Commerce 1979-80; Pres. Gujaret Pradesh Congr. Cttee. since 1975.

Mrs. Marion Dewar,
Canada; Mayor Ottawa.

Gurdial Singh Dhillon,
India; Speaker Lok Sabha 1969-75; Min. Transport 1975-77; x-Pres. Inter. Parl. Union. and Commonwealth Parl. Assn.

Ahmed Dini,
Djibouti; was Pres. Territorial Assembly and National Assembly; x-Cabinet Min.

Nikolai Petrovich Dubinin,
U.S.S.R.; Dir. Inst. Gen. Genetics, USSR Academy Sciences; Lenin Prize 1966; Chrmn, "Man and Environment" div. of State Cttee. for USSR Coun. of Ministers.

Arthur C. Eggleton,
Canada; Mayor Toronto.

Dr. Muhammad El Fasi,
Morocco; Chrmn. Exec. Bd. UNESCO 1964-66; Rector two Univs.; Pres. Assn. African Univs., Assn. Islamic Univs.

Ibrahim Elias,
Sudan; Banker; with Ministry Commerce 1949-56; Under-Sec. Ministry Economy 1965-69; Ministry Treasury 1979-81.

Dr. Taslim Olawale Elias,
Nigeria; Pres. of World Court; Chief Justice Supreme Ct. Nigeria 1972-75; x-Min. Justc.; Pres. Wrld. Assn. Judges.

M. Necati Munir Ertekun,
Cyprus; Lawyer; Judge of Supreme Constitutional Court.

Ioan Evans,
U.K.; M.P.; Chrmn. Foreign Affairs Group Parliamentary Labor Party; Int'l. V. Pres. Parliamentarians for World Order.

Dr. Douglas Everingham,
Australia; M.P.; Minister Health 1972-75; Parliamentary U.N. Delegate 1982; x-V. Pres. Wrld. Health Org. Asn.

Abdulrahim Abby Farah,
Somalia; Under Sec. Gen. of U.N. for Special Political Questions.

A. F. M. Abul Fateh,
Bangladesh; Ambas. to many countries Asia, Africa, Mid-East, Europe; Chrmn. Commonwealth Human Ecology Coun.

Anatole Fistoulari,
U.K.; was Prin. Conduct. London Philharmonic Orch.; Guest Conductor Orchestras in many countries.

Homer Ferguson,
U.S.A.; Lawyer; U.S. Senator 1943-55; Judge since 1956.

Antonio Fonseca-Pimental,
Brazil; Dir. Brazilian Civil Service 1961-63; Mem. Int'l Civil Service Comm. of UN since 1975; Author, "Democratic World Government and the U.N."

A. G. Sembu Forna,
Sierra Leone; M.P.; Cab. Min. 10 yrs. inc.: Transport and Communications; Agric. and Natural Resources; Health; Culture.

Dr. Risieri Frondizi,
Argentina; Prof. Philosophy; Rector Univ. Buenos Aires 1955-66; Pres. Inter-American Union of Latin Am. Univs.

Dr. Ragnar A. Granit,
Sweden; Nobel Prize in Physiology or Medicine 1967; was President Royal Swedish Academy of Sciences.

Amnar Nath Grover,
India; Judge High Ct. Punjab 1957-68; Judge Supreme Ct. India 1968-73; Chrmn. Press Council of India since 1979.

Dr. Max Habicht,
Switzerland; International Lawyer and Prof. Int'l. Law; Legal Advisor to League of Nations, U.N., many world gov't. orgs.

Dr. Louis M. Hacker,
U.S.A.; Prof. Economics and Dean School Gen. Studies, Columbia Univ.; Editor sev. Encyclopedias, Author many books.

George Hakim,
  Lebanon; Min. Foreign Affairs; 1965-67; Ambassador to U.N. and Chrmn. U.N. Grp. Experts on Econ. Dev. Undevel. Countries.
Dr. Jawad Hashim,
  Iraq; Min. Planning 1968-74; now Mng. Dr. Arab Monetary Fund at Abu Dhabi; Chrmn. U.N. Econ. Cttee. Western Asia.
Dr. Gerhard Herzberg,
  Canada; Nobel Prize Chemistry 1971; Distinguished Research Scientist with National Research Council of Canada.
Dr. Akanu Ibiam,
  Nigeria; Gov. Eastern Nigeria 1960-66; x-Chrmn. All-African Church Council; Chrmn. Council of Univ. College at Ibadan.
Dr. George Ignatieff,
  Canada; Chancellor Univ. Toronto; Ambas. U.N. 1946-49; and 1966-68; Rep. on 18 Nation Disarm. Cttee., Geneva.
George X. Ionnides,
  Cyprus; Lawyer and M.P.; Minister of Justice 1970-72 and 1976-78; Min. Interior 1972-74; Min. to Presidency 1978-80.
Dr. Iorgu Iordan,
  Romania; x-Faculty Dean and Rector, Bucharest Univ.; Pres. UNESCO Cttee.; Mem. Romanian Acad.; Mem. many Int'l. Assns.
Ahmed E. H. Jaffer,
  Pakistan; Civic Leader and Businessman; x-M.P.; Pres. Muslim Cmnwlth. Mvmt., Pres. Pakistan Br. English Speak. Union.
Hon. Bal Ram Jakhar,
  India; Speaker of the Lok Sabha many terms; President, Commonwealth Parliamentary Assn.
Dr. Henri Janne,
  Belgium; Sociologist; was Minister Education and Culture; Hon. Rector Univ. Brussels; x-Pres. Royal Acad. Sciences and Letters.
Mohamed Khir Johari,
  Malaysia; M.P.; was Min. Education, of Agric. and Cooperatives, of Trade and Indust.; Sec.-Gen. United Malays Nat'l. Org.; Pres. Asian Rural Reconstruction Confs.
Jamsahib Nawab Alhaj Amir Ali Khan,
  Pakistan; Member Federal Advisory Council.
Sir Muhammad Zafrulla Khan,
  Pakistan; Pres. U.N. General Assembly 1962-63; Pres. of World Court 1970-73; x-Min. Foreign Affairs.
Prince Yaqub Mohammed Khan,
  Hong-kong; Head of Asia Times, and Travel Executive.
Prof. James Kirkup,
  U.K.; Poet; Prof. English Lit. Kyoto Univ., Japan; Prof. several univs. U.K., USA; Author "The Cosmic Shape," many other books.
Suchart Kosolkitiwong,
  Thailand; Pres. International Federation of Religions; Organizing World Eternal Peace Conferences.
Ciro Dominico Kroon,
  Curacao, N.A.; Banker; Min. Social and Econ. Affairs and Public Health; Prime Minister, Neth. Antilles 1968-69.
Maria Kuncewiczowa,
  Poland; Writer and Professor; Founder, Center for Writers in Exile.
Mme. Irene De Lipkowski,
  France; was M.P. and Mayor Orly; Pres. Int'l. Alliance of Women.
Dr. Fritz Lipmann,
  U.S.A.; Nobel Prize in Medicine or Physiology 1953; Prof. Biology.
Mochtar Lubis,
  Indonesia; Publisher and Editor Daily Indonesian Raya, and The Times of Indonesia; Golden Pen of Freedom Award 1967.
Dr. Hans Olaf Lundstrom,
  Sweden; Exec. Dir. World Bank 1978-82; x-Cab. Min. Finance, Econ. Affairs; x-Deputy Gov. Bank of Sweden.
Hassan M. Makki,
  Yemen Arab Repub.; Deputy Prime Min. for Economic Affairs; was Prime Minister, Foreign Min., Ambassador to U.N.

Prof. Ivan Malek,
Czechslovakia; Microbiologist; V. Pres Czech Academy Sciences; V. Pres. Int'l Union Biological Scs.; Lenin Prize 1967.

Dr. Ignacy Malecki,
Poland; Dir. Inst. Basic Tech. Problems, Polish Acad. Scs.; V. Pres. Int'l. Council Scientific Unions; Pres. Pugwash Cttee.

Paul Malekou,
Gabon; was Minister Labour and Social Affairs, of Education, Youth and Sports, of Public Works and Transportation, of House and Urbanism.

Dr. Jose Mallart,
Spain; Educator, Psychologist, Author; Member Exec. Cttee. Int. Assn. Applied Psychology.

Dr. Rashmi Mayur, Ph. D.,
India; Director, Urban Development Inst.; President, Global Futures Network; U.N. Consultant.

Mamoon-Al-Rashid,
Bangladesh; Chrmn. and Mng. Trustee Comprehensive Rural, Educational, Social, Cultural and Economic Centre.

Marcel Marceau,
France; Master Mime.

Hon. Bakeer Markar,
Sri Lanka; M.P.; Speaker of Parliament for many years.

Keba Mbaye,
Senegal; World Court Judge; Appeal Judge Supreme Court Senegal; Pres. World Fed. UN Assns.; V. Char. Int. Inst. Human Rights.

Mustafa Medani,
Sudan; with Ministry Foreign Affs. since 1958; Ambas. to UN, W. Germany, many other countries; Del. UN Human Rights Conf.

Dr. Zhores A. Medvedev,
U.S.S.R.; Sr. Scientist and Head Various Labs and Insts. USSR; now with Nat'l. Inst. Medical Research, London.

Mrs. Leela Damodara Menon,
India; x-M.P.; Mem. U.N. Human Rights Cttee.; V. Pres. All-India Women's Conference.

Dr. Charles Mercieca,
U.S.A. (from Malta); Founder and Exec. V. Pres. Int'l. Assn. Educators for World Peace; University Professor.

Ram Niwas Mirdha,
India; M.P.; was Home Min., and Deputy Chrmn. Rajya Sabha; Chrmn. Parliamentary Group for World Government.

S.P. Mittal,
M.P.; Sec. Gen. Asian Forum Parliamentarians; Sec. India Parl. Grp. World Gov't; Chrmn. Indian Assn. Parl. on Population and Dev.

Jules Moch,
France; M.P. 1946-58 and 1962-67; Minister Public Works in Four Cabinets; Perm. Del. UN Disarmament Cttee. at Geneva 7 years.

Shettima Ali Monguno,
Nigeria; Min. Int. Affairs 19655-67. Fed. Commr. Industries 1967-71; Pres. OPEC 1972; UN Del. Nine Sessions.

Haity Mousatche,
Brazil; Prof. Physiology and Dept. Head Univ. Brazil, and Univ. Centro Occidental, Venz; V. Pres. Brazil Soc. Advance Sc.

Hon. F. Matale Mulikita,
Zambia; Educator, Politician, Businessman; was Minister Foreign Affairs, Labor and Social Services, Health, Power, Transport and Works, Education.

Joseph J. Mungai,
Tanzania; Member Parliament; was Minister Agriculture; Led delegations to Commonwealth Parliamentary Association Conferences.

Joseph B. Mwemba,
Zambia; Teacher, Farmer, M.P., 1973-78; Min. of State for Labour and Social Services 1974-79; Ambas. U.N., 1966-68.

Jayant V. Narlikar,
India; Prof. Astrophysics, Tata Inst. Fundamen. Research; Author, "Structure of the Universe," and other books.

Dr. Joseph Needham,
U.K.; Biochemist and Historian of Science; Prof. at Univrs. in many countries; Pres. Int'l. Union History of Science.

Mrs. Savitry Nigam,
India; M.P. 1952-67; Sec. Congress Party in Parliament; Pres. Indian Housewives Fed.; Chrmn. Indian Fed. UN Assns.

Lord Philip Noel-Baker,
U.K.; Nobel Peace Prize 1959; Chrmn. Parliam. Labor Prty. Foreign Affairs Group; Co-Chrmn. World Disarm. Camp.

Odvar Nordli,
Norway; Prime Minister 1976-81; now Pres. Parliament; Leader Parliam. Labor Party; Min. Labor and Municipal Affairs 1971-72.

Sam Nujoma,
Namibia; Co-founder and Pres. S.W. Africa People Organ. (SWAPO); arrested several times; leading freedom movement from exile.

Fr. Bob Ogle,
Canada; Member of Parliament.

Dr. J. O. J. Okezie,
Nigeria; Min. Health, Agric. and Nat. Resources, 1970-75; Med. Supt. Ibeku Central Hosp.; Sec. E. Nigeria Science Assn.

Dr. H. M. A. Onitiri,
Nigeria, Economist; Sr. Lecturer Univ. Ibadan; Dir. Nigerian Inst. Social and Economic Research since 1974.

Charles D. Onyeama,
Nigeria; World Court Judge 1967-76; High Court Judge, Lagos, 1975-64; Supreme Court Justice 1964-66; was M.P.

Osman N. Orek,
Cyprus; was Prime Min., Turkish Fed. State Cyprus; Sec. Gen. Cyprus-Turkish Nat'l. Union Party; now Lawyer in Turkey.

Mondher Ouanes,
Tunisia; Advocate; Pres. Assn. Lawyers of Tunisia; V. Pres. Union of Arab Legal Professions, headquartered in Baghdad.

Prof. Arvid Pardo,
Malta; Ambas. U.N. 1965-71; Proposed oceans and seabeds as common heritage mankind; Prof. Ocean Law, Univ. S. Cal.

Babhubai J. Patel,
India; Chief Min. Gujarat 1975-80; Minister in Bombay and Gujarat Gov'ts. since 1952, many posts; Univ. V. Chancellor.

Dr. I. G. Patel,
India; Gov. Reserve Bank India since 1977; x-Exec. Dir. for India of Int'l. Monetary Fund; x-Sec. India Ministry Finance.

Dr. Linus Pauling,
U.S.A.; Nobel Laureate Chemistry 1954; Nobel Peace Prize 1962; Lenin Prize 1970; now research on Vit. C and Cancer.

Louis Perillier,
France; Author, "Verification, Key to Disarmament".

Anwar Iqbal Quereshi,
Pakistan; Economic Advisor to Gov't. Pakistan, Int'l Monetary Fund, Saudi Arabia; Pres. Pakistan Econ. Assn.

Dr. Walpola Rahula,
Sri Lanka; Educator; Chancellor of University of Kelaniya.

Dr. G. N. Ramachandran,
India; CSIR Distinguished Scientist; Prof. Physics and Dean Faculty Sciences, Univ. Madras, 1952-67; V. Pres. Indian Academy Sciences.

Dr. Kamarazu N. Rao, M.D.,
India; Pres., Int'l. Medical Sciences Acad.; was Pres., World Fed. Public Health Assns. and Sec-Gen., Population Council of India, WHO Consultant.

Dr. V. K. R. V. Rao,
India; M. P. 1967-77; Cab. Min. 1967-71; Founder-Dir. Inst. of Economic. Growth, and Inst. Social and Economic Change.

Jules A. Razafimbahiny,
Madagascar; Ambas. to many countr. Europe, USA, E.E.C.; Pres. Pan-African Inst. Develop.; With UN Dev. Prgm.

Hon. Mahinder Singh Saathi,
India; mayor of Delhi; was labor leader; works for Hindu-Sikh Unity.

Dr. Abdus Salam,
Pakistan; Nobel Prize in Physics 1979; Dir. Int. Cntr. Theoretical Physics, Trieste; Sec. Confs. Peacefl. Uses Atom. Energy.

Dr. Frederick Sanger,
U.K.; Nobel Prize Chem. 1958; Resrch Biochem. Cambridge Univ.

Dr. Paul E. Santorini,
Greece; Scientist, Engineer, Philosopher; Author several books on Emergence of Universe and of Life in Universe.

Prof. Margaret Schlauch,
Poland; Prof. and Author; Corress. Mem. Polish Acad. Sciences.

Mrs. Nandini Satpathy,
India; M.P. 1962-72; x-Min. Information and Broadcasting; Chief Min. Orissa 1972-76; U.N. Delegate 1970.

Jose Sette-Camara,
Brazil; V. Pres. World Ct.; x-Mayor Brasilia; Ambas. to Switz. 1963-64, to U.N. 1964-68; Mem. U.N. Int'l. Law Comm.

Amadou Seydou,
Niger; Ambassador at various times to France, U.K., Italy, Spain and Switzerland.

Prof. Finn Seyersted,
Norway; Sec. Ministry Foreign Affairs 1945-53; Ambas. Argentina 1968-73; Prof. Int'l. Law, Univ. Oslo since 1973.

Shri K. K. Shah,
India; Mem. Rajya Sabha 1960-71; Gov. Tamil Nadu 1971-76; Cab. Min. 5 years; Sec. Indo-African Soc.; Pres. Indo-Arab Soc.

Rishikesh Shaha,
Nepal; was Gen. Sec. Nepalese Congress; Amb. UN 1956-60; Min. Finan. and Plan. 1961-62; M.P. 1967-70; Univ. Prof.

Dr. Alexandras Y. Schtromas,
Lithuania, now in U.K.; Prof. Political Sc.; was Dir. Legal Research at Vilnus; Author many books, articles.

Dr. Salimuzzaman Siddiqui,
Pakistan; Dir. Research Inst. Chem. Univ. Karachi; x-Chrmn. Pakistan Coun. Scientific and Industrial Research.

Sarv Mittra Sikra,
India; Chief Justice Supreme Ct. India 1971-73; Pres. Indian Law Inst., Indian Br. Int'l. Law Assn., Indian Soc. Int'l. Law.

Jon Silkin,
U.K.; Writer, Editor, Author "The Peaceable Kingdom," "Nature With Man," others.

Dr. Nagendra Singh,
India; Judge at World Court since 1973, was V. Pres.; Prof. Int'l. Law several Univs.; Pres. Indian Society Int'l. Law.

Ross Smyth,
Canada; x-Pres. World Federalists of Canada; Pub. Affrs. Mgr. (rt'd.) of Air Canada.

Lord Donald Soper,
U.K.; Methodist Min.; Alderman, London Co. Council 1958-65.

Dr. Sompong Sucharitkul,
Thailand; Amb. Japan, France, Italy, Greece, Portugal, Benelux; Mem. Permanent Court Arbitration since 1978.

Dr. Bogdam Suchodolski,
Poland; Mem. Presidium Polish Acad. Scs.; V. Pres. Int. Acad. History Science; V. Pres. Wrld. Future Stud. Fed.

Dr. Ivan Supek,
Yugoslavia; Dir. Inst. History and Philosophy Sc., Yugoslav Acad.; x-Rector Univ. Zagreb; M.P. 19963-67; Pres. Yugoslav Pugwash Grp.

Kurt Swinton,
Canada; Educator; x-Pres. Encycl. Brittan.; on Bd. Toronto 2000 Futurists.

Bahjat Talhouni,
Jordan; Pres. of Senate; Prime Minister four times; Foreign Min. 1967-68; Chief of the Royal Cabinet four times.

Tun Tan Siew Sin,
  Malaysia; Min. Commerce and Industry 1957-59; of Finance 1959-74; V. Pres. and Pres. Chinese
  Malay. Assn. 1957-74; Chancellor Malaysian Nat. Univ.; Rubber Planter.
Ben Toruk,
  So. Africa; was Sec. So. African Congress Democrats; Pol. Prisoner 3 yrs.; now Faculty 3rd World
  Studies, Milton Keynes Univ., U.K.
Baron Jakob Von Uexkull,
  Isle of Man, U.K.; Exec.

Note

This list of Provisional World Parliament Honorary Sponsors was
drawn from the following WCPA web site, http://
www.wcpagren.org/sponsors.html, [Accessed September 17, 1998].

APPENDIX H

The Clinton Administration's Role in Education

Hillary Clinton has served as the current administration's most out-spoken advocate for education reform. She began lobbying for the implementation of the new education policies while her husband was still governor of Arkansas. The presidential election, however, would secure her role as the "First Lady of Education." As the president's wife, she would have more influence in shaping her husband's policies than anyone else. Recognizing this fact, Marc Tucker, president of the National Center on Education and the Economy (NCEE), sent a detailed letter to Hillary immediately after the 1992 election. In his letter, Tucker called for a radical, transformational outcome-based education scheme to remold the entire American system. He proposed nothing short of a national system of control over all jobs and education that would literally extend from the cradle to the grave, and would be mandatory for everyone.

Tucker's pro-United Nations organization is arguably the most powerful education policy-making establishment in the United States. Hillary serves on the Center's board of trustees, alongside such powerful globalists as David Rockefeller Jr., Mario Cuomo, and John Sculley. She pursues the NCEE's agenda on education reform from the White House.

On the first page of his letter to Hillary, Tucker stated:

> I still cannot believe you won. But utter delight that you did pervades all the circles in which I move. I met last Wednesday in David Rockefeller's office with him, John Sculley, Dave Barram and David Haselkorn. It was a great celebration. Both John and David R. were more expansive than I have ever seen them—literally radiating happiness . . .

> The subject we were discussing was what you and Bill should do now about education, training and labor market policy. Following that meeting, I chaired another in Washington on the same topic . . .

> Our purpose in these meetings was to propose concrete actions that the Clinton administration could take—between now and the inauguration. In the first 100 days and beyond. The result, from where I sit, was really exciting. We took a very large leap forward in terms of how to advance the agenda on which you and we have all been working—a practical plan for putting all the major components of the system in place within four years, by the time Bill has to run again.[1]

On the last page of his letter, Tucker laid out the strategy for getting the Rockefeller-backed agenda implemented through "Bill." He wrote:

> Radical changes in attitudes, values and beliefs are required to move any combination of these agendas. The federal government will have little direct leverage on many of the actors involved. For much of what must be done, a new, broad consensus will be required. What role can the new administration play in forging that consensus and how should it go about doing it?

> At the narrowest level, the agenda cannot be moved unless there is agreement among the governors, the President and the Congress. Bill's role at the Charlottesville summit leads naturally to a reconvening of that group, perhaps with the addition of key members of Congress and others.

> But we think that having an early summit on the subject of the whole human resources agenda would be risky, for many reasons. Better to build on Bill's enormous success during the campaign with national talk shows, in school gymnasiums and the bus trips. He could start on the consensus-building

progress this way, taking his message directly to the public, while submitting his legislative agenda and working it on the Hill. After six months or so, when the public has warmed to the ideas and the legislative packages are about to get into hearings, then you might consider some form of summit, broadened to include not only the governors, but also key members of Congress and others whose support and influence are important. This way, Bill can be sure that the agenda is his, and he can go into it with a groundswell of support behind him.[2]

Marc Tucker's disturbing letter demonstrates the degree to which President Clinton is directly influenced by global insiders. Fortunately, some of the administration's plans for education during its first term were effectively countered by concerned citizens lobbies, who took the president and his wife to task. Other aspects of the Clinton education agenda, however, have been widely accepted. With big money and a powerful New Age lobby behind them, the White House and its team of social engineers expect their education reforms to be fully implemented by early in the new millenium.

Notes

1. Mark Tucker, in a letter to Hillary Clinton dated November 11, 1992. This letter was written on the stationery of the National Center on Education and the Economy. I tried to reach the organization at the Washington address appearing on its letterhead. However, the center is no longer located there. Its current address is unknown.

2. Ibid.

APPENDIX I

Quotes by Robert Muller

The following statements by former U.N. Assistant Secretary-General Robert Muller shed light on his interfaith perspective, pantheistic/ Chardinian view of Christ, and his intentions for the U.N. and the world. Unless otherwise indicated, all quotes are from his book *New Genesis: Shaping a Global Spirituality.*

Uniting Around the U.N.

Many religions have special invocations, prayers, hymns and services for the United Nations. The most important examples are those of the Catholic, the Unitarian-Universalist, the Baptist and the Baha'i faiths. It is a common practice of the Unitarian-Universalists to display the United Nations flag in their houses of worship. So does the Holy Family Church, the parish church of the UN . . . (p. 45)

I have a Christ in my office. My colleague next door has a statue of Shiva. U Thant had a Buddha in his room. Each of us, be he from North or from South, from East or from West, has his own way of expressing faith in the human race and destiny. (p. 48)

There are many also in the United Nations for whom the cooperation of all nations towards common goals and values is a kind of new religion, a supreme path or way. They see in the UN the same perennial human dream which has obsessed all great religions and philosophies, namely, the establishment of a peaceful, just, happy, harmonious world society. But there is one difference: while in the past all religions and philosophies were born within specific local, cultural contexts, today we are witnessing the birth of a new philosophy, ideology or ethics which originates from a central place of synthesis where all dreams, aspirations, claims and values of humankind converge. This is new. It constitutes one of the greatest and most exciting attempts at total fulfillment in the entire evolution of the human race. There has never been anything like it. It is a magnificent story, the beginning of a profound worldwide transformation of the human society, a new paradigm of the coming age. (pp. 46–47)

A Divine Instrument

How happy the Gautama Buddha, Jesus and Mahomet would be if they could see the United Nations! (p. 94)

The United Nations is the school where they [the religions] all learn from each other . . . and define what is good and bad for the whole human race. . . . This is why we must listen attentively with all our minds, hearts and souls to what the great religions and spiritual leaders have to say. . . . This is why we must also be grateful to anyone who gives the work of the United Nations a spiritual interpretation, thus following the examples of Dag Hammarskjöld and U Thant, who saw in the United Nations the renewed story of the total dimension of human life. (p. 43)

We have the UN Meditation Room, which is visited by hundreds of thousands of visitors each year. We have also a UN Meditation Group led by an Indian mystic. One could tell several moving stories of the spiritual transformation the UN has caused, to the point that this little speck on earth is becoming a holy ground. (p. 46)

The "Indian mystic" who leads this meditation group is Muller's close friend and ally, Sri Chinmoy. Muller subscribes to Chinmoy's view of the UN as "the chosen instrument of God . . . a divine messenger carrying the banner of God's inner vision and outer manifestation."[1] He comments,

In particular I would agree with the prophecy of that spiritual believer in the United Nations, Sri Chinmoy, when he said: "At the end of its voyage, there is every possibility that the United Nations will be the last word in human perfection. And then the United Nations can easily bloom in excellence and stand as the pinnacle of divine enlightenment." (pp. 43–44)

Becoming The Planet of God

Someday our planet will be a world spiritual democracy . . . at some point in our evolution the question of the proper representation of the people in the management of our globe will certainly pose itself, as will the spiritual quest for our proper place in the universe and in the eternal stream of time. There is urgent need to determine the cosmic or divine laws which must rule our behavior on earth. (p. 10)

For the first time in evolution, the human species has assumed a collective responsibility for the success of planet Earth in the universe. Interdependence, globality and a total view of our planet and the environment are now facts of life. . . . We must stand in awe before the beauty and miracle of creation. Perhaps this will be the new spiritual ideology which will bind the human race. We must lift again our spirits and hearts into the infinite bliss and mystery of the universe. . . . We must elevate ourselves again as light, cosmic beings in deep communion with the universe and eternity. We must re-establish the unity of our planet and of our beings with the universe and divinity. . . . We must see our planet and ourselves as cells of a universe which is becoming increasingly conscious of itself in us. That is our royal road out of the present bewilderment. (p. 37)

Little by little, a planetary prayer book is thus being composed by an increasingly united humanity seeking its oneness. . . . Once again, but this time on a universal scale, humankind is seeking no less than its reunion with the "divine," its transcendence into ever higher forms of life. Hindus call our earth Brahma, or God, for they rightly see no difference between our earth and the divine. This ancient simple truth is slowly dawning again upon humanity. Its full flowering will be the real, great new story of humanity, as we are about to enter our cosmic age and to become what we were always meant to be: the planet of God. (p. 49)

Note

1. "Public Education . . . The Shaping of Global Citizens!" *Hope For The World Update* (Noblesville, IN: Hope For The World, Spring 1997, newsletter), p. 4.

APPENDIX J

Co-sponsors of the 1993 Parliament of the World's Religions

The following pages reveal the organizations that helped sponsor the 1993 Parliament of World Religions. Although many of the sponsors came from Chicago and the Midwest for reasons of proximity, a significant number of these institutions represented larger national or international interests. Some of the names on the list may come as a surprise.

Co-sponsors of the 1993 Parliament of the World's Religions

Council
for a
Parliament
of the
World's Religions

Post Office Box 1630
Chicago, Illinois 60690-1630
U.S.A.

Office: 105 West Adams, Suite 800
Telephone: 312 629-2990
Fax: 312 629-2991

American Academy of Religion, *Atlanta, Georgia*
American Buddhist Congress, *Chicago , Illinois*
American Ethical Union, *Evanston, Illinois*
American Humanist Association, *Amherst, New York*
American Islamic College, *Chicago, Illinois*
American Jewish Committee, *New York, New York*
American Jewish Congress, *Chicago, Illinois*
Anthroposophical Association in America, *Chicago, Illinois*
Anti-Defamation League of B'nai B'rith, *Chicago, Illinois*
Anuvrat Global Organization (ANUVIBHA), *Jaipur, India*
Association of Unity Churches, *Lee's Summit, Missouri*
Roman Catholic Archdiocese of Chicago, *Chicago, Illinois*
Bahá'í International Community, *United Nations, New York*
Bharatiya Temple, *Flint, Michigan*
Brahma Kumaris World Spiritual University, *Mount Abu, India and Chicago, Illinois*
Buddhist Council of the Midwest, *Evanston, Illinois*
Buddhist Peace Fellowship, *Berkeley, California*
C.I.R.C.E.S. International, Inc., *Plainfield, Indiana*
Call to Action, *Chicago, Illinois*
Catholic Theological Union, *Chicago, Illinois*
Center for Respect of Life and Environment, *Washington, D.C.*
Center for the Study of Values, *DePaul University, Chicago, Illinois*
Center for Yoga and Christianity, *Pacific Grove, California*
Chicago Association of Reform Rabbis, *Chicago, Illinois*
Chicago Center for Religion and Science at Lutheran School of Theology, *Chicago, Illinois*
Chicago Disciples Union (Disciples of Christ), *Oak Park, Illinois*
Chicago Theological Union, *Chicago, Illinois*
Chicago Theological Seminary, *Chicago, Illinois*
Church of Jesus Christ of Latter-Day Saints, *Salt Lake City, Utah*
Christian Laity of Chicago, *Evanston, Illinois*
Church of the International Society of Divine Love, Inc., *Austin, Texas*
Church of the New Jerusalem - Swedenborgian, *Bryn Athyn, Pennsylvania*
City of God, *Moundsville, Virginia*
Common Ground Center, *Deerfield, Illinois*
Community Renewal Society, *Chicago, Illinois*
Conscious Choice Magazine, *Chicago, Illinois*
Covenant of the Goddess, *Berkeley, California and New York, New York*
Earthkind, U.S.A., *Washington, D.C.*
EarthSpirit Community, *Medford, Massachusetts*
Episcopal Diocese of Chicago, *Chicago, Illinois*
Evangelical Lutheran Church in America, *Chicago, Illinois*
Evangelical Lutheran Church in America - Metropolitan Chicago Synod, *Chicago, Illinois*
Federation of Jain Associations in North America, *Cincinnati, Ohio*
Federation of Zoroastrian Associations of North America, *Hinsdale, Illinois*
Fellowship in Prayer, Inc., *Princeton, New Jersey*
Fellowship of Isis, *Enniscorthy, Ireland*
First Baptist Church, *Evanston, Illinois*
First Presbyterian Church of Lake Forest, *Lake Forest, Illinois*
First Unitarian Universalist Church, *Ann Arbor, Michigan*
Focolare Movement, *Chicago, Illinois*
Free Diast Communion, *Middletown, California*
Gayatri Pariwar-Yugnirman, *Hardwar, India and Niles, Illinois*
General Convention, The Swedenborgian Church, *Newton, Massachusetts*
Gobind Sadan, U.S.A., *New York, New York*
Greater Chicago Broadcast Ministries, *Chicago, Illinois*
Greek Orthodox Diocese of Chicago, *Chicago, Illinois*
Guru Gobind Singh Foundation, *Rockville, Maryland*
Hindu Temple of Greater Chicago, *Lemont, Illinois*
Human Society International, *Washington, D.C.*

14

Exhibit 2-A

Council
for a
Parliament
of the
World's Religions

Co-sponsors of the 1993 Parliament of the World's Religions

Human Society of the United States, *Washington, D.C.*
Hyde Park/Kenwood Interfaith Council, *Chicago, Illinois*
Illinois Conference of Churches, *Springfield, Illinois*
Institute for Ecumenical and Cultural Research, *Collegeville, Minnesota*
Institute for 21st Century Studies, *Arlington, Virginia*
Institute for World Spirituality, *Chicago, Illinois*
Institute of Jainology, *London, United Kingdom*
Institute of Muslim Minority Affairs, *London, U.K. and Jeddah, Saudi Arabia*
Interfaith Ministries, *Wichita, Kansas*
International Assembly of Spiritual Healers and Earth Steward Congregations,
  Seattle, Washington
International Association for Religious Freedom, *Frankfurt, Germany*
International Association for Religious Freedom, United States Chapter, *Abingdon,*
  Pennsylvania
International Church of Metaphysics, *Windyville, Missouri*
International Coordinating Committee on Religion and the Earth, *Greenwich, Connecticut*
International Council of Community Churches, *Palos Heights, Illinois and Durham,*
  North Carolina
International Mahavir Jain Mission, *Blairstown, New Jersey*
Inter-Religious Federation for World Peace, *Ashtead, United Kingdom and New York , New York*
Islamic Research Foundation for the Advancement of Knowledge, *Louisville, Kentucky*
Jain Society of Metropolitan Chicago, *Bartlett, Ilinois*
Jewish Community Realtions Council, *Chicago, Illinois*
Joseph Cambell Society, *New York, New York*
Kashi Church Foundation, *Sebastian, Florida*
Kiwanis Club of Downtown Madison, *Madison, Wisconsin*
Lakeside Buddha Sangha, *Evanston, Illinois*
Lyceum of Venus of Healing, *Ayer, Massachsuetts*
Maha Bodhi Society of India, *Calcutta, India and Mt. Lavinia, Sri Lanka*
McCormick Theological Seminary, *Chicago, Illinois*
Meadville-Lombard Theological School, *Chicago, Illinois*
Monastic Inter-Religious Dialogue, *St. Joseph, Minnesota and Lisle, Illinois*
Muslim Community Center, *Chicago, Illinois*
National Association for Humane and Environmental Education, *East Hadden,*
  Connecticut
National Association of Diocesan Ecumenical Offices (NADEO), *St. Louis, Missouri*
National Conference of Christians and Jews, Chicago and Northern Illinois Region,
  Chicago, Illinois
National Council of the Churches of Christ in the USA, *New York, New York*
National Spiritual Assembly of the Bahá'is of the United States, *Washington, D.C.*
National Spiritual Association of Churches, *Lily Dale, New York*
Native American Center, *Madison, Wisconsin*
Noble Thoughts Development Foundation, *Glendale Heights, Illinois*
North American Conference on Christianity and Ecology, *Washington, D.C.*
North American Interfaith Network, Inc., *Buffalo, New York*
Office of Religious and Cultural Affairs of the Central Tibetan Administration,
  Dharamsala, India and New York, New York
Presbyterian Church (USA), *Louisville, Kentucky*
Presbytery of Chicago/Presbyterian Church (USA), *Chicago, Illinois*
Religious Education Association, *New Haven, Connecticut*
Ribbon International, *Centerport, New York*
Saint Benedict Center Interfaith Dialogue Group, *Madison, Wisconsin*
Saint Isidore's Roman Catholic Church, *Bloomingdale, Illinois*
Science of Spirituality (Sawan Kirpal Ruhani Mission), *Naperville, Illinois*
Self-Realization Fellowship, *Los Angeles, California*
Shalom Ministries, Inc., *Chicago, Illinois*
Sikh Religious Society of Chicago, *Chicago, Illinois*
Spertus College of Judaica, *Chicago, Illinois*
Spiritual Assembly of the Bahá'is of Chicago, *Chicago, Illinois*   15

Exhibit 2-B

Co-sponsors of the 1993 Parliament of the World's Religions

Council
for a
Parliament
of the
World's Religions

Spiritual Growth Network, *Lexington, Kentucky and Danville, Illinois*
Sri Aurobindo Association, *Berkeley, California*
Sri Chinmoy Centre, *Chicago, Illinois*
Sukyo Mahikari, *Brooklyn, New York*
Swedenborg School of Religion, *Newton, Massachusetts*
The Center for Women, the Earth, the Divine, *Ridgefield, Connecticut*
The Graymoor Ecumenical and Interreligious Institute, *New York, New York*
The Jabala Center, *Bloomingdale, Illinois*
The Liberal Catholic Church, *Evergreen Park, Illinois*
The Monthly Aspectarian, *Morton Grove, Illinois*
The Organization for Universal Communal Harmony (T.O.U.C.H.), *Chicago, Illinois*
The Temple of Understanding, *New York, New York*
The Theosophical Society, *Pasadena, California*
The Theosophical Society in America, *Wheaton, Illinois*
Union of American Hebrew Congregations, *New York, New York*
Unitarian Universalist Association of Congregations, *Boston, Massachusetts*
Unitarian Universalist Association - Central Midwest District, *Oak Park, Illinois*
United Church of Christ - Chicago Metropolitan Association, *Chicago, Illinois*
United Lodge of Theosophists, *Los Angeles, California*
United Methodist Church - Northern Illinois Conference, *Chicago and River Forest, Illinois*
Unity School of Christianity, *Unity Village, Missouri*
Universal Peace Sanctuary, *Seattle, Washington*
Vaishnava Center for Enlightenment, *Okemos, Michigan*
Vedanta Society of Madison, *Madison, Wisconsin*
Vishwa Hindu Parishad of America, *Berlin, Connecticut*
Vivekananda Foundation, *Alameda, California*
Vivekananda Vedanta Society, *Chicago, Illinois*
Wat Dhammaram (Thai Buddhist Temple), *Chicago, Illinois*
Winnetka Congregational Church, *Winnetka, Illinois*
Women of Faith Resource Center, *Chicago, Illinois*
Won Buddhism of America, *Flushing, New York*
World Alliance of Reformed Churches, Geneva, *Switzerland and LaGrange Park, Illinois*
World Congress of Faiths, *London, United Kingdom*
World Inter-Faith Education Association (Canada), *Victoria, British Columbia*
Yoga Journal, *Berkeley, California*

Exhibit 2-C

APPENDIX K

Ceremony of Induction and Extreme Oath of the Jesuits

[When a Jesuit of the minor rank is to be elevated to command, he is conducted into the Chapel of the Convent of the Order, where there are only three others present, the principal or Superior standing in front of the altar. On either side stands a monk, one of whom holds a banner of yellow and white, which are the Papal colors, and the other a black banner with a dagger and red cross above a skull and cross-bones, with the word *INRI*, and below them the words *IUSTUM, NECAR, REGES, IMPIOS*. The meaning of which is: *It is just to exterminate or annihilate impious or heretical Kings, Governments or Rulers*. Upon the floor is a red cross upon which the postulant or candidate kneels. The Superior hands him a small black crucifix, which he takes in his left hand and presses to his heart, and the Superior at the same time presents to him a dagger, which he grasps by the blade and holds the point against his heart, the Superior still holding it by the hilt, and thus addresses the postulant.]

Superior

My son, heretofore you have been taught to act the dissembler: among Roman Catholics to be a Roman Catholic, and to be a spy even among your own brethren; to believe no man, to trust no man. Among the Reformers, to be a Reformer; among the Huguenots, to be a Huguenot; among the Calvinists, to be a Calvinist; among the

Protestants, generally to be a Protestant; and obtaining their confidence to seek even to preach from their pulpits, and to denounce with all the vehemence in your nature our Holy Religion and the Pope; and even to descend so low as to become a Jew among the Jews, that you might be enabled to gather together all information for the benefit of your Order as a faithful soldier of the Pope.

You have been taught to insidiously plant the seeds of jealously and hatred between communities, provinces and states that were at peace, and incite them to deeds of blood, involving them in war with each other, and to create revolutions and civil wars in countries that were independent and prosperous, cultivating the arts and the sciences and enjoying the blessings of peace. To take sides with the combatants and to act secretly in concert with your brother Jesuit, who might be engaged on the other side, but openly opposed to that with which you might be connected; only that the Church might be the gainer in the end, in the conditions fixed in the treaties for peace and that the end justifies the means.

You have been taught your duty as a spy, to gather all statistics, facts and information in your power from every source; to ingratiate yourself into the confidence of the family circle of Protestants and heretics of every class and character, as well as that of the merchant, the banker, the lawyer, among the schools and universities, in parliaments and legislatures, and in the judiciaries and councils of state, and to "be all things to all men," for the Pope's sake, whose servants we are unto death.

You have received all your instructions heretofore as a novice, a neophyte, and have served as a coadjutor, confessor and priest, but you have not yet been invested with all that is necessary to command in the Army of Loyola in the service of the Pope. You must serve the proper time as the instrument and executioner as directed by your superiors; *for none can command here who has not consecrated his labors with the blood of the heretic; for "without the shedding of blood no man can be saved."* Therefore, to fit yourself for your work and make your own salvation sure, you will, in addition to your former oath of obedience to your Order and allegiance to the Pope, repeat after me

The Extreme Oath of the Jesuits

I, M——— N———, Now, in the presence of Almighty God, the Blessed Virgin Mary, the blessed Michael the Archangel, the blessed St. John the Baptist, the holy Apostles St. Peter and St. Paul and all the saints and sacred hosts of heaven, and to you, my ghostly father, the Superior General of the Society of Jesus, founded by St. Ignatius Loyola, in the Pontificate of Paul the Third, and continued to the present, do by the womb of the Virgin, the matrix of God, and the rod of Jesus Christ, declare and swear, that his holiness the Pope is Christ's Vicegerent and is the true and only Head of the Catholic or Universal Church throughout the earth; and that by virtue of the keys of binding and loosing, given to his Holiness by my Saviour, Jesus Christ, he hath power to depose heretical kings, princes, states, commonwealths and governments, all being illegal without his sacred confirmation and that they may safely be destroyed. Therefore, to the utmost of my power, I shall and will defend this doctrine and His Holiness' right and custom against all usurpers of the heretical or Protestant authority whatever, especially the Lutheran Church of Germany, Holland, Denmark, Sweden and Norway, and the now pretended authority and churches of England and Scotland, and branches of the same now established in Ireland and on the Continent of America and elsewhere; and all adherents in regard that they be usurped and heretical, opposing the sacred Mother Church of Rome. I do now renounce and disown any allegiance as due to any heretical king, prince or state named Protestants or Liberals or obedience to any of their laws, magistrates or officers.

I do further declare that the doctrines of the churches of England and Scotland, of the Calvinists, Huguenots and others of the name Protestants or Liberals to be damnable, and they themselves damned and to be damned who will not forsake the same.

I do further declare, that I will help, assist and advise all or any of his Holiness' agents in any place wherever I shall be, in Switzerland, Germany, Holland, Denmark, Sweden, Norway, England, Ireland, or America, or in any other kingdom or territory I shall come to, and do my uttermost to extirpate the heretical Protestants or Liberals' doctrines and to destroy all their pretended powers, regal or otherwise.

I do further promise and declare, that notwithstanding I am dispensed with, to assume any religion heretical, for the propagating of the Mother Church's interest, to keep secret and private all her agents' counsels from time to time, as they may entrust me, and not to divulge, directly or indirectly, by word, writing or circumstance whatever; but to execute all that shall be proposed, given in charge or discovered unto me, by you, my ghostly father, or any of this sacred convent.

I do further promise and declare, that I will have no opinion or will of my own, or any mental reservation whatever, even as a corpse or cadaver, (*perinde ac cadaver*,) but will unhesitatingly obey each and every command that I may receive from my superiors in the Militia of the Pope and of Jesus Christ.

That I will go to any part of the world whithersoever I may be sent, to the frozen regions of the North, the burning sands of the desert of Africa, or the jungles of India, to the centres of civilization of Europe, or to the wild haunts of the barbarous savages of America, without murmuring or repining, and will be submissive in all things whatsoever communicated to me.

I furthermore promise and declare that I will, when opportunity presents, make and wage relentless war, secretly or openly, against all heretics, Protestants and Liberals, as I am directed to do, to extirpate and exterminate them from the face of the whole earth; and that I will spare neither age, sex or condition; and that I will hang, burn, waste, boil, flay, strangle and bury alive these infamous heretics, rip up the stomachs and wombs of their women and crush their infants' heads against the walls, in order to annihilate forever their execrable race. That when the same cannot be done openly, I will secretly use the poisoned cup, the strangulating cord, the steel of the poinard [sic] or the leaden bullet, regardless of the honor, rank, dignity, or authority of the person or persons, whatever may be their condition in life, either public or private, as I at any time may be directed so to do by any agent of the Pope or Superior of the Brotherhood of the Holy Faith, of the Society of Jesus.

In confirmation of which, I hereby dedicate my life, my soul and all my coporeal [sic] powers, and with this dagger which I now receive, I will subscribe my name written in my own blood, in testimony thereof; and should I prove false or weaken in my determination, may my brethren and fellow soldiers of the Militia of the Pope cut off my hands and my feet, and my throat from ear to ear, my belly opened and sulphur burned therein, with all the punishment that can be inflicted upon me on earth and my soul be tortured by demons in an eternal hell forever!

All of which I, M——— N———, do swear by the blessed Trinity and blessed Sacrament, which I am now to receive, to perform and on my part to keep inviolably; and do call all the heavenly and glorious host of heaven to witness these my real intentions to keep this my oath.

In testimony hereof I take this most holy and blessed Sacrament of the Eucharist, and witness the same further, with my name written with the point of this dagger dipped in my own blood and sealed in the face of this holy convent.

[He receives the wafer from the Superior and writes his name with the point of his dagger dipped in his own blood taken from over the heart.]

Superior

You will now rise to your feet and I will instruct you in the Catechism necessary to make yourself known to any member of the Society of Jesus belonging to this rank.

In the first place, you, as a Brother Jesuit, will with another mutually make the ordinary sign of the cross as any ordinary Roman Catholic would; then one crosses his wrists, the palms of his hands open, the other in answer crosses his feet, one above the other; the first points with forefinger of the right hand to the center of the palm of the left, the other with the forefinger of the left hand points to the center of the palm of the right; the first then with his right hand makes a circle around his head, touching it; the other then with the forefinger of his left hand touches the left side of his body just below his heart; the first then with his right hand draws it across the throat of the other, and the latter then with his right hand makes the motion of cutting with a dagger down the stomach and abdomen of the first. The first then says *Iustum*; the other answers *Necar*; the first then says *Reges*. The other answers *Impios*. [The meaning of which has already been explained.] The first will then present a small piece of paper folded in a peculiar manner, four times, which the other will cut longitudinally and on opening the name JESU will be found written upon the head and arms of a cross three times. You will then give and receive with him the following questions and answers.

Ques. From whither do you come?
Ans. From the bends of the Jordan, from Calvary, from the Holy Sepulchre, and lastly from Rome.
Ques. What do you keep and for what do you fight?
Ans. The Holy faith.
Ques. Whom do you serve?
Ans. The Holy Father at Rome, the Pope, and the Roman Catholic Church Universal throughout the world.
Ques. Who commands you?
Ans. The Successor of St. Ignatius Loyola, the founder of the Society of Jesus or the Soldiers of Jesus Christ.
Ques. Who received you?
Ans. A venerable man in white hair.
Ques. How?
Ans. With a naked dagger, I kneeling upon the cross beneath the banners of the Pope and of our sacred Order.
Ques. Did you take an oath?
Ans. I did, to destroy heretics and their governments and rulers, and to spare neither age, sex nor condition. To be as

a corpse without any opinion or will of my own, but to implicitly obey my superiors in all things without hesitation or murmuring.

Ques. Will you do that?

Ans. I will.

Ques. How do you travel?

Ans. In the bark of Peter the fisherman.

Ques. Whither do you travel?

Ans. To the four quarters of the globe.

Ques. For what purpose?

Ans. To obey the orders of my General and Superiors and execute the will of the Pope and faithfully fulfill the conditions of my oath.

Ques. Go ye, then, into all the world and take possession of all lands in the name of the Pope. He who will not accept him as the Vicar of Jesus and his Vicegerent on earth, let him be accursed and exterminated.

Note

This Jesuit oath is located in the Library of Congress, Washington, D.C., Library of Congress Catalog Card # 66-43354. A nearly identical version of this oath may be found in the U.S. House Congressional Record, 1913, p. 3216. The oath was originally made public in the year 1883.

Resources

New Age/One-World Movement

Ankerberg, John, and John Weldon. *Encyclodedia of New Age Beliefs*. Eugene, OR: Harvest House, 1996.

Kah, Gary. *En Route to Global Occupation*. Noblesville, IN: Hope International Publishing, 1999.

Kah, Gary. editor, *Hope for the World Update* (newsletter). P.O. Box 899, Noblesville, IN 46061.

Kah, Gary. *Countdown to Daniel's Final Week*. Noblesville, IN: Hope for the World, 2000. Videotape.

Kah, Gary. *The New World Religion*. Noblesville, IN: Hope for the World, 2000. Videotape.

Kah, Gary, website: www.garykah.org.

Ecumenism

Arms, Phil. *Promise Keepers: Another Trojan Horse*. Houston, TX: Shiloh Publishers, 1997.

Hunt, David A. *A Woman Rides the Beast*. Eugene, OR: Harvest House, 1994.

Christian Discernment

Lutzer, Erwin. *Christ Among Other Gods—A Defense of Christ in an Age of Tolerance.* Chicago: Moody Press, 1994.

Martin, Walter. *The Kingdom of the Cults.* Minneapolis, MN: Bethany House, 1985.

McKenney, Tom. *Please Tell Me . . . Questions People Ask About Freemasonry—And the Answers.* Lafayette, LA: Vital Issues Press, 1994.

The Mormon Dilemma. Hemet, CA: Jeremiah Films, 1988. Videotape.

Tanner, Jerald and Sandra, Norman L. Geisler, Francis Beckwith, Philip Roberts, and Ron Rhodes. *The Counterfeit Gospel of Mormonism.* Eugene, OR: Harvest House, 1998.

Evolution *vs.* Creationism

Ankerberg, John, and John Weldon. *Darwin's Leap of Faith: Exposing the False Religion of Evolution.* Eugene, OR: Harvest House, 1998.

Brown, Walter. *In the Beginning.* Phoenix, AZ: Center for Scientific Creation, 1995.

Ham, Kenneth. *The Lie: Evolution.* Green Forest, AR: Master Books, 1989.

Environment

Coffman, Michael. *Saviors of the Earth.* Chicago: Northfield Publishing, 1994.

Education

Kjos, Berit. *Brave New Schools.* Eugene, OR: Harvest House, 1995.

Economics/Technology

Griffin, G. Edward. *The Creature from Jekyll Island: A Second Look at the Federal Reserve.* Westlake, CA: American Media, 1994.

Jeffrey, Grant R. *Surveillance Society.* Toronto, ON: Frontier Research Publications, Inc., 2000.

Index

Special Newsletter Notice

Gary Kah publishes a research newsletter to keep interested readers informed of developments on the matters discussed in this book. The *Hope for the World Update* is a highly-documented publication that displays many of its findings in the form of exhibits. Each issue puts the evidence in front of the reader.

If you would like to receive these timely newsletters, please complete this form and send it, along with your check or money-order, made payable to Hope for the World, to

Hope for the World
P.O. Box 899
Noblesville, IN 46061-0899
U.S.A.

To show our appreciation, we will send subscribers a special 28-page report on education *free of charge*. Subscribers will also receive a *complimentary* cassette that will positively impact their lives!

If you would rather not remove this page, please feel free to photocopy it. You may also write to the above address, or phone (317) 290-HOPE to order your subscription. When ordering, please mention that you heard about our newsletter in this book and would like to receive your complimentary report and cassette.

Subscription Response Form

Yes, I would like to receive your newsletter, *Hope for the World Update*. Enclosed is my check or money-order for $35.00 (U.S.) for a one-year subscription. Please send me your complimentary education report and inspirational cassette tape.

Name _____

Address _____

City and State _____

Postal code _____

Country _____

Telephone _____

Additional Materials by Gary Kah

Countdown to Daniel's Final Week – VIDEO – $23.00* Qty_____
Gary's latest production! This eye-opening presentation was taped before a live audience in April 2000. Approximately 60 minutes long, this video details current developments in the push for world government and the creation of an interfaith religious system. Putting the evidence on display, Gary has inserted video footage of Pope John Paul in his role as a global interfaith leader, including clips of the pope's recent Middle East trip. Gary also outlines the present work of Mikhail Gorbachev, the United Nations, and the UN-affiliated United Religious Initiative. This vital message is tactfully presented so that you can share it with your friends – whatever their position on interfaithism and globalism may be.

The New World Religion – VIDEO – $23.00* Qty_____
This video was taped before a live audience in March 1999, and draws heavily from Gary's book *The New World Religion*. In this one-hour presentation, Gary shares information on the effort underway to unify the world's religions through various ecumenical/interfaith initiatives. He speaks directly on this end-times spiritual deception foretold in Scripture. This video is a *must* to help you understand the dangers of the growing one-world movement. You will want to share this message of discernment with your family and friends!

En Route to Global Occupation – BOOK – $13.00* Qty_____
This #1 Christian Best-Seller has a message that is crucial to the political, economic and spiritual future of this country. Since its release in 1992, *En Route* . . . has sold over 200,000 copies, and has been read by an estimated half million people. It is the result of more than seven years of research and is filled with documented facts and reproductions of actual letters (from the World Constitution and Parliament Association), proving that the drive toward global government is for real. This book also contains much of Gary's personal story.

To receive these valuable resources, please complete this form and send it, along with your check or money order, made payable to Hope for the World, to: Hope for the World, P.O. Box 899, Noblesville, IN 46061-0899, U.S.A.

*All prices include shipping and handling. Check *must* be in U.S. dollars.

You may also write to the above address, or phone (317) 290-HOPE to order any of these items.

Name _____

Address _____

City and State _____

Postal code _____

Telephone _____

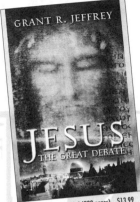

ISBN # 0-921714-56-4 (288 pages) $13.99

ISBN #0-921714-60-2 (288 pages) $13.99

ISBN #0-921714-62-9 (288 pages) $13.99

From

FR⊕NTIER RESEARCH
P U B L I C A T I O N S · I N C
BESTSELLING TITLES

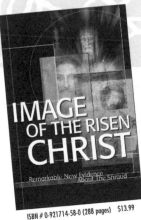

ISBN # 0-921714-58-0 (288 pages) $13.99

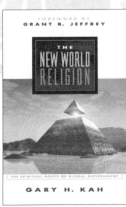

ISBN # 0-967009-80-4 (320 pages) $12.99

ISBN #0-921714-28-9 (276 pages) $13.99

AVAILABLE IN CHRISTIAN BOOKSTORES EVERYWHERE
(OR BY CALLING) IN USA: 1-800-883-1812   IN CANADA: 1-800-853-1423

(Prices may vary in Canada)

Frontier Research Publications

Grant Jeffrey Ministries

Available in Christian bookstores everywhere

Quantity	Code	Description		Price	Total
		Softback Books			
	BK-3	Messiah – War in the Middle East & The Road to Armageddon		$12.99	
	BK-4	Apocalypse – The Coming Judgment of the Nations		$12.99	
	BK-5	Prince of Darkness – Antichrist and the New World Order		$13.99	
	BK-6	Final Warning – Economic Collapse and Coming World Government		$13.99	
	BK-7	Heaven – The Mystery of Angels		$12.99	
	BK-8	The Signature of God – Astonishing Biblical Discoveries		$13.99	
	BK-9	Yeshua – The Name of Jesus Revealed in the Old Testament (Yacov Rambsel)		$11.99	
	BK-10	Armageddon – Appointment With Destiny		$12.99	
	BK-11	His Name is Jesus – The Mysterious Yeshua Codes (Yacov Rambsel)		$12.99	
	BK-12	The Handwriting of God – Sacred Mysteries of the Bible		$13.99	
	BK-14	The New World Religion (Gary H. Kah)		$12.99	
	BK-16	Jesus, The Great Debate		$13.99	
	BK-17	Image of the Risen Christ (Dr. Kenneth E. Stevenson)		$13.99	
	BK-18	Surveillance Society – The Rise of Antichrist		$13.99	
	BK-19	Journey Into Eternity – Search for Immortality		$13.99	
	BK-20	Triumphant Return – The Coming Kingdom of God		$13.99	
		ANY THREE BOOKS OR MORE	**EACH**	$11.00	
		Hardcover Books			
	HC-H	Heaven – The Mystery of Angels		$15.99	
	W-50	Mysterious Bible Codes		$29.99	
	W-51	Flee The Darkness (Grant R. Jeffrey and Angela Hunt)	*Fiction*	$27.99	
	W-52	By Dawn's Early Light (Grant R. Jeffrey and Angela Hunt)	*Fiction*	$27.99	
	W-53	The Spear of Tyranny (Grant R. Jeffrey and Angela Hunt)	*Fiction*	$19.99	
		Videos			
	V-19	Surveillance Society – The Rise of Antichrist		$19.99	
	V-20	Jesus, The Great Debate		$19.99	
	V-21	Triumphant Return – The Coming Kingdom of God		$19.99	
		Double-length Videos			
	V-17	The Signature of God – Astonishing Biblical Discoveries		$29.99	
	V-18	Mysterious Bible Codes		$29.99	
		Total this page (to be carried forward)			

continued overleaf

Quantity	Code	Description	Price	Total
		Total from previous page		
		Audio Cassettes		
	AB-14	The Signature of God (2 tapes)	$15.99	
	AB-15	Mysterious Bible Codes (2 tapes)	$15.99	
	AB-17	Jesus, The Great Debate (2 tapes)	$15.99	
		Computer Programs		
	BC	Unlocking the Bible Codes (on CD-ROM; for IBM-compatible computers only)	$44.99	
	PIB	**Product Brochure**	No charge	
		One low shipping and handling fee for the above (per order)	$4.95	$4.95
		Zondervan Prophecy Marked Reference Study Bible Grant R. Jeffrey, General Editor		
	KJV	Hardcover	$34.99	
	KJV	Bonded Leather: Black	$59.99	
	KJV	Bonded Leather: Burgundy	$59.99	
	KJV	Top Grain Leather: Black	$69.99	
	NIV	Hardcover	$34.99	
	NIV	Bonded Leather: Black	$59.99	
	NIV	Bonded Leather: Burgundy	$59.99	
		Shipping and handling fee for Bibles (per order)	$5.95	$5.95
		Oklahoma residents add 7.5% sales tax		

Additional shipping charges will apply to orders outside North America. **Grand Total** [ ]

All prices are in U.S. dollars

PLEASE PRINT

Name _____

Address _____

City _____ Province _____ Postal code_____

Phone _____ Fax _____

Credit card number_____

Expiry date_____

U.S. orders: mail along with your check or money order to:
Frontier Research Publications
P.O. Box 470470
Tulsa, OK 74147-0470

Canadian orders: call or write for pricing to:
Frontier Research Publications
P.O. Box 129, Station "U", Toronto, Ontario M8Z 5M4

U.S. credit card orders: call 1-800-883-1812

Canadian credit card orders: call 1-800-853-1423

Prices effective July 1, 2001